GOD'S WORD
IN A
YOUNG WORLD

TO

MARY

who has made so much possible by 'staying by the supplies'
(1 Samuel 30:24)

GOD'S WORD IN A YOUNG WORLD

The Story of Scripture Union

Nigel Sylvester

Scripture Union
130 City Road, London EC1V 2NJ

Published by Scripture Union Publishing
130 City Road, London for the
Scripture Union International Council

International Office: 130 City Road, London EC1V 2NJ

Regional Offices
Africa Region: PO Box 52443, Nairobi, Kenya
Americas Region: Apartado 5323, Lima, Peru
British Isles Region: 130 City Road, London EC1V 2NJ
East Asia/Pacific Region: Room 04-04, 7 Armenian Street, Singapore 0617
PO Box 3, West Pennant Hills, NSW 2120, Australia
Europe Region: Postfach 1129, D-5277 Marienheide, Germany
South Asia Region: St. John's Parsonage, Bangalore 5, India

National Offices
Australia: 241 Flinders Lane, Melbourne, Victoria 3000
Anzea Bookhouse, PO Box 115, Flemington Markets, NSW 2129
Canada: 300 Steelcase Road W., Unit 19, Markham, Ontario, L3R 2W2
England: 130 City Road, London EC1V 2NJ
New Zealand: 62 Ghuznee Street, PO Box 760, Wellington
Northern Ireland: 12 Wellington Place, Belfast, ST1 6GE
Republic of Ireland: 9 Northumberland Avenue, Dun Laoghaire, Co. Dublin
Scotland: 280 St. Vincent Street, Glasgow G2 5RT
South Africa: Millard House, 83 Camp Ground Road, Rondebosch 7700
United States of America: 1716 Spruce Street, Philadelphia, Pa 19103

ISBN 0 86201 259 7

Photographs by Gordon Gray, Maurice Ambler, Carol Acworth, Jean-luc Ray, P. J. McNully, Nigel Sylvester.

Phototypeset in 10/12 Baskerville by Nuprint Services Ltd, Harpenden, Herts.

Printed and bound in Great Britain at the Pitman Press, Bath.

Contents

Foreword

There are several reasons why I welcome Nigel Sylvester's fascinating history of Scripture Union.

The first is *personal*, namely that it was a Scripture Union staff worker, the Rev E. J. H. Nash, who showed me the way to Christ. First, his preaching of the gospel aroused within me the desire to know Christ personally. Next, he taught me the way of salvation. Then, when I had come to Christ, he both nurtured me by prayer and counsel with astonishing faithfulness and led me into Christian service by giving me opportunities for which I was scarcely ready. I have paid my tribute to him in the symposium *Bash: A Study in Spiritual Power* (1983).

My second reason is *theological*. Two of Scripture Union's fundamental emphases are the value of children and the importance of daily Bible reading. In both these SU is following Jesus Christ. For he was and is the great lover of children, who invited them to come to him and warned us neither to hinder nor to stumble them. He also stressed that the life and health of human beings depend not only on material bread, but on the Word of God.

Thirdly, I admire SU's *strategic* principles. When its English-born and English-based work began to spread to other countries, it could easily have degenerated into an imperialistic mission, exercising control from a distant headquarters in London. But the crucial step to internationalise and decentralise was taken in 1960. Now SU is a family of autonomous movements and regional councils. One result has been the rise of gifted and dedicated national leaders.

My fourth reason is *cultural,* namely SU's sensitive adaptation to changing culture. It all began when an aristocratic English gentleman traced out a Bible text (in the Authorised Version, of course – there were no others) in the sands of Llandudno, North Wales, for the benefit of upper-class children who were on holiday there. Many similar Victorian enterprises, refusing to change, have long since outgrown their usefulness and perished. In the well-known phrase, the 'movement' became a 'monument'. Not so Scripture Union. Instead, it has become a worldwide movement, reaching out to young people of every background, developing an extremely diverse programme, responding to contemporary needs in each culture, and using modern educational methods.

I warmly commend *God's Word in a Young World.* Nigel Sylvester (who in his modesty hardly mentions himself, although he has had an influential ministry in SU, first in Africa , then in Britain, and now as International Secretary) has brought the story to life. His book is very far from being a dull catalogue of names and dates; he has a deft touch in tracing the development of SU, and he wisely builds his story round some of the leading SU personalities in each country. So long as SU remains deeply rooted in the Scriptures, and sensitive to the needs of a constantly changing world, it has under God a great future.

John Stott
January 1984

Introduction

Writing this book about the history of Scripture Union has been a fascinating and inspiring task, and I would like to thank the International Council for encouraging me to do it. I was not an ideal choice, but one or two others we approached had declined, so I offered to make the attempt. I have never done anything like it before, and fitting it in between travelling and other responsibilities, it has been five years since I started. I am sorry it has taken so long.

With so much material available, particularly for the last twenty-five years, the process of selection has been one of the most difficult aspects. My apologies to any readers who feel that something vital has been left out. It was important that I tried to keep the book to a reasonable length.

One of the disadvantages of being personally involved, in the latter part of the story, is that of objectivity. I have no doubt that my selection of material to some extent reflects my own point of view, and this must be allowed for. Where my own name would have appeared in the text, I have avoided clumsy circumlocutions like 'the present writer' and followed Luke's example, in Acts, of using the first person.

All writing of history involves interpretation, this book included. Indeed I have deliberately tried to reflect on the events recorded and draw out some of the things we can learn from them for the present day. As International Secretary it is, I suppose, impossible for me to write a book like this in a completely unofficial capacity. But it is important to make the point that the views expressed are my own, not necessarily the official views of the Council.

No one could begin writing about the history of Scripture Union without the help of John Pollock's *The Good Seed,* which tells the story in a fascinating and comprehensive way up to 1958. I have drawn on it extensively in the early sections of the book. It is a special pleasure to me to pay tribute to John, as it was he who led me to Christ when I was a student at Cambridge. The working papers for this book have been kept in the archives in London, and were an enormous help to me in finding my way round the original sources.

A list of some of the other published sources appears on page 251. There are references to CSSM and Scripture Union in so many Christian biographies and autobiographies in the last 100 years that I have only listed the main ones. I have also had access to hundreds of reports, newsletters, minutes and magazines from Scripture Union around the world which would take far too long to mention. But I am grateful to all those who have supplied information, or sent comments and suggestions on sections of the manuscript at various stages.

Finally I would like to thank my successive secretaries, Jenny Brewster and Liz Tydeman, who have typed and retyped with commendable patience; and my courteous editor, John Grayston, who prevented me, among other *faux pas,* from reporting that in 1886 Henry Hankinson found 'an active committee with 10,000 members in New South Wales'. As John remarked, that would be a bit large even for Scripture Union!

Nigel Sylvester
Rickmansworth, February 1984

Part I

Bold Pioneers 1867–1900

1

A Tale of Two Beaches

The ancient bus jolts off the asphalt highway, churning up clouds of dust as it stops beside the low, white building of the Scripture Union camp site, on the coast of Peru. Forty children, clambering over each other and over their few possessions, hop down the steps. For a moment they gaze astonished at the space which stretches in all directions. Then they scuttle off like crabs towards the beach.

BORN IN A PRISON

They have come for a camp for children from the women's prison in Lima. Born in jail, or brought in with their mothers because there is no one else to look after them, they only know a world bounded by the four walls of a prison courtyard or a cell. Lilly Escobar, the wife of a member of the Scripture Union Regional Council, visited the prison and saw the need. She decided something must be done, and so, with Scripture Union, she arranged to have a camp for them. 'It was chaotic and exhausting,' a visitor recalls. 'That first dash for freedom was typical of the kids' behaviour throughout the week. Mealtimes were mayhem, bedtime ditto. There was no time off for the helpers.'

'We just don't know how Lilly keeps going,' one of the helpers commented. 'The kids just wear you out.'

'So why do you do it, Lilly?'

'Oh, for lots of reasons. The kids need a good holiday. They need to know there's a world outside the jail. They need to know that they matter to God, and they will never believe that if we just tell them Bible stories in the prison. Here we try to love them in action, whether we're changing their pants, or stopping them killing each other, or talking to them about Jesus. We try to help them in the long-term as well. If the mother has a long sentence we try to get them accepted into a Christian children's home.'

A TEXT IN THE SAND

Over 100 years earlier, some other children played on a beach. They were not brought up in jail in Peru, but in prosperous homes in Victorian Britain, and were enjoying family holidays. Josiah Spiers, a young office worker, also on holiday, watched some of the children making a garden with pebbles and seaweed; he suddenly had an idea. 'These children could be making a text of Scripture with the stones.'

Josiah Spiers' friend Tom Bishop described what happened next.

> He ran to the nearest shop and bought a ball of string and some pegs. 'Who'll help me to write a text?' he said to the nearest group of children. 'I will, I will,' answered a dozen voices, and soon an eager band of volunteers was busily at work. The pegs were fixed in the sand, the string was tied to them so as to make straight lines. Josiah Spiers borrowed a spade and traced the words 'God is Love' in the sand while the children ran off to collect white stones to form the letters. As the work went on, quite a crowd of children and grown-up people gathered round. Soon the text was finished. 'What shall we do next?' the children asked. Mr Spiers had not expected anything further, and was rather surprised. 'Shall I tell you a story?' he suggested. 'Oh, yes, a story! A story!' cried fifty voices at once. Quickly everyone moved a few yards up the beach and the children sat down on the sand to listen. When one story was finished, they asked for another and another. In this totally unplanned way the first Seaside Service was held.

The date was 26 August 1868; and the place Llandudno, a quiet resort in North Wales built eighteen years earlier to cater for the new fashion of holidays by the sea.

It was from this small beginning that Scripture Union grew into a worldwide movement.

SPECIALLY FOR CHILDREN

The story really started the year before, in London. One summer evening in 1867 Josiah Spiers took a group from his Sunday School to a special meeting for children in John Street Chapel. He had no idea that at the meeting he would find his life's work and that he was about to start a movement which would spread all round the world and affect the lives of millions.

The large church was crowded with over 1,000 people. But it was quite different from any service Spiers had ever seen. 'Children should be seen and not heard,' the Victorians used to say. When they went to church, children were put in the galleries. They could not see but they were out of the way. Now Spiers found them in the main part of the church, with adults in the galleries. Usually the children had to sit stiff and still, listening to long, grown-up sermons. They had to sing hymns they could not understand, and learn long passages of the Bible by heart. Here they were encouraged to relax and enjoy themselves. The hymns had simple words and were set to lively tunes. The preachers' stories were interesting. Some of them were even amusing.

A young American called Payson Hammond was leading the service. A few years earlier, while training in Scotland to be a missionary, he made a revolutionary discovery – revolutionary in those days at least. He discovered that, even when they were quite young, children could have a personal, living relationship with Christ. They could do so if only someone told them about him in a way that they could understand. Instead of speaking from the pulpit, he stood informally on a platform. 'Throwing off the stiffness of preaching for the simplicity of asking questions,' a newspaper reported, 'he told stories, and announced hymns the congregation had not heard before, set to music in a lively and attractive way.'

Gradually the children relaxed and started to enjoy the service. This strange young American was making the teaching of the Bible, which they had thought so difficult, clear and interesting. The prayers were quite short and used words they might have chosen themselves; so they felt they could join in. The hymns were bright and cheerful so they could enjoy them and remember them. After the last hymn, in another startling innovation, Hammond invited the children to stay behind for counselling, individually or in small groups.

Many of the adults present were shocked at Hammond's methods. Some of them thought that children were quite unable to understand the great truths of salvation, so it was dangerous to ask them to accept Christ. Others thought the cheerful hymns were almost irreverent. After only four evenings at John Street Chapel, Hammond moved on to other London churches. But already hundreds of children had professed their faith in Christ. Even more significant for the future, a few adults had seen the possibilities of his methods. One of them was Josiah Spiers.

Spiers had attended every evening after work. He was deeply impressed with the lively, informal approach, the attractive use of stories and music and above all with the call for a response. 'I think,' he wrote, 'it is just the kind of service we require in connection with our Sunday Schools.' Without wasting any time, he arranged for a meeting near his home the following Sunday. At 8.00 pm fifteen children aged 7–12 met in the house of an artist, Thomas Hughes, in Islington, North London. Spiers, Hughes and another friend led the service. Though it did not have a name yet, the Children's Special Service Mission, later to become Scripture Union, was born.

During the next few months events moved quickly. Each Sunday the interest of the children was so great that Spiers and his friends decided to meet again the following week. Then they arranged an extra meeting each Wednesday. By November they had decided to hold the services regularly and fifty were attending. Next month they had so many children that they moved into a large school room, rented for Sunday evenings 'at the rate of £12 a year, but only for the ensuing quarter certain.'

Meanwhile Hammond's meetings had sparked off similar services in other parts of London. The largest of these was at Surrey Chapel, south of the River Thames. One of the leaders there was Tom Bishop, a young civil servant in the Customs House who became the other key figure in the future growth of the Mission. Tom Bishop helped with the services and counselled the children. But his main gifts were those of a writer and organiser, and he used them with great effect in the coming years. It was the teamwork, which lasted for forty-two years, of Josiah Spiers, the magnetic speaker, and Tom Bishop, the skilful and far-sighted administrator, which built the CSSM and Scripture Union into a national, and then an international, force.

The two men met in April 1868, and Bishop soon joined the committee Spiers had formed to organise the Islington meetings. On 30th May the name Children's Special Service Mission was officially adopted. It was a clumsy name but it described the work accurately. Also Parliament had recently passed the Special Services Act, which allowed Anglican churches to use services not in the prayer book for certain purposes. The Mission was taking advantage of the new law. In an age when denominational feelings were strong, such consideration for church rules was important. But the services had been interdenominational from the start. Spiers and his friends managed to gain the confidence and good will of Anglicans and nonconformists alike and soon 'children connected with about 20 different churches, chapels and Sunday Schools were attending.'

By the first annual meeting, on 3rd July 1868, an average of 300 children were coming to Spiers' weekly services, and 687 names were on the register. Great efforts were made to keep in touch with the children individually. As soon as a child attended for the first time, one of the leaders wrote him a letter. 'About 1200 letters have been written during the past year,' said the first Annual Report, 'nearly 400 in reply to the children's own letters.' And already the young mission was clear about its main objective: 'Many of the children have given decided evidence of conversion, and of others we are very hopeful.'

WIDER CONTACT

Until Josiah Spiers' holiday it remained a small, local, little-known society. But that first unplanned and informal service at Llandudno was repeated every day until he went home. Each morning the children came running up to him as soon as he appeared on the beach, insisting on some more stories. On the Sunday afternoon a more formal beach service was arranged, announced by the Town Crier. Spiers stood in a boat, which was filled with children, and some 300 or 400 listened from the shore.

The beach services were a major step forward for two reasons. First, Spiers had found a way of making contact with the wealthier sections of society, whose children avoided Sunday School and had special spiritual needs. Secondly, the beach services gave Spiers and the CSSM some useful publicity. The first year at Llandudno he made many friends among adults as well as children, and received a number of gifts for his work in London. Soon afterwards invitations began to arrive to conduct children's services in other parts of the country. As he had recently received a small legacy, sufficient to be able to manage without a salary, Spiers resigned his job: for the next forty years, until his death, he gave the whole of his time, without pay, to the CSSM.

2

A Prince of Speakers

No sooner had Josiah Spiers taken the decisive step of giving up his job than the children's services ran into a storm of controversy. In November Payson Hammond came back for further meetings at Islington and at the famous Charles Spurgeon's Metropolitan Tabernacle. As Tom Bishop recalled, with typical understatement, some years later:

> Mr Hammond's methods were in some ways open to criticism. Many things which he did were not thought wise by those workers who were nevertheless inspired by his example and teaching to undertake more definite work for the conversion of children than they had ever done before. The meetings at the Metropolitan Tabernacle indeed led to a somewhat excited correspondence in the newspapers, and a good many prejudices were raised against Children's Services, which hindered our work for many years afterwards.

In spite of these problems and criticism of 'sensationalism' and 'playing on the emotions of the children' which he faced himself from time to time, Spiers had a full programme. Most of each summer he spent at the seaside. In 1871, for example, he was on tour almost without a break from early June to the middle of October, with meetings in eleven different centres. Friends came to help whenever they could, but often he was on his own. The rest of the year he travelled all over the country, wherever he was invited. On Mondays he set off by train to some distant part of the country. Tom Bishop made all the arrangements, corresponding with local sponsors in the evenings after work. Each Saturday, if at all possible, Spiers returned to London. For several years he was still the leader of the 'Central Services' of the mission at Islington which not only helped children in the neighbourhood, but also served as a model to show others what could be done.

CHILDREN'S SPECIAL SERVICE MISSION.

SPECIAL SERVICES FOR CHILDREN AND YOUNG PEOPLE

WIIL BE HELD (D.V.) BY

JOSIAH SPIERS, Esq.

Superintendent of the Central Services of the Mission, St. Jude's, Mildmay Park, London,

IN

THE CASTLE HALL

TAUNTON,

ON

Sunday evening, 29th March,
Monday evening, 30th March,
Tuesday evening, 31st March,
Wednesday evening, 1st April,
Thursday evening, 2nd April, 1874.

To commence each evening **at Half-past Six** o'clock.

Young People of all classes will be welcomed, and Teachers and Parents are affectionately invited to come with their Children.

It is not desirable that little children under eight years of age should attend, unless accompanied by their parents.

Handbill advertising one of Josiah Spiers' missions.

VIBRATING WITH ENERGY

Contemporary accounts show that Spiers had a remarkable gift for speaking to children. He was shy and timid with adults, and often rather vague in conversation. But once he was on his feet, speaking to a group of children 'he took instant command, his whole figure vibrating with humour and energy'. 'He was childlike without being childish', one of his close colleagues remarked, 'a prince of speakers to children.' 'He had a most arresting style of speaking – with great gusto – and held the children's attention every minute of the meeting, stories, hymns, choruses following in quick succession, and new programmes and ideas every night.' He used no elaborate visual aids but told his stories with great dramatic effect, using some simple piece of equipment, a stick, a cushion or a doll, to illustrate a point. 'Mr Spiers' influence over the children is almost magical', a newspaper reported from Bristol in 1874, after he had taken three children's services a day there for a week, with a total attendance estimated at 10,000. The year before, the local newspaper at Derby commented on the good behaviour of the children during the services. Its reporter found it very surprising 'when it is considered that at the evening meetings there has never been fewer than 1,200 children present, many of them belonging to a morally neglected class of boys.'

The unusual character of the meetings no doubt helped to attract such large crowds and hold their attention. In spite of their piety and their respect for family life, the Victorians had little understanding of children, and less of how to bring them up in the Christian life. Children from wealthier homes were expected to go with their parents to church, dressed in their 'Sunday best', and sit quietly through the long adult services. In most such homes there would be family prayers, but again they would be formal and tedious, mostly very difficult for children to understand. Sunday Schools were quite widespread, but children from wealthier homes did not mix with the 'lower classes' by attending. There too, however, the atmosphere was strict and formal. Much of the time was spent learning the catechism or passages of the Bible by heart. Josiah Spiers' methods were a striking contrast. Even his message had a different emphasis. At both church and Sunday school, and in family prayers, the emphasis was frequently on the severity of God in punishing sin. 'I had been in contact with good people who were hard', wrote a woman who heard Spiers when she was a child. 'So often the text "Thou God seest me" had been told me that I dreaded God. The secret of Spiers' influence was his love for us. It was like a new aspect of Christianity for me.'

In a strictly segregated society it was remarkable that he was able to find a welcome among rich and poor alike. 'Mr Spiers has devoted much of his time during the past winter to the children of the very poorest class', reads the annual report for 1871. Yet he was equally able to make friends with the children from more wealthy homes whom he met on the beaches in the summer, or in the increasing number of 'drawing room meetings' arranged for them. As time went on he felt more and more called to work with these 'neglected children of the upper classes'. He used to say that there were missions to the poor, but none to the rich and was deeply concerned by what he called their 'paganism'. Even though his own background was a different one, he was accepted by such children and their parents 'largely through his extraordinary simplicity, naturalness and humility', to use the words of one who later joined the staff.

RELIGION IS A HAPPY THING

His message was plain and straightforward: the love of God shown in the Lord Jesus Christ, Christ's death for us on the cross; his resurrection from the dead; his presence at the meeting, waiting to forgive the sins and to fill the life of any child who would trust him. Although 'our little ones who are taken from us in helpless infancy, are "safe in the arms of Jesus"' he had no doubt that 'children are sinners and need a Saviour', and spoke strongly on the subject. But he did not dwell morbidly on sin. His great emphasis was on the love of Jesus, the sin of not loving him in return, and the forgiveness available because of his death on the cross for those who come to him. 'Jesus loves me this I know, for the Bible tells me so', 'There's a friend for little children' and 'I am so glad that Jesus loves me', with their bright and cheerful tunes, were some of the hymns he most often chose to teach the children. They show where his emphasis lay. Children enjoyed the services so much that some adults became suspicious. 'I am afraid', wrote Bishop 'a good many ministers have an idea that at the Children's Services we feed the children with nothing but *sweets*. We certainly do not give them the roast beef of theology, nor the sauce and pickles of eloquence; but we do give them a Christian child's natural food – the sincere milk of the word.' But at the same time 'we strive to make it felt that religion is a happy thing, and to associate it in the children's minds with all that is bright and joyful.'

The atmosphere of the services was bright and attractive, but they had a very serious purpose and managed to combine humour and cheerfulness with reverence and solemnity. And they avoided the unhealthy excitement and undue pressure which had worried many adults at Payson Hammond's meetings. The whole service was designed to convey biblical truth to the children, 'breaking up the Gospel into little pieces, suitable for the reception by the little ones, in the same manner as their parents would break up a crust of bread for them'. Bishop often used to quote Spurgeon: 'Our Lord said "Feed my lambs" not "Feed my giraffes". So do not put the spiritual bread on upper shelves; put the food within their reach. Be childlike in your language, but never be childish.' 'We try to make the teaching so direct, and so personal, that all shall see clearly that we aim at nothing less than their real conversion to God.'

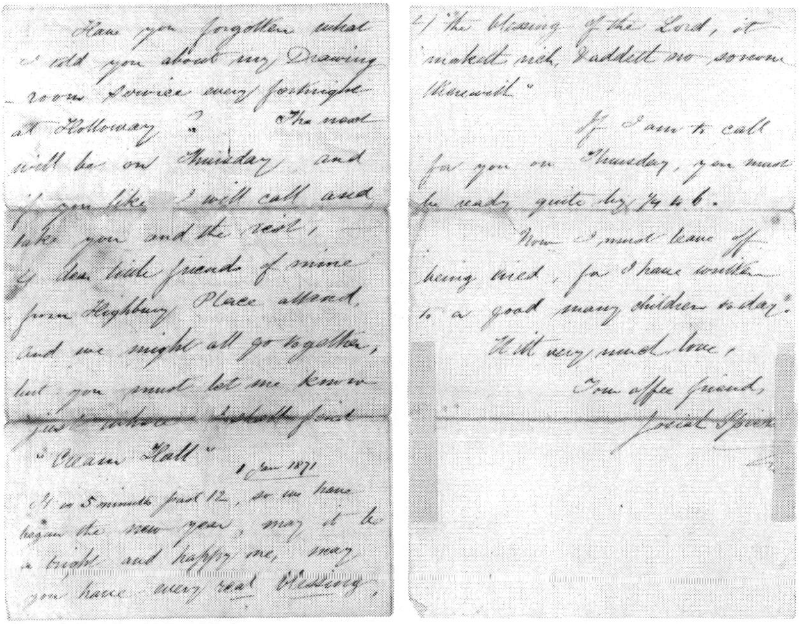

Part of one of Josiah Spiers' many letters to children.

INDIVIDUAL COUNSELLING

At the close of each service those children who wished 'to give themselves to the Saviour' were invited to stay for a brief meeting when teachers could talk with them in small groups, or one by one. 'We look on this as the most important feature of the services', wrote Bishop. The after-meetings aroused some suspicion until adults stayed to see what actually happened. 'I am thankful to say', wrote Spiers, 'that the suspicions almost always vanish when the objectors stay and take part. We believe in great stillness and order: where there is much noise or excitement we expect little real good will be done.'

Before they left, the teacher wrote down the name and address of each child, and a Christian friend in the area was asked to keep in touch with him or her. Spiers would write himself to those he had spoken to personally. He wrote hundreds of such letters each year, all by hand, knowing that 'children treasure up letters and read them over and over again'. Where possible follow-up classes were arranged. Each helper had no more than five children to look after, through prayer, personal conversation, letters and when possible through weekly meetings.

SPIERS' STRATEGY

Within a few years, Spiers had worked out his strategy. In a letter printed in 1876 he explains 'the *terms* upon which I am willing to hold services for the dear little ones:

1. It must be a "mission", not just one or two services. I never care to go anywhere for less than five days, and much prefer eight or ten, as we always see much more blessing when the mission can be extended beyond the week.
2. The series of meetings must be held in one building and commence at 7.0 p.m. each evening.
3. The meetings must be held in public and quite undenominational halls, unless it is utterly impossible.
4. The mission must be quite of an unsectarian character – that is, all the different denominations of the Church of Christ being urged to unite in getting the children together and leading them to the Saviour.

5. Each service will be followed by a time for counselling in small groups.
6. Let friends who arrange these missions have as many prayer meetings as possible beforehand.
7. No payment will be taken for services; only travelling expenses required.'

BASIC PRINCIPLES

Already he had discovered a number of principles which became permanent features of the CSSM, though they needed to be worked out more fully as it grew and developed. One was the place of teaching in effective evangelism. He avoided one-off meetings, with an instant appeal for decision. He preferred to spend several days, so that the children could understand what they were doing when they responded to Christ.

Secondly, right from the start the Mission kept clear of denominational controversy. In a day when the barriers between the churches were much higher than they are in most countries today, CSSM insisted in being genuinely interdenominational, uniting for a single purpose of 'leading the children to the Saviour'.

Thirdly, the pioneers of the CSSM insisted that there should be no clash with the regular institutions of Christianity. Their task was not to take the place of other agencies but to assist them. 'Recognising the supreme importance of the Christian home, the Christian ministry and the Sunday School, we desire not to supercede these agencies, but to *supplement* their work', one of the early annual reports explains.

Fourthly, they recognised the limitations of the new methods, however good. 'What is the real power in these Evangelistic Services? Not, as some imagine, the power of excitement, or the power of the speaker, but the power of the Holy Spirit in answer to *prayer*.'

GOING ON SATISFACTORILY

What effect did all this have in the long-term? Spiers ran hundreds of such missions. How much lasting influence in the lives of the children did they really exert? It is of course impossible to answer such questions precisely, but the indications are encouraging. Spiers' books *True Stories* (1890) and *More True Stories* (1907) are packed with examples of boys and girls who came to Christ after one of his meetings. There was the little girl of five who said to him 'in a very loud whisper' after one of the early beach services: 'Mr Spiers, I don't love Jesus but I *should* like to be one of His little lambs. Will you please pray for me?' 'I can tell you', Spiers adds, 'that this little girl, who is now of course a grown-up lady, has been greatly used in bringing poor sinners to Christ.' There were the five children at Rhyl, brought by their mother so that he could 'talk to them and pray with them'. 'The two eldest especially appeared to be in earnest about getting saved, the boy thirteen and the girl fourteen years of age; and no doubt they did that day receive Jesus into their hearts by faith. That boy is now a grown-up young man. The last time I heard of him he was preaching to the workers employed on his large farm in a distant land, while the sister has for years been labouring to bring the poor women and children of India to Christ. Oh, what numbers are now working as missionaries in India, China, Japan or Africa; as ministers of the gospel, open-air preachers, Sunday School teachers, deaconesses and local secretaries of the Scripture Union; whom I remember having received Jesus as their Saviour when they were boys and girls!' There was even an 'old man, over seventy who stayed to the after-meeting one night. After talking to him for some time, I asked him to kneel down and seek the Lord's pardon for all his sins. But he had great difficulty in bending those knees, so unused to prayer.'

The records of Spiers' early meetings at Islington provide some statistics on how effective was his follow-up system. When they professed conversion, children were asked to join the 'Christian Instruction Class'. In its first three years, 234 children were joined 'under the guardianship of about sixty teachers. From the reports received, it appears that 199 of these young people are going on satisfactorily; nine have been lost sight of; and only twenty-six are reported unsatisfactory in their conduct.' A similar note of encouragement was frequently sounded by Tom Bishop at the annual meetings. 'We are particularly thankful', he wrote in 1879, 'that so many lads and young men who were led to decisions for Christ at the Children's Services, have now become earnest workers, and some of them are holding Sunday Evening Services amongst the roughest and poorest children.' There is little doubt that many hundreds of individual boys and girls at the services in these early years found a personal faith in Christ that was to stay with them all their lives. At the same time 'many ministers had been led to take a deeper interest in children.' Indeed, the small group of men who had banded together a few years earlier to run some local children's services in London was beginning to have a national influence.

3

Expanding Influence

When the CSSM was started, Spiers and Bishop were young and unknown. Spiers was thirty at the time, Bishop only twenty-eight, and they were men without influence, doing routine jobs in business and the civil service. Yet within a few years, in John Pollock's words, 'the CSSM was becoming a national institution' and 'they were slowly changing an aspect of British religion'. How was it that their influence spread so far and so fast?

MEN OF VISION

One reason was that they had a group of men around them who shared their vision. The forty or fifty 'members of the Mission' and particularly the committee were convinced that the work of CSSM was urgent and important. Most of them were actively involved in it in their spare time. Two, Samuel and James Tyler, ran the South London 'Central Services' at Surrey Chapel. Another, Henry Hankinson, helped Spiers at Islington. Many of them gave at least part of their holidays to help with the rapidly growing work at the seaside. In later years, others who could afford it, like William Shrimpton, would travel abroad at their own expense to share the message. Over the years many gave up business careers to give their whole time to CSSM, several of them without a salary.

Moreover they threw themselves into this task with immense enthusiasm and dedication. They had the vigour and determination of young men, and Spiers at least was an outstandingly able children's speaker. Perhaps their strongest asset, however, was their immense sense of conviction. They were certain that the time was ripe to develop children's services all over the country, and that the need was urgent. This conviction is demonstrated in the words of Tom Bishop:

> They are the missing link in our Sunday School system. So often the Sunday School class leads the child to a certain point, and no further. They come regularly to Sunday School, but they do not come to Christ. At thirteen or fourteen they go to work, and fancy

themselves too big for Sunday School – and so we lose them. It seems as if we have come to a time when the results of past years of labour have to be gathered in. The work in these Children's Services is a *reaping* work. The Sunday School has sown the seed, and sown it well. We are largely reaping the fruits of other men's labours.

MULTIPLYING THE WORKERS

Another reason for their expanding influence was that they did not try to do everything themselves. At the beginning, of course, there were no full-time staff. The central services in London, and those that started up in other parts of the country, were run entirely by voluntary helpers who found time for it in their busy lives. Spiers reckoned that it was an important part of his work to find and train others, and spoke at 'many meetings for teachers and workers'. Almost every year the annual report pleads for 'more labourers, the great need of the Mission. We especially want efficient men to commence and carry on new services'.

In 1873 Bishop wrote to a number of friends in London inviting them to join the 'Children's Evangelistic Band'. Members would be expected to give 'two or three evenings in a certain week each month' to take a series of children's services. So many were willing to help that he formed the sixty-eight volunteers into seven 'divisions' in different parts of the city, each with a 'leader, three or four others of some age and experience in the work, and four or five younger men'. The lists still survive, in Bishop's neat handwriting. Among the names is that of Gibbard Hughes, who at the age of eleven, had been one of those present at Josiah Spiers' first meeting in his father's house in Islington, six years before. He was later to run a large and effective Bible Class in North London for many years. Regular meetings for the band were arranged for prayer and training. With all this new help in London, Spiers was able to turn his attention to other parts of the country.

The emphasis on finding and training others brought impressive results. 'Ten years ago, Sunday evening and week evening services for children were hardly known', wrote Bishop in the 1877 report. Yet 'when our list was last revised there were 100 Sunday evening and 125 week evening services carried on regularly' in London alone. There were another ninety-four regular meetings in Liverpool, 'with an average attendance of 17,500 children and a staff of 740 teachers', and others in many other towns.

OVER FIVE MILLION LEAFLETS

Print was the main medium of communication in the late nineteenth century. The invention of steam driven printing presses and the spread of education had opened people up to the printed page to an entirely new degree. So CSSM made good use of print to spread its ideas. Tom Bishop wrote frequent letters to the Christian press explaining the work of the Mission and answering its critics, and produced a series of pamphlets encouraging people to run children's services and showing them how to do it.[1]

Much of the advice has a surprisingly modern ring. 'The hymns should be bright and cheerful, and set to lively tunes. Those should be chosen which contain the clearest elements of Gospel truth. The prayers should be short and simple, and in words the children can join in and make their own. *Silent* prayer is most important.' In leading the service 'it is a great mistake to talk in a louder voice than is necessary, or in an artificial voice. *Talk* to the children rather than preach to them.' 'Be careful', writes Samuel Tyler, 'not to set up for children the standard of *adult* piety.'

At the same time they were producing leaflets for the children themselves. The literature side of the work grew rapidly. In 1877 Bishop could look back on eight years of publishing and report on 'the large number of publications which the Mission has been instrumental in distributing.'[2]

By 1879 850,000 pieces of literature were being circulated in English each year, and a total of over 5 million had gone out in ten years. It was a formidable achievement for a group of men with no publishing experience, and no staff except a clerk who came to Bishop's home in the evenings.

[1] Bishop's titles included, *A Plea for Children's Services* (1870), *Practical Hints for the Conduct of Children's Services* (1873) and *A Fold for the Lambs* (1873) on follow-up. Spiers joined in with *The Value of a Child's Soul* (1873) and Samuel Tyler with *Hindrances to the Growth of Christian Life in the Young* (1873). By 1877 220,000 of these pamphlets for Christian workers had been distributed, and Bishop could comment: 'Its wide circulation is gradually bearing fruit, and leading Christian people to take a deeper interest in the conversion of the young.'

[2] He listed 2,200,000 hymn sheets, 280,000 children's booklets, 750,000 children's picture leaflets, 49,000 *Walking in the Light,* to start children reading the Bible, and 90,000 tracts for use at Conversational Meetings, as well as 220,000 pamphlets for Christian workers.

FROM LENINGRAD TO AUCKLAND

It was mainly literature which extended the Mission's influence abroad. The idea of special children's services had already been taken to other countries in a limited way. For example, some visitors from St Petersburg (now Leningrad) heard Spiers and Bishop on the beach in 1870, and started children's services there on their return. Thomas Kitt, who had worked with Spiers at Islington, started them in Auckland, New Zealand in 1873; and W M Roger wrote from Ontario, Canada in 1875, saying that he was doing his best to spread the ideas that he had learned from Spiers on a visit to England the year before.

In August 1875 Bishop, with Samuel Tyler, went to Germany for his summer holiday to tell people about the children's services in England and to 'stir up others to undertake a work similar to that which has been so much blessed in this country.' First they spent a weekend in Amsterdam, where a regular Sunday evening children's service was commenced. For three weeks they travelled up the Rhine, speaking to teachers' meetings and Sunday Schools, including one meeting for 1,000 children at Heilbronn, and giving away large numbers of tracts. 'My greatest difficulty was to carry about from place to place the books and papers I needed. As Heidelberg is a Protestant town with six clergymen who are all decided rationalists, I gave away nearly all my tracts there.' After a brief visit to Basel, where he had 'a meeting in the Vereinshaus of 800 children and another of 200 teachers', Bishop returned home. But he was back in Germany the following summer, when he also visited Paris and found a Mr Heriot who had thirty-five weekly children's services, attended during the winter by 2,500 children per week. Bishop realised that in other countries 'the circumstances are widely different, and it is not easy for a stranger to tell them what they should do.' But he saw the need for Christian literature for children, which was 'almost unknown abroad' at that time. When he got back to England he spoke to the Committee about it. Spiers wrote to a number of friends, asking if they would contribute to a special 'Continental Fund', and a substantial sum was quickly gathered. The Earl of Shaftesbury and Frances Ridley Havergal, the hymn writer, were among the early contributors.

In 1877 Bishop spent six weeks on the Continent to arrange for translation and distribution. He personally handed the first German children's leaflets to 'Christian workers who would distribute them wisely and prayerfully'. A year later, leaflets had been printed in Dutch, French, German, Italian, Portuguese, Swedish and Spanish. By 1879 nearly 600,000 leaflets had been printed, translations into

Czech, Hungarian, and Slovenian were in preparation, and 'Mr Hudson Taylor has taken our tracts to China with him, in the hope of getting them translated into Chinese.'

SOUND ADMINISTRATION

As the literature work expanded, the Mission needed better administration. It could not be run any longer from Bishop's home, supervised entirely by him in the evenings after he returned from work. In November 1878 a small office was opened in London, and Henry Hankinson was appointed to run it.

Henry Hankinson had worked closely with Spiers at the Children's services at Islington, and had been a member of the committee almost from the beginning. He had considerable business experience, and spoke several languages fluently, a most useful gift when the overseas work was growing so strongly. He was called Secretary and Bishop Honorary Secretary. Together they ran the administration for the next forty-two years. Although they both did a certain amount of speaking, and a great deal of writing, the firm administrative base which they provided was their greatest contribution to the Mission. Without it, as the CSSM and SU were to see so clearly in other parts of the world in later years, Spiers' outstanding speaking ability and the time and effort put in by others would have been very much less effective. Together Bishop and Hankinson set standards of wise organisation, competent publishing, efficient correspondence and sound finance which were of immense value.

FINANCIAL CRISIS

Although the workers were all voluntary, and local groups organising meetings covered their own costs, the Mission still needed money. Funds had to be found for the printing of hymn sheets and handbills, for the children's leaflets, many of which were given away free, and for secretarial expenses. To start with the committee paid most of the costs out of their own pockets. Soon gifts came from other friends as well, and they tried to sell sufficient hymn sheets and tracts to cover the cost of those that were given away.

The big question was whether to make any appeal for money. Opinion was divided on the subject in Christian circles in England at the time. Some men like William Booth, of the Salvation Army, and in America the famous evangelist D L Moody, believed it to be right to make strong appeals for the funds they needed for their work. Others,

19

The Committee met at 114 Church Road, Saturday May 1st 1869
at 8 o'clock P.M.
Present Mr Spiers, in the Chair, Messrs. Hughes, Bishop & Tweltaff.
The Meeting was opened with prayer.
The Minutes of the last Meeting were read and confirmed.
The Secretary reported the state of the funds as follows:—

Contributions from April 11th to 27th — 1.16.4.	Expenditure from April 17th to 27th — £2.8.6p.
	Balance — ~~3.12.5½~~
Leaving a balance due to the Sec. of — ~~3.4.7½~~	Books — 1.3.6
	Hymns — 0.5.0
£2.0.8p	~~5.0.11½~~
	£3.17.0p

An enquiry was entered into as to the amount of Debts unpaid which with the balance make a total of about ten pounds. The necessity of active measures to obtain a larger amount of Subscriptions was seen to be imperative, especially as the Summer season is approaching, when Sea side Services for Children will be of much importance for the advancement of the work.
Mr Bishop stated that Dr Brock & Dr Edmonds had declined the Vice Presidency of the Mission.
Mr Bishop also informed the Meeting that the Lambeth Auxillary of the Sunday School Mission had

Extract from the first CSSM minute book (1869).

like Hudson Taylor who had just started the China Inland Mission (now the Overseas Missionary Fellowship), took a contrary view. 'God's work done in God's way will never lack God's supplies', he said, and made it a principle that the CIM would never ask for money, except in prayer to God.

On 1st April 1871 the CSSM committee reached a unanimous decision:

> Since the Lord has been graciously pleased during the last year to supply the wants of the Mission without our having made any appeal for funds... and has repeatedly sent funds in a remarkable manner in answer to special prayer, the Committee feel guided to come to the following Resolution: That as a general rule the Committee will not ask any person for subscriptions for carrying on the ordinary work of the Mission.

In future they would not send reminders to their supporters unless they asked for them. There would be no collections at the Islington services, though a box for gifts would be available. But 'we will make known to friends of our work any special new effort for which funds may be required'. As John Pollock comments, 'It was a decision to proceed on a qualified faith basis.'

Exactly five years later they changed their minds. The work was growing fast. In 1873 Spiers held 'a series of large services in important towns' including a mission at Derby attended by over 2,000 children. 'These of course involve considerable expenditure in hymn sheets and children's books.' Many people from all over the country were asking for help as well. The same year they published four new pamphlets for Christian workers and for a few months a full-time office worker was employed. But income did not grow quickly enough, and by June 1874 the Mission was in debt. The treasurer out of his own pocket lent the cash to help them through but a year later the debt was four times as high, equivalent to half the annual gift income. Not surprisingly, the treasurer wanted to resign. Something was going seriously wrong.

During the next nine months strict economies were made, stocks of literature were drastically reduced, and the office worker made redundant. 'By April (1876) the Mission was free from debt, and the Committee held a special meeting, to which other leading workers in the Mission were invited, for prayer and conference as to our future course of action.' Spiers insisted that it had been a mistake to get into debt in the first place. After a lengthy discussion they unanimously agreed not to incur debt in future, 'but to spend only what had been contributed beforehand, and at the same time to inform our friends more frequently of the objects of the Mission for which funds might be needed.'

It was on these two principles, of never spending money until it had been received, and of sharing the needs of the work discreetly with its friends that the steady growth of the CSSM, and its extension into other areas, was grounded.

4

A New Dimension

Three years later CSSM took a step which led to the development of a whole new dimension to its work. It all started with Annie Marston, a young woman from Keswick, in the north of England, where the famous convention had started a few years before. Annie wanted to encourage the girls in her Sunday School class to read the Bible, but found that they did not know where to begin. If they did try to start they soon got stuck in some difficult part of the Old Testament and gave up. So she chose passages for them to read each day, wrote lists of them every week, and gave them to the children each Sunday. The following Sunday they discussed what they had been reading, and Annie tried to answer their questions about difficult passages.

A CIVIL SERVANT'S RESPONSE

The children were enthusiastic. 'Very soon they became so eager', she recalled, 'and their questions were so many and sometimes so important, that it was impossible to get through in the time.' When some of the children moved to a higher class, they wanted to continue their Bible reading. At this stage Annie wrote to the CSSM 'telling them of the delight of these children in their daily reading, and asking if the Mission could not take up the work of printing and circulating lists of daily Bible portions for children.' It was a new idea however in those days that children would want to read the Bible except in school or with their parents. Tom Bishop was not attracted by the idea. 'It is not good for children to be asked to make promises they will not keep', he wrote. 'It would be impossible to exercise supervision over the members... If it failed it would have been better not to have tried it; if it succeeded it would involve great expense for the CSSM and additional workers.'

During the next few months Annie, in her own words, 'fired another shot at the CSSM' from time to time. Eventually her patience was rewarded. In December 1878 Bishop was off work for a few days with a sore throat and had more time to think. The office in London had just been opened, so it was possible to consider a fresh advance. He decided to put the idea to the committee. To his surprise, they liked it, and agreed to start as soon as possible. They called the new organisation the Children's Scripture Union, and the first membership card appeared on 1st April 1879.

THE SCRIPTURE UNION SYSTEM

As the committee worked out the details, they made several decisions that set a stamp on the Scripture Union Bible reading system for years to come. They agreed 'to include all such parts of the Bible as are suitable for children' and to read through a book of the Bible consecutively. Old Testament and New Testament books would be taken alternatively, and passages were to be 12–15 verses in length.

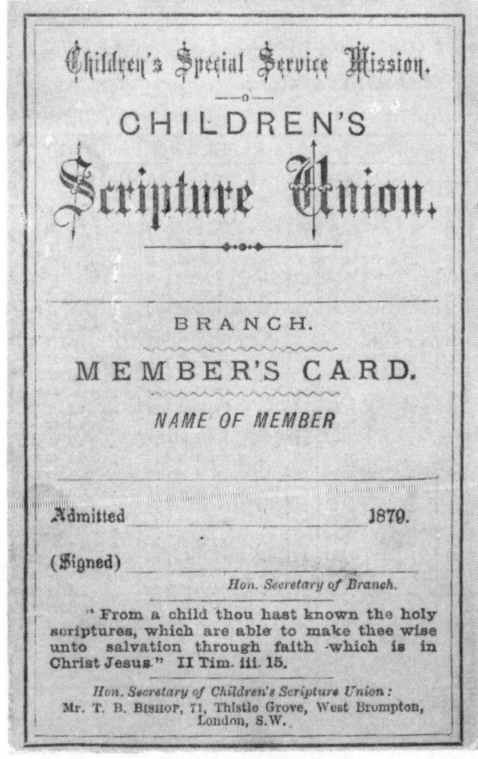

Children's Special Service Mission.

CHILDREN'S

Scripture Union.

BRANCH.

MEMBER'S CARD.

NAME OF MEMBER

Admitted 1879.

(Signed)

Hon. Secretary of Branch.

"From a child thou hast known the holy scriptures, which are able to make thee wise unto salvation through faith which is in Christ Jesus." II Tim. iii. 15.

Hon. Secretary of Children's Scripture Union: Mr. T. B. Bishop, 71, Thistle Grove, West Brompton, London, S.W.

The first SU card, 1879.

Bishop had at first suggested three series of readings for different ages of children, but the committee decided that everyone should read the same passages, though separate cards were printed headed 'Scripture Union for Young People' for older teenagers. The card stressed 'the importance of reading the Bible thoughtfully and with prayer', and recommended choosing a verse or a few words from each day's portion to think about during the day. Even the shape of the card, with its triple fold and vertical columns of readings, and, across the top, the 'prayer before reading', 'Open Thou mine eyes...' (from Psalm 119) are still used in many countries over a hundred years later.

Other aspects were different. 'If you cannot, or do not, keep up the reading of the daily portions, this Card must be returned', says the 1879 card. The condition was left off the following year, but members were still expected to take the commitment seriously. 'I missed reading my passage on Thursday morning', wrote a Quaker boy, 'but I beg thee to allow me to keep my card, as I want to try again to keep it up. This is the first time I have missed and I mean it to be the last.' Subscriptions of one penny a card were invited 'to cover the cost of postage and printing', but cards were sent free to those who could not afford 'even this small sum'. Cards were sent out in packets of six or more through branch secretaries, who were strongly encouraged to arrange regular meetings for their members. Reports soon came in of branch meetings all over the country, some of them with over 100 members.

WORLDWIDE INTEREST

The response to the scheme was remarkable. Six thousand cards had been issued by 1st April, and 30,000 by June. In 1880, 54,000 cards were distributed and 500 branch secretaries had been enrolled. An eleven-year-old Yorkshire girl had a branch with ninety-one members, and branches were formed in day schools, in Sunday Schools, and wherever children could be contacted. For example, one enterprising friend started a branch for the children employed in the London theatres, a poor and exploited class in those days. Within a year there were 147 members out of 'about 300 girls and a few boys' on the London stage. Regular meetings were held, with a tea provided. A small lending library was set up for them, and plans were discussed for a reading room in Soho, a summer outing to the country, and 'perhaps a convalescent home at the seaside for those who had been ill'.

The scheme quickly spread to other countries as well. During 1879 the lists of readings were published in Christian magazines in Germany, Sweden and Spain. The next year the cards were printed in German, French, Spanish, Italian, Swedish and Czech, and branches were formed in Australia, Canada and India. Five years later cards were being published in nineteen languages including Arabic, Chinese, Japanese, Bengali, Hindi, and Tamil, and total membership was reckoned at 40,000 overseas, with a further 160,000 in Britain. By the time the Scripture Union was ten years old worldwide circulation had reached 470,000 in twenty-eight languages, and encouraging reports were coming in from many countries.

At first the lists of readings were published without any attempt to explain them. So the regular weekly or monthly branch meetings to discuss the passages were all the more important. Only six months after the Scripture Union began, however, Bishop launched another big project, a regular monthly magazine for children and young people. It was called *Our Own Magazine,* and included articles each month illustrating or explaining the current readings. It was an immediate success. After a year it had reached a regular circulation of 20,000, and after five years 55,000. At one penny per copy it paid its way. The stories and illustrations appear quaint and old-fashioned today, but were modern and contemporary in their day. Bishop did not approve of fiction, and insisted that all the stories should be true ones, though the names were usually changed. Every issue had at least one story or article which explained how a child could receive Jesus as Saviour. 'It is generally acknowledged', the 1880 annual report could claim, 'that the paper has filled a vacant place in children's literature.'

THE FIRST NOTES

It was in 1886 that the first Scripture Union notes appeared. The initiative came from a twenty-two-year-old medical student at Cambridge, Charles Hartford-Battersby. While helping at a beach mission the previous summer, he had met a number of Christian boys from boarding schools. There were no SU meetings in schools in those days and he wanted to do something to help them. He wrote to Tom Bishop suggesting a monthly magazine, with notes on the SU reading each day and other features. This time Bishop and his committee were quick off the mark. Four months later the first issue of *Our Boys' Magazine* appeared, edited by a group of five Cambridge students, checked by Bishop, and published by the CSSM. Six months later

The first issue of 'Our Own Magazine', 1879.

daily notes also appeared in *Our Own Magazine*, written by Henry Hankinson at his home, late at night or early in the morning.

TWOFOLD GROWTH

It is an interesting fact that the two ideas that started off the whole SU Bible reading ministry both came from two young people, Annie Marston and Charles Hartford-Battersby. It was a decisive turning-point in the history of the Mission. It gave a new dimension to the ministry among children by offering valuable help to thousands who were not in touch with any of the CSSM's existing activities. But it was soon to extend the Mission's influence into the adult world as well, as more and more people of all ages started to read the daily portions. It soon became clear, moreover, that the two aspects of the work, evangelism and Bible reading, fitted together perfectly. The history of the movement over the next hundred years illustrates the way that each side of the work complemented and assisted the other.

The rapid growth of SU membership in its early years was to a great extent because it was part of the CSSM, which was already well-known and widely respected. Spiers' travelling and speaking, and Bishop's letters and leaflets had built up a wide circle of friends. Many of them became branch secretaries. The practice of daily Bible reading was seen as the best possible follow-up for evangelism. So wherever Spiers and his colleagues went they recruited new members. When SU decided to send the cards abroad, the friends Spiers had made through his missions quickly raised the money.

Equally, the launching of the SU Bible reading system helped the existing children's work. It was an ideal way of nurturing children who had responded to Christ and it helped them to make the Mission and its work much more widely known. The seaside services felt the benefit immediately. 'In 1878 only five places had been visited by eight workers'. In 1879, the year SU was started, 'twice as many seaside towns were visited and twice as many workers engaged', though no doubt this increase was also because 'special prayer meetings for more workers were held in May and June'. Seven years later no less than sixty beach missions were held. There had been a twelvefold increase in ten years.

The launch of Scripture Union was important, too, in carrying the influence of the CSSM around the world. The cards and later the notes soon circulated in an increasing number of countries and languages. It was the Scripture Union, more than any other aspect of its work, which turned the CSSM into a worldwide movement.

5

Circling the Earth

In the 1880s, SU in England was still mainly for children. It was not until 1885, when founder members were starting to read the Bible through a second time, that a few cards were printed for adults. But in Japan Scripture Union had already been launched as an adult movement two years earlier. It all happened through the initiative of an American schoolgirl.

Adelaide Whitney had been introduced to SU by another schoolgirl at the age of thirteen, when she was visiting England. A few months later she returned to Tokyo, where she lived with her brother, W N Whitney, a doctor and a translator at the American Legation. She tried to persuade some of her foreign friends to join but had no success. One day she told an elderly Japanese Christian, Mr Sen Tsuda, about her discouragement. 'Why don't you ask *us* to join?' he replied. 'The oldest Japanese Christian is only a few years old in the faith. The short readings will be just right for us.' With Dr Whitney's active help they decided to launch *Seisho no Tomo* (Friends of the Bible) on 10th November 1883 at a crowded meeting at the Meiji Knaido to commemorate the 400th anniversary of the birth of Martin Luther. 'After three addresses had been delivered, Mr Tsuda rose and explained to the assembled people the plan of the Union, and told them that a man was stationed at the door to distribute application forms.... For the week following the signed applications were constantly coming to us.' One of those who joined was an old lady of eighty, who had been a Christian for five years, 'but was sorry she had not begun earlier.' Another was sent by a man who said that until he attended the meeting 'he was entirely ignorant of the nature of Protestant Christianity', but was 'much moved in my inmost heart' at the meeting.

ORGANISING SECRETARY AT FIFTEEN

Still only fifteen years old, Adelaide Whitney acted as national secretary. As the whole Bible was not yet translated into Japanese, she chose a special selection of New Testament readings. In the first month 304 members joined, and 2,000 attended a meeting for 'members and friends' the following April. Within five years there were 12,300 members, with 314 branch secretaries. A monthly magazine was published, eleven pages in Japanese and one in English, with a circulation of 2,000, and forty different children's leaflets. In 1888 a travelling secretary, Mr Iwase, was appointed 'to preach the gospel and visit the various branches', the first staff worker outside England. Two years later 'an evangelist with leaflets and a soup cart' was working in the Tokyo slums, in connection with the Akasaka Memorial Hospital. Adelaide Whitney continued as secretary until her death, in 1896, at the age of twenty-eight. *Seisho no Tomo* continued to grow, a second travelling secretary and a children's evangelist were appointed a few years later, and in 1908 they even started regular beach services: 'Mr Miyahara came to play the cornet and lead the singing', and up to 150 children were present.

EARLY DAYS IN AUSTRALIA

Meanwhile SU had made a good start in Australia. In 1879, within a few months of the first card being printed, the Rev H B Macartney, of Caulfield, near Melbourne, wrote asking for 'electrotypes' so that he could print a local edition. A magazine he had started called *The Missionary* promoted the idea, and he appointed local secretaries to handle distribution. For Victoria itself he chose one of his own church members, Mrs J W Veal, who was to be the energetic honorary secretary for the whole state for the next twenty-nine years. In 1880 only 737 cards were distributed, but a year later 1221 members had joined in New South Wales alone, and there were others in Victoria, Queensland, Tasmania and New Zealand. In 1884 William Shrimpton, a member of the committee in London, visited Australia and New Zealand, and spoke at a large number of meetings. In New South Wales alone membership rose from 2,000 to 7,000 within a year. He left behind lengthy instructions for branch secretaries, which combined precise administrative details with fervent spiritual exhortation. Two years later Henry Hankinson, sent from London on a visit to recover his health, found 8,000 members in 150 branches in Victoria, and an active committee and 10,000 members in New South Wales.

During the next few years SU in Australia continued to grow. The first beach services were arranged in 1888 at Manly near Sydney, and in 1889 at Brighton, Victoria. But in the 1890's, partly as a reflection of the economic problems of the country, the impetus faded. In New

South Wales membership peaked at 22,500 in 1892 and was down to 14,000 by 1900. The local committee had never been strong on organisation. As they grew older they failed to recruit a single new member, and their affairs became hopelessly muddled. Money that should have been sent to London to pay for supplies was used for other purposes, and as the years went by this unnecessary debt steadily increased. In Victoria, by contrast, membership continued to grow until 1897, when it reached 20,000, beach services were carried on for a time, and bills were paid promptly. But here too they failed to recruit younger helpers. When Macartney left the country in 1898, Mrs Veal became the dominant force. As she grew older, she became increasingly reluctant to delegate and kept SU firmly to her own Church of England circle. So membership steadily declined.

SIX INDIAN LANGUAGES

Meanwhile Scripture Union was also getting going in India. Three children who joined after a beach service at Eastbourne, in England, wrote to tell their father, Robert Williamson, a merchant in Calcutta. He arranged with Tom Bishop to print the card in Bengali, and there were sixty members in 1881. By 1884 F W Brownrigg of the Indian Civil Service, a former beach mission worker from England, arranged for the cards to be printed in Hindi and Urdu. They were also printed in Oriya, Marathi and Tamil, and 'a number of members copy them out in manuscript in Telegu'. Two other former beach mission workers, A N C Storrs and L G Scott Price, now CMS missionaries, helped to start the Tinnevelly Children's Mission in South India. Originally part of CSSM, it later became independent. By 1893 it had a full-time Tamil evangelist, called Luke John, SU branches in sixty-nine villages, and a monthly magazine containing articles on the current SU readings.

REPORTS FROM NEAR AND FAR

When Bishop addressed the SU's Tenth Anniversary meeting in 1889, quoting Shakespeare he could describe the Scripture Union as, 'Truly! A girdle round the earth.' With nearly half a million members reading in twenty-eight languages, it was beginning to have a world-wide influence. In France there were eighty branches with 13,000 members. A young girl writes from Doubs: 'I am a member of the *Union Biblique d'Enfants,* and thanks be to God for it, for it is since I have been that I have found my salvation.' In Germany Baron von

A children's picture leaflet in Bengali (1884). By 1900 over eighteen million of these leaflets had been printed in fifty languages. Unfortunately, no-one saw the need to choose pictures to suit the culture of the readers.

Gemmingen published 10,000 cards and 'a monthly paper *Das Jugend Oelblatt* ('The Olive Leaf for the Young') containing articles and questions on the Scripture Union portions.' Holland had 7,000 members in eighty-five branches. A pastor from Belgium wrote about a little girl of fourteen at Jumet who used to go down to the coal pit at 5.00 am and returned between 9.00 and 10.00 at night, too tired to eat the poor supper left for her, but never started in the morning without reading her portion. In Europe cards were also printed in Italian, Spanish, Portuguese, Swedish, Norwegian, Czech, Hungarian, Finnish and Danish. In Denmark there were 3,000 members and each received a monthly letter.

A leaflet printed the same year shows how far the SU readings had spread. Several reports from Palestine and Syria showed that the Arabic cards and 'Children's Picture Leaflets' were widely used. From Bethlehem a German missionary wrote that the leaflets had 'often been the means that the word of God entered, when it would have been impossible to have got through in any other way.' In Madagascar, 8,000 cards were printed in Malagasy and the portions were read each day in 700 schools. A correspondent reported that 'the gradual growth of our school children in Scripture knowledge is most marked and pleasing', and that the work would be 'very much stimulated' by a gift from a branch in England that would make it possible for them to sell 1,000 Bibles to the children at half-price. From Ode Ondo in Nigeria there was a report of sixty members 'reading their Yoruba translations regularly with the help of English cards and holding monthly meetings, one for adults and one for children'. From Jamaica: 'Five new branches have been started with about 60 or 80 members each – the Scripture Union is fast outgrowing my management.' In South Africa, where William Shrimpton had made another effective tour a few years earlier, 'Mrs Barclay of Cape Town has kindly undertaken to be general secretary in Cape Colony, and is arranging for meetings of the Cape Town local secretaries.' Other brief reports were included from places as diverse as Colombo, Rangoon, Penang, Toronto, Christchurch and Wellington in New Zealand, Shanghai, Monte Video, Honolulu ('the cards sent this year were lost in the post') and the remote Pitcairn Islands in the South Pacific ('The members on the island number 26. On Sunday all the children come to my house, a cottage surrounded with ripe orange trees which are now loaded with fruit').

Sadly there was only passing reference to the United States, although the report in 1882 had stated that 'the Rev W F Crafts of the Church of Christian Endeavour, Brooklyn, New York, had kindly consented to act as general secretary for the Scripture Union...Special cards had been printed for the United States under the name of "The Boys and Girls Department of the Christian Alliance for Bible Reading and Memorizing: Auxiliary to the Children's Scripture Union", with General S L Brown as the treasurer.' Possibly there was no mention of this arrangement in 1889 or later because Crafts had hijacked the idea. In 1888 he published his own Bible reading system 'Reading the Bible with Relish.' It contained daily portions covering the whole Bible consecutively in a year, questions for daily meditation copied direct from SU and other material, even including a blank marriage certificate! The first attempt to introduce SU into the USA had evidently failed.

Some SU cards from the 80s and 90s.

6

Widening Strategy

Back in Britain CSSM's influence grew rapidly in the 1880s. We have already noticed the remarkable upsurge in the number of seaside services. Missions in other parts of the country increased almost as sharply, from thirty-eight in 1879 to 110 ten years later. SU membership, and the number of regular meetings for its members, also went up year by year. In 1887 Bishop could report that, 'we are glad to know that of the 2700 local SU secretaries, a goodly number arrange a regular weekly, fortnightly, or monthly meeting for their members.' The same year the chairman of the committee, Henry Hutchinson, resigned from business to become Travelling Secretary. By 1889, the mission had four paid staff workers, three full-time honorary 'agents', and four clerks in the office.

STUDENTS ON THE BEACHES

A key development in the early 1880s was the strong link that CSSM forged with the universities. At Cambridge a group of students had recently formed the Inter Collegiate Christian Union (CICCU), out of which the International Fellowship of Evangelical Students (IFES) was later to develop, and D L Moody had recently held a highly effective mission. One of the founders of the CICCU, W F T Hamilton, helped Spiers at some of the seaside services one summer. He was so impressed that he asked one of Spiers' colleagues, Edwin Arrowsmith, to come to Cambridge to recruit helpers for beach missions.

Edwin Arrowsmith, now aged 31, had been a foundation member of the Children's Evangelistic Band, when he was in partnership with his father in a parquet flooring business in fashionable Bond Street. He proved to be a speaker and leader of exceptional ability, and his name ranks next to Spiers and Bishop among the CSSM pioneers. As soon as he received Hamilton's invitation, he saw the immense possibilities of the universities as a source of manpower for the seaside work. A few came in 1881 and, for his 1882 mission at Scarborough, Arrowsmith had a full team of university students. From that time on it became a regular pattern of Christian Union life at Cambridge for parties of students to spend a few weeks each summer helping at the seaside services.

The link was to be extremely beneficial and strategic. For one thing it made it possible to reach the older teenagers, most of whom had ignored Spiers' children's meetings. Arrowsmith had a way of speaking which got through to people of all ages. Writing to his mother in 1878 from Llandudno he said,

> It has been really wonderful to see the attention of the crowds. I have never had the smallest interruption and young men who came to scoff have often remained to pray. It has been most instructive to see the young men and girls come round directly it became dark, and remain riveted to the spot, often for a couple of hours, and receive the little books I gave away. Numbers came to hear who would never think of going to a place of worship...you can see it by the expression on their faces when you are showing the simplicity of God's plan of salvation. On two or three occasions there were between 500 and 600 children present, and over 1,500 adults.

When he had a team of students with him, there was even more interest, especially if some of them were members of one of the university sports teams. A rowing 'blue', in particular, had the drawing-power of a pop-star a century later. 'Mr Arrowsmith was a clever fisher of men', wrote Cecil Tyndale-Biscoe, the cox of the Cambridge boat, later to become a well-known missionary in Kashmir. 'He made me see that as a Cambridge blue I could be of great help in attracting public school boys to his services on the beach. I made him promise that he would not ask me to preach; anything in the athletic line but no preaching.'

With a strong team to help him (the young men and women housed in separate buildings and only allowed to meet at beach services), Arrowsmith organised the mission with thoroughness and imagination. Spiers had held services on the beach, quite informally. Arrowsmith set out to 'reach every visitor in the place, old and young, and to bring them to face their condition before God'. 'Boys are hard to catch', he used to say. 'You have to bait your hook.' The building of an impressive sand pulpit, lantern processions, boating, cricket matches, tract distribution, everything was organised in detail, with a single object in view. He set a pattern for beach missions which, in broad outline, still continues in many places 100 years later.

All this made the Mission, and its ideas, more widely known. From the first the seaside services had been a shop window through which people who knew nothing about the CSSM could catch a glimpse of what was going on, unobserved, in churches and public halls all over the country all through the year. The presence of a strong group of university students as helpers at the mission, and the improvement in the programme that could be made with a larger team, strengthened the impression that was made.

A TRAINING GROUND FOR CHRISTIAN WORKERS

The link with the CSSM also benefitted the work at universities. Describing a slightly later period of evangelical life at Cambridge, Oliver Barclay writes:

> 'The rise of the CSSM and Scripture Union was an important factor. It was not only the encouragement of personal daily Bible study that helped, but the involvement with holiday seaside missions and camps. These were an enormous encouragement and many young converts were taken off immediately to beach missions with a Cambridge team and there pushed into public witness for the first time. A sense of spiritual responsibility for the boys who had been in your tent in the summer camp was a school of pastoral and evangelistic training for which many lived to be grateful, and it had in its turn an effect on evangelism in the University.... Over the years the CICCU has owed an enormous debt to this work (and vice versa).'

There were dangers however:

> 'Sometimes it has been over-influenced by the thrill of children's evangelism towards neglecting depth and critical thought.' (*Whatever happened to the Jesus Lane Lot?* IVP, p.49)

It was Arrowsmith, in John Pollock's words, 'who ensured that the CSSM should go down in history not only as a nursery of the Church, winning the children, but as a training ground of Christian workers.' In his old age he used to joke about the 'bishops I have put on the bench' – those who had worked with him as young men at the seaside. He was a superb trainer of young men and women. 'I want you to promise that when you think you are losing the attention of the audience, you will please stop,' he told Gerald Lander, later to be

Bishop of Hong Kong. 'How many of those dear little children understood what you meant when you said "involuntarily"?' he asked Frank Millard, after his first attempt at a beach talk. Some did not like such directness. But those who wanted to learn benefitted enormously.

One of Arrowsmith's helpers underlines his influence: 'What the CSSM has been to the Christian life of the Universities is difficult to measure. Its robust manliness, which showed that the simplest presentation of the gospel message was compatible with a delight in every healthy form of sport; its absolute allegiance to the Bible, as manifested by the Scripture Union, the mainspring of its work, and the truly non-denominational character of its work, all gave it an influence which was most remarkable.'

INTO THE BOARDING SCHOOLS

It was the link with Cambridge that led to the next major advance, which was into the 'public schools', the boarding schools for boys from middle and upper class families, where most Oxford and Cambridge students at that time were educated. As early as 1880 special cards were printed for the Public Schools Scripture Union. Membership increased during the 80s, partly through contacts at the seaside services, and partly through the boys' own efforts at recruiting among their friends. Two years later 2,000 cards were printed, and there were branches in many leading schools, one having sixty members. In 1886, as we have already seen, a group of Cambridge students took the initiative in starting *Our Boys' Magazine*. It was not easy to live a consistent Christian life in the tough world of a nineteenth-century boarding school, and the magazine aimed 'to help them to all that is good and right'.

Then in 1888 George Pilkington, a brilliant Cambridge scholar and athlete, was appointed to the CSSM staff to take missions in public schools. He had been converted from fierce agnosticism through the CICCU, and only a few years later was to be killed on missionary service in Uganda. His academic reputation and colourful personality gave him many openings in the schools, and numbers of boys were converted.

Willie Holland, later to be a missionary in Allahabad, was one of those who 'gave his heart to God' when Pilkington was running a mission at Durham Grammar School.

It was his utter manliness that first struck me. He was a thorough man, ringing true from top to bottom. He was a man of God, one who knew God and believed in God. I remember when I first saw him, as he came swinging round the corner – the great tall strapping figure; the beaming face – almost as red as his scarlet tie – his hat far enough back to show his broad forehead; a huge calf-skin Bible under his arm, and a club of a walking stick in his hand. I never saw him without that Bible! But a Uganda calf ate it, all but a few pages of Revelation.

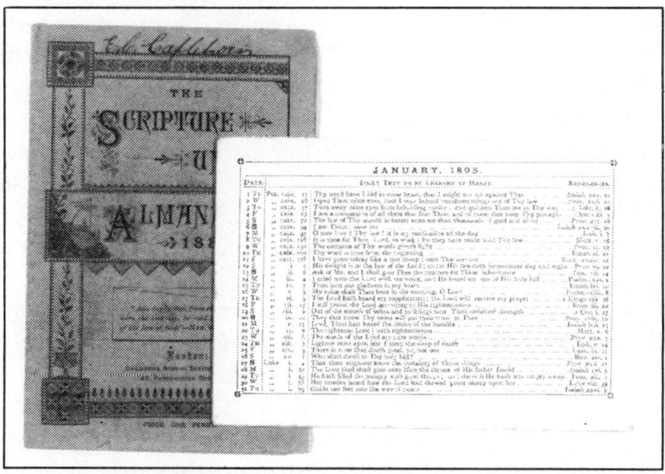

The Almanac chose a text from the SU reading each day for the members to learn by heart.

THE FIRST CAMPS

Three years later, two Cambridge theological students, Stanley Power and C H Clissold, came up with another idea: an evangelistic camp for public school boys. 'Our plan was as follows: to collect together as many as possible under canvas, to provide for them all the sports and amusements dear to the heart of boys, and while in the midst of these enjoyments to influence more by example than by words.' It was an original idea to arrange a camp with an evangelistic purpose. The first Universities Camp for Public Schoolboys was held at Rustington, near Littlehampton, on the south coast of England, in August 1892. Fifty-five boys were present, with Major Liebenrood in charge, and Canon John Taylor Smith (soon to be Bishop of Sierra Leone) as chaplain. The tents were pitched within a few minutes' walk of the sea. 'The days', Taylor Smith reported 'were spent in bathing, boating, cricketing, fishing etc., and the evenings always closed with family prayer. On the last night some of the most unlikely ones, who had come to camp as a joke told how they had found Christ that week.'

The Universities Camps were not at first officially part of CSSM, but were closely linked with it. Staffed by Christian army officers, university students and one or two young clergymen, the combination of a cheerful open-air holiday, energetic games, semi-military discipline, and spiritual challenge was on exactly the right wavelength for the boys and it proved immensely popular. Three camps had to be organised in 1883 and four in 1884, taking 254 boys and staffed by fifty-nine officers. 'Fifteen trim tents in a crescent shape on a high cliff facing the sea, with the beautiful Isle of Wight away in the distance', wrote Major Seton Churchill. 'Glorious days of sport! Beautiful stretches of wood for rambling naturalists and decent roads for the cyclists!...Many a young life surrendered on those summer nights; many a quiet prayer, many a glorious meeting place with Jesus on those quiet cliffs.'

The growth of the camps and the continued contact with the public school boys at beach missions strengthened the work in the schools themselves. By 1899 SU could report that:

> In every school we try to have a boy as secretary, responsible for the running of the branch. He distributes the cards; he looks after the members as far as he can, and in many schools he has some kind of quiet meeting every Sunday...What we aim to do is to have a branch organised in every school, with, if possible, a little meeting at which the boys can feel they are united in fighting against evil and serving the Lord Jesus.

Although little is said about it in the reports, a similar work was going on in girls' schools. In 1899 Mrs F Barclay Wilkinson spoke at a conference for SU secretaries, and told how, 'in answer to prayer, especially the prayers of the girls themselves, openings for meetings in some of the most unlikely places have been granted.' Soon afterwards 'the large and increasing number of engagements for Mrs Wilkinson' led the committee to appoint first one and then a second colleague.

TO REMOTE VILLAGES

The 1890s also saw a new branch of the Mission formed to take the gospel to children in England's isolated and neglected villages. Back in 1885 a young solicitor's clerk called Samuel Hewlett had been converted from a godless background, at the church where Tom Bishop worshipped. In the summer he helped with seaside services, and was soon working full-time in the CSSM office. One day he read in a magazine about two Cambridge students who had 'hired a gipsy caravan and spent their vacation touring villages and preaching the gospel.' Gipsies were the only people to use caravans at that time, and this further example of student inventiveness sparked off a fresh development of CSSM work. Hewlett was deeply impressed by what they wrote about the spiritual need of the villages, and prayed that 'if it be the Lord's will I should follow up this effort.' In early summer 1892 he set off in a baker's cart, with tracts stored where the bread had been, and texts painted on the side. He travelled 160 miles, visiting forty villages in the course of three months, with friends joining him to help with the preaching from time to time.

The following year 'instead of paying flying visits to a number of places it was found wiser to settle down in one place for a number of days.' Like Spiers, he found a mission more useful than several one-off meetings. During the winter, with the help of an anonymous gift of £100, a horse-drawn caravan had been built, vividly painted with gospel texts. Late one Saturday night, in May 1893, after a prayer meeting with some of the students, Hewlett set off from Cambridge. With him was a young lawyer called George Goodman, who, with his brother Montague, was to be prominent in CSSM work for the next fifty years.

The tour that summer was 'deeply encouraging'. The first day out George Goodman led to the Lord a young railway porter called Willie Knott, who developed a gift for languages and later became a missionary to the Jews. At one Suffolk village a local farmer, James Cutting, was so impressed that he soon became a full-time honorary worker. Hewlett was a man of tremendous zest and enthusiasm. The day they met Cutting they drove through the village, sitting 'on the platform of the van, Will Perkins with his silver cornet, Arthur Lyon with a concertina, myself driving the horse and making a joyful noise'. But it was not mere froth. 'I have never known a person who could so move a village in a week, or a fortnight, until the whole place turned out to him', wrote Montague Goodman. 'He had tremendous power, and won many children to the Saviour.'

So the Caravan Mission to Village Children was born. It had a separate fund, but was 'under the auspices of the CSSM' which made a large annual grant for salaries. By 1901 there were five caravans and 'one large tent (without a van) in charge of Mr Edmund Clark', the man who was later to put CSSM on its feet in Australia. The six full-time staff were assisted by a large number of young men like the Goodmans, who helped during the holidays at their own expense, and a team of '490 correspondents (mostly ladies) who write each month to 1315 village children and send them our monthly tract for Christian young people, *Words of Life and Beauty*'. The Caravan Mission continued as a separate organisation until 1923, when it had fifteen evangelists. At that stage it merged fully with the CSSM.

By contrast an attempt by Bishop to harness new technology by forming a 'Cyclists' Children's Mission' to go out into the villages, with 'lady cyclists' assisting by giving tracts to the children, apparently came to nothing, for we hear no more about it. Even the best idea is fruitless without someone to give time and energy to it.

GOLDEN BELLS AND CHORUSES

In 1890 the committee took a major step of faith in agreeing to publish the Mission's first two books, as distinct from pamphlets. Both were immediate successes. Spiers' *True Stories, New and Old* was extraordinarily popular, 173,000 selling in the first fifteen years, a further 14,000 being given away, by the author, at his own expense. *More True Stories* followed in 1907. Written just as he spoke, they recalled incidents from his missions or illustrations from his messages. Spiers also compiled *Golden Bells,* the Mission's first full-length children's hymn-book. Though, in John Pollock's words, 'typical of the low state of hymnody in England', it was immensely popular, selling four million copies by 1925, when a revised, and much-improved, edition was produced.

CSSM led the way in Christian music for children. In the 1890s it invented 'choruses' – short verses with easy tunes, each containing some scripture or simple piece of teaching. Some were refrains of hymns already known, but most were specially written. George Goodman seems to have started the idea, and he printed a booklet of sixty-eight choruses for the Herne Bay beach mission in 1897. They were particularly suitable for children who could not read, but since they stayed in the mind long after the mission was over, were popular and valuable teaching aids for older children as well. The idea spread widely, and soon many seaside missions produced their own leaflets. In 1921 the first CSSM Chorus book was published, with over 300 items. 'After this', John Pollock comments, 'chorus singing became, throughout the world, a recognised part of Christian work among the young, and a happy pastime for grown-ups'.

THE DEBATE ABOUT THE BIBLE

Right from the start the pioneers of the Mission had been willing to experiment. With camps, cyclists, caravans and choruses, CSSM was showing itself well able to adapt its methods so as to reach out effectively to a wider circle. The critical question was whether it would also alter its message. It was a time when a number of Christian organisations were doing so, a notable example being the Student Christian Movement, the national organization of which the CICCU was the Cambridge branch. The CSSM, like the SCM, might easily have moved in the same direction.

The debate centred on what Tissington Tatlow, the SCM general secretary, called 'the modern view of the Bible', which accepted the Higher Criticism originating in Germany. As Oliver Barclay comments:

> The issues were not all black and white. A more *scholarly* approach to the exposition of the Bible was in itself, good, and the older evangelicals were often too superficial. But along with this there came in, and was welcomed, a *rationalistic* approach. People began to argue that we should acknowledge only those parts of the Bible that were intellectually acceptable...Often the new rationalistic approach meant accepting highly speculative, but clever, reconstructions of the Bible which appealed to the current evolutionary philosophy of religion. Anything in the Bible that did not fit with such a scheme was deemed to be an error...The rationalistic (not rational) principle meant that all revealed truth was to be accepted only if it could be justified only at the bar of reason. (*Whatever happened to the Jesus Lane Lot?* p.52)

Gradually the new ideas spread through the student world and the leadership of the churches.

> Liberalism seemed to be a way of making Christianity more acceptable and relevant to the new scientific generation. Most of those who went liberal did so believing that they had to move from the old position because of modern discoveries. They also believed that the shift would enable them to win over those who were abandoning their faith because of the sceptical and rationalistic spirit of the age. As has often happened before, they absorbed the ideas they set out to combat...The SCM was progressively taken over by liberal theology so that evangelicals found it imposible to

> maintain their position within it... It was soon possible for people to argue that anyone holding to the traditional orthodoxy was simply not an educated man. (*Whatever happened to the Jesus Lane Lot?* pp.56, 57)

In the CICCU, where the majority of students continued to accept the historicity and the authority of the Bible, and to proclaim the evangelical message, the issue came to a head in 1910, when it decided to disaffiliate from the national SCM.

This theological ferment naturally affected the CSSM. But as far back as 1894 Bishop had seen the way theological thought was moving. He drafted a long, clear statement of the Mission's position. 'The divine inspiration and supreme authority of the Scriptures has been a leading principle of our work... We have always shown clearly that we accept "all Scripture" as "given by inspiration of God" and as "profitable for doctrine, for reproof, for correction, for instruction in righteousness".' A solid reason for holding to this position was 'the estimate which the Lord Jesus Christ placed upon His Father's Word. We find that He treated the facts recorded in it as true in every particular, and that He regarded each utterance in it as infallible.' Nor is it possible to divorce the teaching of the Bible from its historical accuracy: 'We hold strongly that the doctrines rest upon the facts, and that we have no right to expect any true morality or Christian life apart from the full acceptance of the facts and doctrines.'

For twenty years the statement was printed in the annual report. It helped to maintain and clarify the Mission's theological position, and to influence those who were in contact with it. In view of the close links with Cambridge, it seems likely that this clear and definite statement helped to give the student leaders there the strength and perception they needed when they were under pressure from the national SCM to broaden their basis of faith. The students' decision to break with SCM policy and retain an evangelical position was unpopular with the SCM national leadership. But it had a profound influence on the development of student work all over the world, as it led directly to the formation of the Inter-Varsity Fellowship (now UCCF) ten years later, and the International Fellowship of Evangelical Students (IFES) in 1947.

7

Retrospect: 1900

Looking back over the first thirty years of the Mission's history, at the turn of the century, Spiers, Bishop and their friends must have found much to encourage them. In the annual report from 1884 onwards, they clearly spelt out their aims: 'The great aim of our Mission has been to use any and every means to lead children and young people to know and love the Lord Jesus Christ as their Saviour... to lead them onwards in the Christian life, and to point out to them, in due time, paths of Christian usefulness.' It is important to note that it was much more than a drive for 'child-evangelism'. The word 'know' is significant because it underlines their belief that teaching and response are both important. Young people were specifically included, not just junior-age children. Follow-up and training in Christian discipleship were important parts of the programme. And useful service was seen as the goal. To a remarkable extent, this aim had been achieved.

First and foremost, of course, there were the thousands of children and young people who had found a living faith in Christ through the Mission's activities. 'Again and again, when I have questioned those who have offered their services (for missionary work)', said one of the committee of CMS about that time, 'I have had the answer: "It was at the CSSM at such and such a place that I first heard the message of God's love to me and I gave my heart to Him."' 'When I was a schoolgirl Edwin Arrowsmith came to Harrogate', wrote Amy Carmichael, who later founded the Dohnavur Fellowship in South India, 'and our school marched in a long, wriggly crocodile to just one single meeting. But in that one meeting, in the minute's silence after the hymn was sung, the Lord Jesus drew me to himself.' Countless numbers of people could look back on a similar experience. The permanent effect in the lives of so many proved how right the pioneers of the CSSM were in their convictions about the conversion of children.

CHANGED ATTITUDES

Secondly, over the years there had been a remarkable change in the attitude of the Christian public to evangelism among children. In the 1892 annual report Bishop could write: 'Looking back to the half suspicious way in which these special efforts were then regarded, and the objections urged by many who could scarcely believe it possible that children could be converted at all, or, if they could, that the work would last; we can only praise the Lord for the wonderful change that has come to pass. Now the difficulty is frequently not to get Sunday Schools to have the services, but to find sufficient men to comply with the applications received.'

TRAINED WORKERS

Then the Mission could thank God for the hundreds of active Christians who had been inspired and trained through service with it. 'I am more than ever convinced', said Bishop Taylor Smith, 'that work in the CSSM is the best preparation for work at home and abroad.' The close contact with Oxford and Cambridge, and the camps and schools groups that had grown out of it, had been particularly significant in this training of Christian leaders. Professor Handley Moule could write from Cambridge in 1894, 'I can only say this that the number of those who are now living true, earnest, decided, good-conveying lives as young Christian men in a university course – the number of those who to my knowledge owe, in the first instance, the message of God to their souls to the work of the CSSM, is a very large number indeed.'

WORLDWIDE INFLUENCE

Finally, through its literature, and through the hundreds who had served in its ranks when they were young and were now scattered all over the world, CSSM and Scripture Union could see the beginnings of its international ministry. 195,000 SU cards in thirty-one languages were distributed abroad that year, and as many as eighteen million leaflets in fifty languages had been sent overseas since the Mission started. Reports published that year included news of Mr Kanaya, travelling secretary in Japan and of William Smith, a 'colporteur' on the staff in Sierra Leone. Children's meetings in Marathi in Pune had resumed 'after the terrible visitation of the plague'. Beatrice Spiers, niece of the founder, had just started as a CSSM missionary in Spain. Luke John was busy with the Tinnevelly Children's Mission in South India. There were 1,500 SU members 'scattered over 9 provinces' of China many of whom 'may be in terrible danger' from 'the Boxer conflagration'. A long visit was planned for the newly appointed

Assistant General Secretary, Martyn Gooch to Australia and New Zealand. A seaside mission and weekly children's services were being held in Durban, South Africa, where the SU branch had English, African and 'Dutch' members.

SPIRITUAL DECLINE

But while there was much to encourage there were already signs that the work in England was beginning to run out of steam. Gooch noted that 'bright and happy as are our seaside services and SU meetings, they are not as largely attended as they used to be', and that 'not the same interest is taken by parents in the spiritual welfare of their children.' This was partly a result of a general decline in religious life in England, and evangelical life in particular. The spread of liberal theology and evolutionary philosophy was undermining confidence in the Bible and its message. The controversies which ensued brought about a polarisation among clergy and ministers. Those who accepted the new ideas became increasingly impatient with those who would not follow them; the evangelicals on the other hand became defensive and less effective.

AGEING LEADERSHIP

For the CSSM these problems were more serious because of the age of its leadership. By 1900 Bishop was sixty-one, yet he was to continue as General Secretary for another twenty years. As he grew older 'he tried to put a stop to new projects because he said he did so want to have a quiet time in the evening of his days.' Of the fourteen members of the committee, twelve had been in the leadership of the Mission for over twenty-five years, and the other two for fifteen. The group of young men in their twenties and thirties who started the mission and 'dared to do things differently' had grown old and conservative without realising it and failed to bring younger men on to the committee.

Yet it was these men, and Bishop in particular, who guided the mission, and kept it on course through the theological storms of the period. For this the worldwide Scripture Union today owes them an enormous debt of gratitude.

For the next forty-five years, however, most of the progress made by the CSSM was in other countries.

Dictated

19

The Children's Special Service Mission.

President—Rev. Edward A. Stuart, M.A.,
Vicar of St. Matthew's, Bayswater, W.
Treasurer—Jas. E. Mathieson, Esq., 47, Phillimore Gardens, Kensington, W.
Honorary Secretary—Mr. T. B. Bishop, 13a, Warwick Lane, Paternoster Row, E.C.
Secretary—Mr. Henry Hankinson.
Organizing Secretary—Mr. Henry Hutchinson.

OFFICE—13a, Warwick Lane, Paternoster Row, LONDON, E.C.

"Our Own Magazine." "The Children's Scripture Union."

Telegraphic Address,
"HANKINSON, LONDON."

13a, Warwick Lane,
Paternoster Row, London, E.C.

May 11th 1895

Dear Mr Wright

With reference to our conversation about the lighting of our premises by electricity, our Committee are prepared to offer you 5% per annum on the outlay to which you would be put in respect thereof; & as they are not able to say definitely, ~~at~~ ~~so~~ so long a distance as six years, whether they will exercise the ~~would take up the~~ option of renewal at the end of

Draft of a letter from T B Bishop, instructing a contractor to instal electricity in the CSSM offices (1895). Note the caution of the civil servant, retaining the right to go back to gas lamps after six years if the newly-invented electric lighting was not satisfactory.

Part II

Gifted Individualists 1900–1945

8

Great Days in India

In 1896, in response to many requests from friends in India, the CSSM took the important step of sending out its first overseas missionary. They chose Bernard Herklots, a young Cambridge graduate, who had already served on the staff in the north of England. Arriving in Calcutta in November, he spent two and a half busy years, travelling all over the country, during which he spoke at over a thousand meetings, before his health forced him to return to England.

In 1901 Roddy Archibald arrived in his place. Brought up in a wealthy and influential Christian home, Roddy Archibald had found a personal faith at the age of nine. His father, Sir William Archibald, was a Master of the Supreme Court in England and had founded the Royal National Mission for Deep Sea Fishermen. In spite of his privileges, life was not easy for Roddy because of a serious stammer. He only overcame it through intense prayer, and throughout his life public speaking was a costly and difficult experience for him. He arrived in India at the age of twenty-five expecting to stay three years. He finally left when he was seventy. It was he who set the work in India on its feet.

MISSIONS IN SCHOOLS

He spent the first two years visiting the English speaking schools, which at that time catered mainly for English and Anglo-Indian children. All his years in India, he was constantly on the move. 'I have no headquarters but my pith helmet; no station but the railway station', he used to say. Because of the great distances he stayed a week or more in each school, usually conducting meetings morning and evening, and playing games with the children in the afternoon. So the pattern of school missions developed, which has been a strong feature of CSSM work in India ever since.

Then in 1904 he spent four months with the Tinnevelly Children's Mission, formed thirteen years earlier by two missionaries with CSSM experience in England. The experience was to influence the rest of his life. He joined the three Tamil evangelists for a series of missions, speaking by interpretation, or listening to one of the others. One of them, I D Samuel, was 'a sweet singer'. He never spoke without composing a Tamil chorus on his theme, which he taught the children. On one occasion Archibald gave him the outline of his talk as they walked over to the church. 'As soon as I had finished speaking, out he came with a chorus, written on the blackboard, taking up every point in the address, and with a tune to suit it. So the words spoken were stamped in song.'

FORTY-FIVE INDIAN EVANGELISTS

During his time in Tinnevelly, Archibald helped to organise their first camp, for 150 specially selected boys contacted at the missions. V S. Azariah, later to become the great Bishop of Dornakal, was one of the main speakers. Archibald and another missionary were the only Europeans in camp. 'It has been a blessed privilege', he wrote, 'to be associated with the three Tamil evangelists. We have had many barriers to meet and overcome. Their simple faith and pure prayer power has been a lesson to me.' Eight years later, Roland Allen would publish his prophetic book, *Missionary Methods – St Paul's and Ours,* which was largely ignored at the time but had such a profound influence later. Already in 1904, Archibald had grasped one of its main points: that the evangelism of India would be carried out most effectively by Indian Christians themselves. He saw the possibilities of a team of CSSM evangelists working among their own people in each language area, and from then on a large share of his time was given to finding and training such men.

The first to be appointed, in 1907, was Rakhal Biswas, from Bengal 'who knew his Bible better than any Indian I ever met', as Archibald commented. Then came A V George from Travancore and C B Perera from Ceylon (Sri Lanka). 'During the last 40 years', Archibald wrote in 1948, 'no less than 45 Indians served on our staff in 11 language areas.' Particularly in Kerala, many of them served for a few years and then went on to positions of leadership in their churches.

'CSSM came to be regarded as a training ground for the clergy', one of them remarked. Archibald's influence on the Indian church, through the staff he trained and through children converted through his missions was so significant that in 1976 a special issue of the all-India Christian magazine *Light of Life* was produced to mark the 75th anniversary of Archibald's arrival in the country. It included articles about five well-known Christian leaders all converted through him. As the editorial put it: 'His ministry left a marked imprint on lives all over the country.' (*Light of Life,* September 1976, p.2)

LEADER AND FRIEND

Archibald's method of training was to take his Indian colleagues touring with him. He prayed with them and showed them how to use the magic lantern and to use simple visual aids. They helped him by interpreting when he was giving his talks or counselling the children. So they not only absorbed his methods but his spiritual depth and understanding. They learned from one another and each grew in the process.

To modern eyes the weakness of his approach was its paternalism. Finances were paid almost entirely from London. Only one local committee was formed, in Kerala, from 1926 to 1933. When this was disbanded, because of various difficulties, he did not form another. Although he consulted other people, Archibald took the decisions himself. In this, of course, he was very much a child of his day. But he set a pattern that made it difficult in later years for CSSM and SU in India to grow up into a self-governing movement. His qualities as an evangelist and trainer, as a man of God and a leader of men, however, more than made up for this authoritarian approach. He was ahead of his time in his lack of colour prejudice and the closeness of his friendships with his Indian colleagues. The Tamils called him *Annachi* – 'elder brother'. 'We could sit quietly by and watch with perfect confidence our Indian brothers conduct the meetings, bringing home to the minds of boys spiritual truths in a way we could never hope to emulate', he wrote. Such confidence was rare in those days, when the power of the British Raj was at its peak.

Another quality which stands out is his gift for personal evangelism which he considered 'after prayer, the most fruitful, the most joyous and at the same time the most difficult work in the world.' 'My own decision for Christ', said Bishop A J Appasamy at the inauguration of his diocese in 1950,

> was made in the meetings held by Mr R T Archibald. He had a wonderful way of appealing to young people. He played with us and sang with us; we had access to him at all times; we were wholly taken up with the love which he showed for us. We looked forward to his meetings after the close of school. He pleaded with us to yield ourselves to Christ. He taught us to love the Bible and to study it with care, working over the great verses with ink so that

they stood out clearly and impressively. He kept in close touch with us in after years, both by remembering us in his prayers and by writing letters to us.'

Subodh Sahu, now a well-known evangelist, describes a picnic that Archibald invited him and his friends to join, at the start of a week's mission. Subodh was fifteen at the time, but too shy and lonely to join in the games with the other boys. He was suspicious too about the picnic. Why should this foreigner invite them? There must be a trap. As they crossed the Mahanodi River by boat, he stood on the deck alone, looking out over the water. 'Suddenly two arms were round me, large hands gripping the deck rail either side of mine. Fearfully I looked up into this foreigner's eyes and literally saw love beaming down at me. My confidence welled up, and I realized the man had no ulterior motive; he simply loved me.' (*Light of Life*, September 1976, p.2) In that first conversation Archibald said little. But he had won Subodh's interest. 'I was open like a sunflower to all that he had to say.' On the last night of the mission, he stayed behind after the meeting, with several other boys. One by one Archibald spoke to them and led them to Christ. For Subodh at least it was the turning point of his life.

Sometimes his approach was far less gentle. In his book *Monsoon Daybreak*, R R Rajamani describes how he was walking back to the school dormitory after one of Archibald's sessions of games.

'Suddenly I felt a hand on my shoulder and turned to see Mr Archibald. "Why are you so bad, Rajamani?" he asked me.

'I looked up startled, my eyes squinting into the afternoon sun, my toes curled nervously in the gritty red sand of the playing field. I could not evade the penetrating look of those kind eyes. For once in my life I was at a loss for a reply. Then all at once my eyes filled with tears. "True, sir!" I burst out. "I know I am bad; but I cannot help it." "Go to a quiet place. Kneel down there and try to recall all the wrong things you have done from your earliest days, all your disobedience, all your sins against your parents, everything. Tell them all to the Lord Jesus." That was all he said.'

He went to the village church, but it was locked. So he knelt down in the porch. 'Just to please him, I honestly did what he said. Systematically I began to recall all I had done wrong, and to repeat it mechanically out loud – to God. After five or ten minutes it was too much for me, the lies I had told my mother and father, the malice and deceit at school. Suddenly I broke down and burst into tears, crying to God for mercy. But in a few more minutes this too passed, and all at once my heart became filled with unutterable joy. Jesus my Lord knew it all and had forgiven me! I jumped up, with my shirt and veshti all covered with dust, and began to run for sheer joy.'

When he got back to the dormitory, he asked the other boys to forgive him. 'It was not easy at first. They found it hard to believe that I should have so changed as to confess myself in the wrong. However, God had begun to work in several of them as well; so they said they forgave me. That day marked the start of a spiritual revival in the school in which many shared.' (Quoted in *Light of Life,* Sept 1976, pp.10, 11)

Archibald was a prolific letter-writer, seeing it as a good way of helping boys who had started to follow Christ, after he had moved on to other schools. 'Every time I would write to him with half a page he would reply with three or four', Subodh Sahu recalls. Wherever possible, too, he formed them into groups for prayer and Bible study, called 'Kings Swordsmen' for the boys and 'Lightbearers' for girls. Subodh Sahu led the group at Cuttack, and there were still a dozen active members by the time of Archibald's next visit. The boys were particularly impressed when they found out later that the meeting had gone on so long that he had missed his evening meal and had to go to bed hungry.

Each day too, in spite of the heat, he disciplined himself to pray. A doctor from South India, who worked with him, describes how 'he was an early riser, being out of his bed at 4.30 for an unhurried time for the study of God's word.... In the afternoon, after a short period of rest, he was accustomed to spend an hour on his knees.' 'Worship', he would say, 'is the growing point of the soul.'

In 1937 Archibald called a staff conference at Nasik, only the second to be held. Sixteen Indian evangelists were present from ten language areas, together with six others from Britain who were working with Archibald in the English medium schools. When he retired in 1945 at the end of the war, the number of staff was much reduced. But in the workers he had trained he had laid a foundation for indigenous national leadership in the independent India which was about to be born.

Elsewhere in Asia there was only limited CSSM progress during this period. In 1906 the SU card was printed in Korea. 'It is very timely', wrote a missionary from there, 'as we are in the midst of a very gracious revival. There are scores of places that have never been visited by any Korean or foreign teacher where the people are reading the New Testament and, because it says so, are keeping the Lord's day, have burnt their fetishes, and are striving to follow in Christ's footsteps.' To-Ki-Chan, 'though still young, a graphic and winning speaker', was appointed as a CSSM children's evangelist. By 1921 there were 25,000 SU members, and the card 'was used in family worship in thousands upon thousands of Korean homes'. In 1924 Godfrey Webb-Peploe went to China, to start work there along the lines Archibald was using in India; but before he had learned the language his health failed, and he had to leave. In Japan a long succession of staff workers carried on the seaside services and evangelistic tours. In Burma and Malaya SU cards were used. But East Asia would have to wait another twenty years before Scripture Union was to take deeper root.

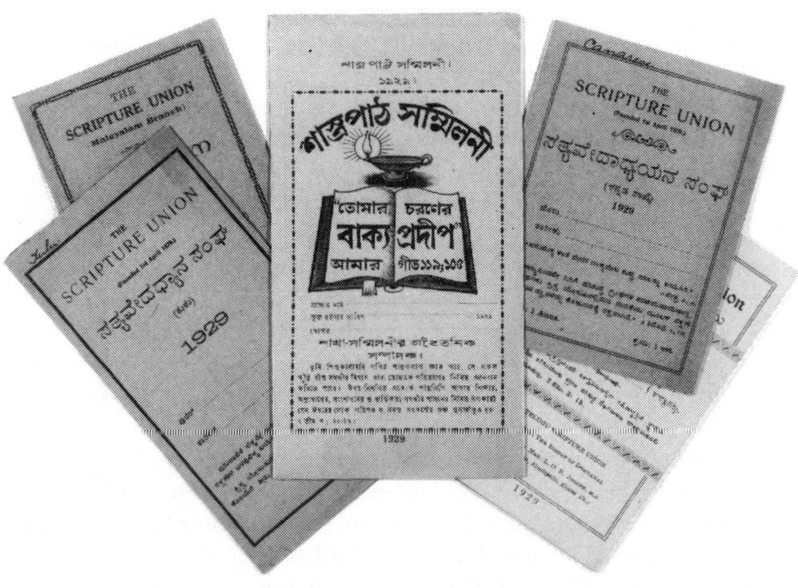

SU cards in five Indian languages (1929).

Josiah Spiers on the beach (1890); from a contemporary drawing.

The first caravan ready to start (1893).

*(Left) Josiah Spiers, (right) Tom Bishop:
The pioneers of CSSM and Scripture Union. Unfortunately, the only photographs of them available which are good enough to reproduce were taken at the end of their lives. When they founded the Mission, Spiers was aged 30, and Bishop only 28.*

Mission team members, 1888 style.

(Left) Hudson Pope, children's evangelist (1905–1960).

(Right) Adelaide Whitney, pioneer of SU in Japan at the age of 13.

Hudson Pope speaking on 'the tabernacle' at a beach service at Bridlington (1908).

Ernst Aebi and family (1948).

Boys' camp at Vennes (1934); Ernst Aebi in the foreground.

(Left) Roddy Archibald, founder of CSSM in India.

(Right) Edmund Clark, pioneer in Australia.

Beach mission reunion in London (1938).

Puddox in South Africa (1958), Puddox is a kind of camp cricket, which CSSM/SU invented and spread around the world.

Off to a picnic at Pigeon Island – with one boy left behind! (New Zealand camp, 1950's).

Great Wood boys' camp in south-west England (1966).

SU Band in Switzerland (1948).

CSSM evangelist in India (1950's).

Old Jordans Conference (1960).
Front row, left to right: Russel Fountain (New Zealand), Otto Dose (South Africa), Armin Hoppler (Switzerland), Derek Warren (England), Jean Cruvellier (France), Alan Kerr (Australia), Stacey Woods (USA).
Middle row: Wilman Sloan (Scotland), Peter Campbell (Scotland), Akira Hatori (Japan), Arthur Rouse (Canada), Claire-Lise de Benoit (Switzerland), John Laird (England), O C Matthew (India), Leonard Bréchet (France), Faulkner Hole (England).
Back row: Michael Hews (England – minutes secretary), Bruce Lumsden (New Zealand), Paul Reed (South Africa), Nigel Sylvester (Ghana), Harold Ling (England – conference secretary), Cecil Johnston (India), Colin Becroft (Australia).

9

Pioneers in Australia

As we have seen, CSSM and SU work in Australia was in a decline by 1900. To try to revive it the Assistant General Secretary from London, Martyn Gooch, paid an extended visit from 1901–03. He carried through a hectic programme of children's missions, beach services and meetings with SU members, branch secretaries and committees. Another Englishman, Bob Drury, joined him for the last eight months, and together they visited all the main schools in New South Wales, Victoria and South Australia. Two years later the first Australian staff worker was appointed, Valentine Soul. For five years he travelled widely, from Adelaide to Brisbane, visiting SU branches. But, while these activities influenced many individual lives and slowed the decline, they did not halt it.

A MAN WITH AN INDIA-RUBBER FACE

A new chapter opened with the visit of Edmund Clark, another of the colourful characters that CSSM was able to recruit at this period. After twelve years as a staff evangelist in England, Clark was sent to Australia and New Zealand to recover his health, which had broken down after his wife died. He found immense opportunities for CSSM work and the response was so great that he was asked to return more permanently. His second visit, from 1922–28, made a lasting impact. He had boundless energy and worked at an intense pace. A typical example was the seven months in Victoria in 1924 when he conductd 17 missions. He wrote:

> I am wonderfully well, and able to do a tremendous amount of work. Every Sunday I have three services, and on weekdays children in the afternoon and adults at night – for ten days in each centre – with an address at a school most mornings and a dinner-hour talk to warehouse boys in the city every Tuesday. Then on my rest days, Thursdays and Fridays in each fortnight, I manage to visit conferences for SU secretaries, ministers and Sunday School teachers with a talk on 'The Value of a Child's Soul'.

In a later age Clark could have been a great success on television. Someone described him as 'a born actor with an India-rubber face, who could easily have been a music hall celebrity', and he made a deep impression as a speaker wherever he went. 'Though only a small man', wrote Alex Brown, who was to succeed him, 'his eyes stood out like organ stops and seemed to penetrate you wherever you were. In the open air he would draw immense crowds of adults as well as children.' He was a superb story-teller, often acting out the parts as he told the story, and had 'a legendary skill for driving home a point by acting out a situation on the spur of the moment'.

Such gifts were particularly suitable for beach services. So was the Australian climate. In 1922 Clark wrote: 'There are hardly any Sunday Schools because during the weekends the people go off in their motor cars to the sea and to the mountains. And unless something is done to reach the children on the beach on the Lord's Day, they will grow up without any knowledge of Christ.' A few months later he ran his first beach mission, at Austinmer, fifty miles south of Sydney. Paul White, then a boy at Sydney Grammar School and later to become the 'Jungle Doctor', was one of the small team of helpers. The following summer three missions were held on the beaches and one at an inland park. A pattern had been set which was to become such a strong feature of the Australian CSSM in the coming years.

Some of the missions were run in conjunction with a camp for schoolboys, who might be his only helpers for the services. 'The staff was just myself and four schoolboys, sleeping in a tent. Numbers attending were even larger than before. On our opening Sunday afternoon we used 350 hymn-sheets', he wrote of Austinmer early in 1924. At other times he ran separate boys' camps which were said to be 'highly popular and somewhat disorganised'. Often he had no helpers and even cooked for the boys himself.

Clark made a long-term impact on the lives of hundreds of young Australians. One of them was Marcus Loane, the future Archbishop of Sydney. 'During my fourteenth year', he writes, 'Mr Edmund Clark conducted a mission at St Paul's, Chatswood, and I was present at nearly every service. On the Sunday evening he brough his sermon to a close with an appeal. He asked any who were willing to receive the Lord Jesus Christ as their Saviour to say openly and publicly, "I do". I can still recall where I was sitting, beside my mother and sister. I knew that God had spoken to me. After a moment of silence, He gave me the grace and courage to say "I do".' (*Tuned in to Change,* p.61f)

Without doubt Edmund Clark was a gifted and effective evangelist, who planted the CSSM firmly on the Australian map. But he had his limitations. He was a strong individualist, who found it very difficult to work with others unless they were prepared to follow his lead. 'If Noah had had a committee', he used to say, 'the ark would never have been built.' So nothing much happened apart from what he did himself.

Nor was he all that good at training younger men. His own technique as a speaker was so good that he was afraid to hand on responsibility to others. Instead of developing their own style, the young men who worked with him became, one of them recalls, 'copyists who would ape his methods, down to the most ridiculous mannerisms, which while perfectly natural with him were asininely idiotic with them'. Nevertheless, when Clark's intense programme caused a further breakdown, in 1928, and he had to return to England, he left behind in Australia a number of young men who had worked with him and caught his vision, and were well equipped to carry on his work.

ON TWENTY POUNDS A YEAR

One of them was Alex Brown, who had found Christ as a boy of six after one of Archibald's meetings in Darjeeling in North India. He joined the staff in 1923, soon after Clark arrived for his second visit, and continued for thirty-three years. It was just as well that he was not put off by a typing error in the letter of invitation, in which the secretary offered him a salary of £20 a year, instead of the £200 that was intended. 'I have always thanked the Lord', he wrote later, 'that it was with the princely sum of £20 a year in my mind that I actually came into the work.'

Brown continued very much along the lines Clark had pioneered: children's missions in churches, camps and beach missions, and schools visits. While Clark was short and plump, Brown was tall and lean. But he was just as energetic, and soon developed into an equally attractive children's speaker. He followed Clark, too, in his emphasis on giving clear biblical teaching in his evangelistic work. 'He wanted to bring boys and girls to a clear decision for Christ, but never by exerting pressure.' It was the long-term results that mattered. As he wrote himself: 'Edmund Clark didn't keep results, of course; neither did I. But the proof of the pudding is in the eating and there are people all over the world now who were brought to the Lord by Mr Clark.' When eventually, in 1928, he persuaded the committee to buy a car for him, he was able to reach out into the country areas. Once a year 'I would seek out some country district where I could find ten schools in a radius of roughly 20 or 30 miles, pitch my tent as near to the centre as possible, and work out a timetable with the school teachers covering the next three months'. So the pattern continued right through till the Second World War.

To follow up Edmund Clark's and Alex Brown's fruitful missions, regular interdenominational Bible classes were started in the late 1920s. In Sydney, Vincent Craven and Stacey Woods, two young men who were to work together later in the development of Inter-Varsity Christian Fellowship in Canada, ran meetings in homes, church halls and in the SU office. Craven had been converted at the age of sixteen at one of Edmund Clark's parish missions, after his father had 'dragged him out of bed and forced him to come to church that night'. He had left school at fourteen but had drive, natural ability and a flair for work with boys. In 1930, at the age of twenty-two, he left business to become General Secretary in Sydney. About the same time similar meetings started in Melbourne using the name 'Crusaders'. A few camps were arranged, both for boys and girls, and some beach missions. So a small start had been made with the various strands of CSSM ministry. But the work was totally unco-ordinated, with Crusaders, CSSM and SU (as a Bible reading system) all run by separate committees, and each of them somewhat suspicious of one another.

THE IRISH DOCTOR

These small sparks of life were fanned into flame by the remarkable visits of Dr Howard Guinness. Guinness, aged twenty-seven at the time of his first visit in 1930, was travelling secretary of the IVF (now UCCF), the evangelical student movement in Britain. He was just as interested in reaching schoolboys with the gospel as university students, and found many opportunities, particularly in the independent schools, which Vincent Craven and his friends in Sydney found hard to penetrate. In Melbourne, too, he found a remarkable response, and the 'Crusader Union of Victoria' was officially founded in June. Guinness made skilful use of leading sportsmen who were Christians to attract boys to the meetings, and confronted them with an uncompromising challenge to sacrificial commitment to Christ. He returned in 1933 for a further tour, accompanied this time by a team of students, and in each State had a packed programme of meetings and interviews.

He wrote to London at the time giving an example of his approach:

I addressed a famous high school of perhaps 450 boys for the last period of school one morning. I endeavoured first of all to interest and amuse them with stories of camp life in England, passing on as soon as their sympathy had been won to stories of great Christian athletes, soldiers, etc. From here, in answer to the question, 'Why are many men so proud of Christ?' it was but a small jump to the story of a war hero who went to a lonely death to save his battalion – and so to Christ. Thus we found ourselves in the middle of the gospel, for we were together at the Cross. My own testimony of conversion and conflict with sin at school helped to bring things nearer home, and then came stories of boys I had met at other schools who had opened their life's door to the Lord Jesus and started to live and witness for Him openly. A letter from a senior prefect a month later told that God was continuing to work in a simply marvellous way. Their daily prayer meetings numbered 20 or 30, and boys were becoming fearless for Christ!

Looking back on these visits John Prince wrote:

Howard Guinness' impact on Australia in 1930 and 1933/4 was truly amazing. His visits took place at a time when evangelical life was at its very lowest point of the century. Liberal theology dominated church life and thought to a degree which made evangelicalism almost disreputable, all the more so because many who attended church out of habit or duty resented the displays of religious enthusiasm of those who carried Sunday observance into weekday life. Yet this was precisely what Howard challenged people to do. His booklet *Sword Drill* encouraged *daily* Bible reading and prayer, while *Sacrifice* called for 100% devotion to the Saviour.

Only in Sydney did the theology of the Church of England make his approach acceptable and the group of evangelical students, which the CSSM work of the twenties had helped to produce, provided a launching pad from which the Crusader Union of New South Wales emerged. Victoria, with its Crusader group already going, forged right ahead. In the other three mainland States it had been merely the planting of a fertile seed which would, in three different climates, struggle to life in three different ways. But already in 1934 the life was there. (*Tuned in to Change* p.102f)

THE START OF REGULAR MEETINGS

The big difference between the twenties and the thirties in Australian CSSM was that voluntary helpers at last began to play a significant part. Austinmer CSSM had been run entirely by volunteers since 1928, and so were the girls' camps, which began in 1930. It was possible to run five beach missions in the summer of 1931–32, with a number of camps for boys and girls as well. They were followed up by regular Bible study groups, weekly drawing-room meetings and Saturday night 'squashes' for teenagers. Vincent Craven himself found opportunities to have regular Scripture classes, under Church of England auspices, in several of the state high schools. He gave clear evangelistic Bible teaching to a large number of boys, some of whom became Christians.

These various activities for young people were all run by separate groups. Apart from the CSSM committee none of them was strong enough on its own to afford any staff, so they were all struggling. In New South Wales a crucial meeting was held early in 1935 to try to bring the strands together. Leaders of CSSM, Crusaders (working in the independent schools), the boys' and girls' camps, and the Bible classes all agreed to ask the CSSM committee to launch an Inter-School Christian Fellowship (ISCF) in the state high schools, which all would support. The name had first been used by Howard Guinness in Canada. A similar organisation had been started in Melbourne the year before, though it was smaller and not officially connected with CSSM.

Progress was quite rapid. The CSSM appointed Heather Drummond to work in the girls' schools while Vincent Craven continued to look after the boys. In the first year seven camps and three well-attended one-day outings were arranged; and regular meetings were held in about ten schools and sixteen private homes in different parts of Sydney.

By the late thirties these various CSSM-type activities were beginning to have an influence in Australian church life. Alex Brown was continuing tirelessly with his effective children's missions and was breaking new ground with original forms of camping, such as a 'bike-hike' through the Outback. Scripture Union membership was slowly recovering too. In 1932 there had been less than 20,000 members in the whole country: in 1937 26,500 cards were distributed and 7,000 *Daily Notes*. There was now a salaried staff of four, all based in New South Wales, and a strong team of voluntary helpers.

There were, however, serious weaknesses. The work was still

extraordinarily fragmented. The leaders of activities for boys and girls co-operated very little with one another. Crusaders in the independent schools and ISCF in the state schools had little contact, and in Victoria each was separate from both CSSM and SU. It was inevitable that tensions and misunderstandings arose. Administration in Sydney had much improved under Vincent Craven's leadership, but the staff were frequently paid late or underpaid. The committee had not matured to the point where it saw staff salaries as something they were honour-bound to provide. As the number of camps and beach missions increased, leaders and helpers were selected without sufficient care, and standards fell. Immaturity led to mistakes, such as the time when CSSM forgot its interdenominational character to the extent that eight campers were baptized by immersion at a Young People's Conference in Sydney. The incident caused criticism from parents and clergy that took many years to live down.

So while there had been progress, there were also problems. As John Pollock commented, 'the true spirit of CSSM had taken root as a hardy Australian indigenous plant. But the great days were yet to come.' (*The Good Seed*, p.146).

Early booklets of SU notes (1923 and 1924).

10

In South Africa and Canada

Meanwhile the SU tree was being firmly planted in South Africa. There had been a few beach services there since 1890, and by 1907 SU cards were published in Xhosa, Zulu and Sesotho. The spread of the SU readings owed much to a remarkable voluntary worker, Miss Jessamy Sprigg. She travelled widely for no less than fifty-four years, speaking in schools and visiting SU branches. The daughter of a former Prime Minister, her name gave her access to schools wherever she went. Frequently her trips covered over 1,000 miles, taking in thirty or forty meetings, speaking to people of all races; yet she kept it up almost until her death at the age of eighty-eight.

In 1907 Oswin Bull, a CSSM enthusiast from England, arrived in Cape Town to work with the Students Christian Association. He encouraged the students to read the SU portions, and produced notes on the SU readings, which were translated into Afrikaans. He also revived the beach services, taking a team of students to Kalk Bay in 1911. Several missions were started and in 1923 a 'Committee for Seaside Services' was formed in Cape Town. They wrote to the CSSM in London to ask for financial help. The London Committee decided to send a staff worker instead. In November 1924 Frank Millard arrived and CSSM in South Africa was properly under way.

A MAN AMONGST MEN

Aged twenty-seven, Millard had studied at Oxford and the Bible Training Institute at Glasgow, and had experience of beach missions under such leaders as Edwin Arrowsmith. Very strong and athletic, he was 'just the man for the free and easy youth of South Africa'. First and foremost he was an evangelist among boys, feeling his best with the nine to twelve age group.

In his camps and missions he made unusual effort to make the boys feel at home even if they had no Christian background. Camps were planned with superb skill and efficiency to provide 'a thoroughly good holiday' for the boys. He insisted on short talks, using words which everyone could understand, and avoiding pious platitudes and religious cliches. Above all he took every opportunity of making friends with the boys, joining wholeheartedly in volley ball, canoeing, swimming and other games. At camp he was always known as 'Hippo' because of the splash he made when he dived into the pool. 'It is only by friendship', he used to say, 'that you earn the right to speak to a boy about Christ.' In the evening the camp concert and sing-song was a regular feature. In fact there was so much fun and laughter at the camps that some Christians doubted if they were really spiritual. But Millard knew what he was doing: 'Remember that although on the surface the work appears to be so light-hearted and carefree, there is in reality a very stern spiritual battle against the powers of darkness.'

Murray Hofmeyr recalls how he and his brother were attracted by the bright singing and attractive programme at the Fish Hoek beach mission, when he was seven years old. He had never been to church in his life, but joined cheerfully in the games and services, and returned the following year. Some of Millard's talks still stick in his mind. Millard kept his name on file, and when he was old enough asked him and several other boys from his school to join him at camp. On Easter Sunday morning, with the sun streaming through the open sides of the marquee, after one of the student leaders had given the talk, he received Christ as his Saviour. It was a lasting conversion, for he became a regular camp and beach mission leader himself in years to come. Later he was to combine a successful career in engineering with active membership of the SU South African Council, and has been its chairman for many years.

Through Millard's camps and missions over the years, hundreds of such boys started to follow Christ. But he had a horror of inducing a superficial response, and was strongly against asking an adolescent to do something at the time to show he wanted to make a decision. 'If he is asked to do something visible, e.g. raise a hand at a meeting, shake hands with a speaker, or sign a decision card, he is all too apt to think: "That is what the speaker meant when he invited me to come to Christ; I'll do that." Consequently he does *that* and never really comes to Christ at all.' He was deeply concerned at the after-effects of a superficial decision, as he believed it frequently led to an antagonism to Christianity in the future. Far better to keep the door open for a genuine response later.

Soon after he arrived, Millard decided to direct most of his efforts to evangelising the white English-speaking section of the community. He was convinced that 'the spiritual approach to the unconverted must be in the home language of the unconverted in the first place'. Moreover he felt that it was the English who were, in many ways, the most spiritually unenlightened. So he decided to concentrate on them.

TWO FALSE STARTS

The Committee however was concerned to reach children of all races. In 1930 Skalk Liebenberg was appointed for work with Afrikaans children, though he left after four years because of his wife's health. Two years later James Walkey arrived from England for work with Africans. Roddy Archibald came from India to train him to speak by interpretation, and they toured Natal and Eastern Cape together. Thirty years later the Methodist Conference handbook, recording the death of one of its leading ministers, the Rev Lumkele Damane, gives us a glimpse of them in action: 'Mr Damane began to change his old habits during a powerful revival meeting held at Adams College, Natal, by two dynamic European preachers, Messrs. Walkey and Archibald. Their main theme was "Jesus breaks every fetter and can set you free".' In view of such success it is particularly sad that within a year of his arrival, James Walkey had died. It was thirty-eight years before anyone was appointed in his place.

FOLLOW-UP

While Millard travelled widely, speaking at schools, leading beach missions, running camps, all the time winning new people to Christ, he left the follow-up mainly to others. Outstanding among them was a Cape Town lawyer, Gordon Mills, who ran a large Sunday afternoon Bible class for young people in his home at Rondebosch. Following Mills' example, several other groups were started in different parts of the Cape, some meeting in homes and some on school premises. In 1938 they came together to form the Schools and Varsities Christian Union. Originally SVCU, though closely associated with CSSM and SU, was a separate organization. The two bodies officially merged, to bring the evangelistic and the follow-up work together, in 1962.

Winsome Campbell's story illustrates how these various activities could fit together in a young person's life.

> 'I first met "Hippo" Millard at a Sunday School Aniversary when I was eight years old. He spoke on the need for us to have a pilot to guide us in our lives, and I gave my life to the Lord. I was very shy but Hippo soon put me at my ease when I spoke to him after the meeting.'

She met the CSSM again at Sea Point beach mission.

'Because I was shy, I stood alone on the promenade watching the children on the beach and listening to every word. Once again my shyness was overcome by friendly interest, and gradually I became fully involved.'

At her first camp, when she was aged thirteen, it rained every day. 'I was so shy that I spoke only when spoken to. I went home muddy but excited, and hardly able to wait for the next camp. We were not allowed an SU group in our school, but most campers in our area belonged to a SVCU Bible class. Gradually I was encouraged to become a junior mission worker and tent leader. While at college and when I was teaching I managed to join four or five camps and missions per year, and my cup of happiness was full.' After seven years of teaching she joined the SU staff full time, and left only on retirement twenty-nine years later.

In spite of Winsome Campbell's story, the main thrust of Millard's work was among boys, and the girls tended to be neglected. The SVCU Bible classes helped to fill the gap. Gordon Mills had four daughters, three of whom were to marry men who later became SU Council members, so there was no danger that he would forget their needs. But the first SU woman staff worker, Kitty Hamilton, was not appointed until ten years after Millard arrived. The first girls' camp was held only in 1935.

In the work to which he felt called, however, Frank Millard was exceptionally effective. His zest for living, his humour, his athletic powers, his practical common sense and superb organisation, coupled with a deep sensitivity to the needs of the boys, were all qualities which God could use. He retired in 1960 'after 36 years of phenomenal accomplishment', as the newsletter put it at the time. The number of people in Christian service in South Africa today who owe their conversion to him, confirms the truth of that assessment.

ACROSS CANADA

The same year that Frank Millard arrived in Cape Town, Victor Ware was appointed CSSM evangelist in Canada. Ware had worked with the Caravan Mission in England for some years and was then living in British Columbia. He started beach missions on the West Coast and Lake Winnipeg, and spoke at churches across the country. An Anglican minister, Norman Barclay, joined him for Eastern

Canada in 1929. The same year Howard Guinness, the Irish doctor who was soon to make a major impact in Australia and New Zealand, blazed across the country. He captured many young people for Christ, and founded the Pioneer Camps. In Canada CSSM was not capable of following up his tour, and the Inter-School Christian Fellowship which grew out of it was linked with Inter-Varsity and the emerging International Fellowship of Evangelical Students.

Ware and Barclay encouraged people to use SU notes, but their main work was with children. The SU side was organised by an elderly gentleman of great energy called Robert Richardson, who took up the task in 1915, when he was already over sixty, and kept it up for the next thirty years. The number of subscriptions grew steadily but Richardson would not work with a committee, and made no plans for the future. In 1939 Ware retired and Barclay suddenly died. Until he died in 1946, at the age of ninety-two, Richardson was the only SU representative in the country.

CHILDREN'S MISSIONS IN UGANDA

In South America, in the West Indies and in many countries of Africa, the cards continued to circulate. A letter from Lagos reported that they had 944 boys and 131 girls as members including 203 Moslems, who were among the keenest members and were often included in the prize-winners at the annual competitions. Regular meetings were held in a number of schools in the city, including the CMS grammar school. By 1939 SU cards were printed in forty-four African languages. In East Africa, Fred Crittenden was appointed children's missioner in 1936. He travelled widely in Kenya and Uganda, speaking to African and European children alike. A particularly fruitful week was spent at Kings College, Budo, near Kampala. 'There was no emotion', he reported, 'but boy after boy came quietly afterwards to talk to me, saying he wanted to get right with God.' He planned to find one or two African colleagues and develop the work on the Indian pattern. But he made such an impression at Budo that he was asked to become private tutor to its most eminent pupil, the future Kabaka of Uganda. John Duncan came from Scotland to take his place, but the 1939 war started soon after he arrived, and he had to move on to other work. It would be another fifteen years before SU would have a staff worker in Tropical Africa again.

11

Europe in the Thirties

Throughout the period 1900–1939 SU cards continued to circulate widely in Europe. The upheaval of the 1914–18 war put a stop to the work for a time in much of Eastern Europe. But it gradually recommenced, and by 1939 the cards were printed in twenty-two European languages, including Bulgarian, Czech, Hungarian, Rumanian and Polish. It was all, however, organised from London. There were local distributors in some places, but there was little personal contact with the readers.

A START IN SWITZERLAND

It was in Switzerland that SU first became a genuinely national movement. The initiative came from Mrs Dunn-Pattison, a wealthy English woman, whose husband had been killed in World War I. In 1923 she came to live at Chateaux d'Oex. She was an energetic Bible teacher, knew CSSM and SU well, and was convinced of its importance. In 1925 she enlisted the aid of an aristocratic Swiss lady, Mme van Berchem. Reluctant to help at first because of her busy life, Mme van Berchem later threw herself wholeheartedly into the task, and explained why: 'After a while I felt vividly the importance of having a work of that sort in our country. I knew, from experience in my own family, the decisive influence on young people of the habit of reading the Bible day by day.... The hearts of children are indisputedly the best soil for the seed of the word of life.... Nothing can replace the teaching of the Bible received during the first years of life.'

The two women needed great determination, for at first the response was slow. Church leaders were suspicious, and they 'received many rebuffs'. But they travelled constantly, visiting individual Christians, holding small meetings in homes, taking opportunities in churches or larger halls, wherever they were invited. Whenever possible they left behind groups of children, meeting regularly with an adult leader, to read the Bible together. *La Ligue pour la lecture de la Bible* was officially formed at a prayer meeting in Chateaux d'Oex in

1925. Cards were translated from English, and a magazine *La Boussole* (The Compass) with notes for children was published.

The most significant feature for the future, however, was that La Ligue was quite independent of the CSSM committee in London. As early as 1924 Mrs Dunn-Pattison had written to Mr Hubbard, T B Bishop's successor, recommending that a Belgian called Philémon Ringoir should be appointed staff worker. The committee in London sent their 'best wishes' but decided that they could not send any money! They were building the new headquarters in Wigmore Street at the time and funds were scarce. It seemed a set-back, but in fact it was the best thing that could have happened. After praying about it with some friends, Mrs Dunn-Pattison decided that God 'intends us to delay no longer but to go forward'. Philémon Ringoir 'launched out in faith' and had 'a fruitful ministry' for a number of years. Although an English woman and a Belgian helped to plant it the new movement was rooted in Swiss soil from the start.

The next major advance was at Vennes, near Lausanne. Dr Pierre de Benoit, Mme Van Berchem's son-in-law, founded the Emmaus Bible Institute there in 1926. La Ligue and Emmaus were closely associated from the start. When Dr de Benoit arranged the first youth camp there in 1929, a hundred boys and girls attended. The following year two camps were arranged.

GYM WAS MY GOD

Both the 1930 camps were led by a young man called Ernst Aebi. Mme van Berchem met him while he was studying at Emmaus, and asked him to translate the English SU notes into German, and to lead the two camps. The response to the notes was disappointing; but the camps were remarkable. Years later, Aebi told John Pollock about them: 'Fifty-five girls out of the seventy gave their hearts to the Lord Jesus through personal talks. Not one as far as I know has back-slidden. The same blessing came on the boys. When I saw that the Lord had given me such a gift I realised that I had received a clear call.' (*The Good Seed,* p.166) At the beginning of 1931 he became general secretary of the Swiss Scripture Union.

Ernst Aebi was a man of immense energy and vitality. 'Gym was my god', he used to say about his life as a teenager. A serious illness when he was seventeen caused him to stop and think. A few weeks later, after a mission service, he accepted Christ. 'I saw my sins, and I remembered the text, "Behold the Lamb of God, which taketh away the sin of the world." I asked him to take away mine. A wonderful change came over me. I knew then that I would be a missionary.'

His missionary service in fact was in his own country. For thirty-one years, until his death, he gave himself totally to the evangelisation of Switzerland and to building up Scripture Union. He had an unusual range of gifts. Warm-hearted and impulsive, he was not only a dynamic speaker and effective personal evangelist, but also a skilled administrator. As well as writing SU notes, and running camps and conferences, he held large evangelistic campaigns in towns and villages all over the country, and great rallies in the larger cities.

A turning point in his ministry came in 1932. God had particularly blessed one of the evangelistic campaigns, and a number of people, young and old, had made decisions for Christ. After he said goodbye to them on the final night Aebi went to bed. But he could not sleep. 'How can these people grow in their faith? What can I do for them?' he asked himself. Eventually he had a vision of what he should do – stop translating English SU notes, and produce his own. Written by Swiss writers and adapted to Swiss needs, they would make it possible for those who had been converted to 'make personal contact with the word of God and to grow, however difficult their circumstances'. The committee was doubtful, for the circulation of the translated notes was very low, but Aebi was determined. *Der Bibellesebund* was launched on 1 January 1933 and proved an immense success. Circulation grew rapidly as a result of the evangelistic campaigns. Pierre de Benoit started French notes in 1934, and total Swiss membership shot up to 18,000 by 1935 and 28,000 by 1940.

Meanwhile Dr de Benoit built a camp site for La Ligue, next to the Bible Institute, on a glorious site looking over Lac Leman (Lake Geneva). A visitor described the vivid scene as the campers met round a huge bonfire on the night before they went home. 'The whole chain of the Alpes de Savoie were shadowed by the cloak of night, Lac Leman glittering with the reflected lights from Evian; the vast dome of the sky; the glowing flames soaring into the night. Suddenly Mr Aebi, with a mighty inspiration from God, gave out his text – the searching words of Christ, "I am come to send fire on the earth."' The number of camps and of campers grew. Soon 1,000 children and young people were coming each summer, from all parts of Switzerland. From 1936–39 large camps for French young people were organised at Vennes as well.

UPHILL WORK IN FRANCE

Aebi had also become responsible for La Ligue in France. An Englishman, Harry Johnson, had worked there from 1922–33, supported by the CSSM committee in London. He travelled by bicycle, with a small harmonium, holding rather ineffective children's missions in his very bad French, and published a translation of the English SU notes. When he resigned, the London committee asked Aebi to take over. A young Frenchman, who had just graduated from Emmaus, Frank Buchet, joined the staff and La Ligue was at last able to take root in French soil. It was an uphill task, but Buchet was encouraged by some remarkable conversions. One young man, who later became an SU secretary, was sent to camp by his father, a 'free thinker', with the words: 'I am sending you my rascal of a son. At the free thinking meeting no-one has been able to do anything with him. I took him to the Catholics but he stayed the same. Now I am bringing him to you; we will see if your God can do anything!' After he was converted however the father was still not pleased. 'We did not send our son to you to be made religious, but merely to improve him. You have abused our confidence and made our home miserable. Take care, Monsieur Pastor.'

To start with France made use of the Swiss camp site and the Swiss notes. But Aebi was convinced that 'the French mentality is quite different from the Swiss' and that a distinctive French Ligue must develop. The first camp on French soil was held at Sumène, in the Cévennes, in 1936 and a French edition of the notes appeared in 1939. These developments were just in time, for they made it possible for the camps and the notes to continue, under difficulties, throughout World War II and the German occupation.

LATVIA AND BEYOND

Far away in Latvia, a Scripture Union evangelist was also at work among his own people. 'Once I was an atheist', said Jacob Vagar on a visit to London in 1939, 'now I am a preacher of the unsearchable riches of Christ.'

In 1920 Vagar, aged thirty, was a captain in the Red Army, based in Odessa. His earlier enthusiasm for communism was beginning to wane as he saw the ruthlessness and brutality around him. Deeply disillusioned and unhappy, he decided to commit suicide. After an official dance one night, he put his revolver to his head to end his life.

He was about to pull the trigger, when he seemed to hear a voice:

'Jacob, you have tried everything, and nothing satisfies you. One thing you have not tried – to live according to the Gospel. Try it and you will be satisfied.' Verses of the Bible, which he had learned at Sunday School as a child, came into his mind: 'Rejoice in the Lord', 'that my joy might remain in you' and then 'Faith comes by hearing, and hearing by the word of God'. He remembered that he had a Latvian New Testament, buried at the bottom of his suitcase. His godly mother had given it to him when he had left home ten years before. As he hunted for it he prayed: 'O God, if you exist, and if the Bible is your word, reveal yourself to me.'

Starting at the beginning he read steadily through, praying for light and faith. Four months later, as he was reading one Sunday morning, a brilliant light seemed to fill his room. He jumped up thinking there was a fire, and the light went out. From that moment he believed. Falling on his knees, he prayed, 'Lord Jesus, I am the sinner you died to save. Save me.'

He immediately applied to leave the army, though he knew he risked imprisonment or death by doing so. But the rules were not as clear in Russia then as they later became. After he had spoken to the army committee about his new-found faith the chairman commented 'it seems an innocent sort of army that Comrade Vagar wants to join' and discharged him. A policeman even told him the way to the house of some Baptists: 'There is often some bright singing in there. Perhaps that is what you are looking for.'

After working for a time as an evangelist in Odessa, Vagar was deported to his native Latvia, which at that time was enjoying a few years of independence. He was employed as a teacher but gave all the time he could spare to evangelism among the children and young people, many of them were orphaned and destitute.

The Latvian Baptist Church was so impressed with Vagar's work that they sent him for Bible training in Britain. There he met the CSSM and was appointed as their first staff evangelist for 'Latvia and beyond'. He returned home in 1931 and for the next nine years travelled from village to village, spending a week in each, holding meetings for adults and children, with definite spiritual results.

Then war came again. Russia occupied Latvia in June 1940, and on 21st August Vagar was arrested. A Latvian who escaped to Sweden wrote to say that he was 'put in the main prison, along with our military and political leaders. In their hour of agony they gathered round to hear of the Saviour. Many were saved. Many of them faced death as children of God.' The following year he was banished for eight years to Russian Turkestan. Nothing was heard of him again.

12

Britain in the Lean Years

Back in Britain, Tom Bishop carried on as General Secretary until he was eighty. The decline in evangelical life, begun in the closing years of the previous century, gathered pace. Naturally it affected the CSSM. Numbers at meetings declined and opposition increased. Bishop made sure that the Mission held firm to the authority of Scripture. But in his old age he also put a stop to any changes in method which might have helped to stem the tide.

Nevertheless two significant developments took place during that time. The first was the formation of the Crusaders Union of Bible Classes. They met in homes and aimed to reach boys not attending Sunday School. The first class to use the name was founded by the Rev A C Kestin in 1900, and the idea spread rapidly. It was under a separate committee, but affiliated to CSSM in 1907. Some years later it branched out to become a great movement on its own, but the combination of straightforward Bible teaching on Sundays with a range of games and other activities during the week, was very much in the CSSM tradition, and the two movements continued to work closely together.

NEW IDEAS IN SCOTLAND

There was good progress, too, in Scotland, where Henry Rankin, a friend of Josiah Spiers, formed an Advisory Committee in 1902. A young Organising Secretary was appointed and an office opened in Glasgow. Decentralisation generated new ideas as well as fresh interest. In 1907 Scotland ran the first CSSM/SU camp for girls in the world, a bold experiment in those days. Eva Wallace, who had joined the staff in 1904 to visit the girls' schools, remarked that the committee's agreement to the suggestion showed that 'Prayer changes things'. 'Driving, cycling, walking and talking, the golden days seemed to fly' and day by day 'those in charge saw that God was setting his seal of approval on the work.'

In the twenties the foundations were laid for the schools and camps work which grew so strongly in Scotland later. Boys and girls were given equal attention, and all types of secondary school were visited. By 1937 Scotland had one man and three women schools workers, compared with only one of each in England. The process of decentralisation was soon carried a stage further by the formation of district committees in Glasgow, Edinburgh and Aberdeen, responsible for all aspects of CSSM and SU work in their area. Monthly rallies were held in several centres, and regular weekly meetings in many of the leading schools.

An example was the group in Glasgow High School, which was started in 1927 by John Laird, when he was a medical student. Ten years later the group reported: 'The boys now run it themselves with the help of outside speakers. Our maximum is 20, while our average is about 14'. In a nearby girls' school, 'some of the members are not very keen. We enrolled eight new members last session, and we know of at least one who came to know the Lord, so we feel it is well worth while carrying on.' The strategy of regular contact with the young people through weekly school meetings, monthly rallies and the strong programme of summer and Easter camps was beginning to work.

IN ENGLISH VILLAGES

Across the border in England the emphasis was on children's missions rather than school groups. The Caravan Mission, under the forceful leadership of R T Garwood, grew rapidly. By 1931 there were twenty-three missioners touring the villages. But it was difficult work. The villages were less responsive than in earlier years, and the staff felt particularly called to preach the gospel in places where there was no local evangelical church. Sometimes they parked their caravans and pitched their tents almost in defiance of the local vicar. At headquarters Garwood had his battles too, as his department depended on a grant from general CSSM funds, and his colleagues did not all share his vision for the village work. 'Remind him he is only a humble village evangelist', was the response when he first suggested that one of the men should have a car. It was several years before the final horse-drawn caravan was phased out.

As well as the Caravan Mission in the villages there was a small team of CSSM evangelists, who led groups of younger voluntary helpers at the seaside in the summer, and for the rest of the year travelled all over Britain holding missions in churches and church halls. One of them, W G Ovens, attracted huge crowds at the beach mission he ran each year at Portrush in Northern Ireland. The strong

SU movement that was to develop there in later years owes much to his lengthy visits each year. Bryan Green and Tom Rees, later to become well-known evangelists for adults, each served on the staff for a number of years. But the outstanding example was Richard Hudson Pope. He joined the staff in 1905 and only finally retired, at the age of eighty, in 1960.

A SUPERB TEACHER

In his first year Pope ran a series of twenty-four missions, lasting a week or a fortnight each, and the pace scarcely slackened as he grew older. 'I wonder if some people hold back from giving their whole life to service among children', he once said, 'because there are no career prospects? After ten years you will still be a children's evangelist. After twenty years, still a children's evangelist. After forty years, still a children's evangelist. There is no future, not down here on earth. But what about that day when the gates of heaven are thrown wide and you march in, and all your children with you?'

Small of stature, with the erect bearing of a soldier, he had boundless energy for his work, and for the boys and girls he was called to serve. As someone wrote: 'He gave workers standards of discipline, behaviour and speaking which deeply influenced the whole tone of the Mission at home and abroad.' He was always serious and earnest when speaking about Christ, but had a warm and friendly personality, with a flair for music, and was full of humour and enthusiasm. So children flocked to hear him, learned to trust him and responded eagerly to what he had come to tell them. He always kept their letters when boys and girls wrote to tell him that they had started to follow Jesus. By the time he retired they filled a large trunk

A feature of Pope's work was that a large proportion of the children he led to Christ continued as active Christians into adult life. Many became Christian workers themselves. When I was travelling round England taking SU meetings, in the 50s and 60s, I kept on meeting people who told me that they had found Christ as children 'when Mr Pope took a mission at our church' years before. An interesting example of the long-term influence is provided by a list of names from a mission in Edinburgh in 1923. It must have been one of the smallest missions he ever conducted: yet of the twenty boys who attended the mission, four became missionaries, three others became ministers and two joined the SU staff. One of them was George Duncan who later became known worldwide as a writer and convention speaker.

Another Scotsman, James Meiklejohn, recalls a beach mission at St Andrews, when he was twelve years old. One Sunday evening 'as there was nothing much else to do' he went, rather reluctantly, to a meeting for teenage boys. 'Led vigorously and tunefully by a very cheerful, oldish man, with a nervous twitch in one eye, I learned my first choruses. That evening for the first time in my life I heard the Christian message in an interesting, understandable and sometimes humorous way.' Whenever he could, for the rest of the holiday, he went to hear Hudson Pope again. Two weeks later, he was at a crowded meeting of forty teenage boys packed into a small living room. Pope spoke on the text 'Christ Jesus came into the world to save sinners.' At the close, Meiklejohn 'knelt at the sofa in the corner where he had been sitting, very conscious of a great sense of need to have a Saviour, but also that two boys from the same school were watching.' The decision he made that night stuck. In years to come he would put in thirty-four years on the SU staff himself.

One of the reasons why Hudson Pope's missions had such permanent results was probably his emphasis on teaching Christian doctrine. 'If you teach at all, you must teach doctrine', he used to say, 'sharply-defined, clear-cut doctrine.' But it must be taught in a way the children could readily understand. During his early training with the Mission he spent a week with George Goodman, at the Caravan Mission in Surrey. Goodman's clear and logical way of presenting Christian truth so impressed Pope that he went home and tore up all his carefully prepared sermon notes and started again. His aim was to make the truths of the Bible clear and plain to a boy or girl. Realising the value of visual aids he effectively developed the skill of making a model that illustrated some aspect of the faith. 'A tremendous lot of thought and care went into the preparation of my models – hours of thought as to the simplest way to present such truths as grace, regeneration, faith, substitution, redemption, etc. But once I have made it, I use the model and the same address hundreds of times over. That does not mean that one need not prepare again. You may safely use the address a hundred times, as long as you pray about it as much the hundredth time as you did the first time.'

He placed great emphasis too on the change that should take place in a child's life after he accepted Christ. 'What is repentance?', he wrote. 'A change of mind leading to a change of direction and conduct; therefore repentance and conversion must always go together.' Those who came to him for counselling or made decisions to accept Christ at his meetings knew what they were doing. For many it was the turning point of their lives.

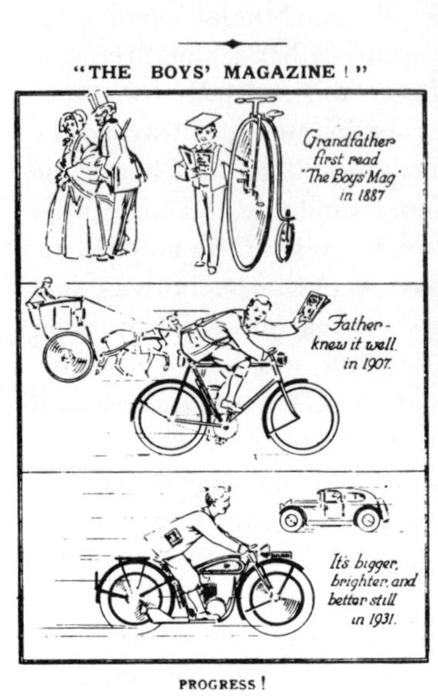

Advertisement for 'The Boys Magazine'.

Handbill for one of Hudson Pope's missions (1914)

THE FIRST SCRIPTURE NOTES

When Tom Bishop finally retired, in 1920, J H Hubbbard was appointed as his successor. So he became the first paid general secretary. He had already been on the staff for twenty years as accountant, and for some years had tried to introduce some new ideas. 'Without consultation or permission', he later wrote, 'we felt our way along, lest the idea should be turned down.' Once he was in charge there was a burst of progress. Notes on the SU readings, which had appeared in *Our Own Magazine* for thirty-five years, and had been printed as a separate booklet by the Officers Christian Union in the 1914–18 war, first appeared on their own as an official SU publication in 1923. Written by the well-known Scottish preacher, Graham Scroggie, they were a great success. Various writers contributed, and by 1927, when Scroggie began a famous five-year series covering the whole Bible, circulation was 60,000.

In January 1921 Hubbard launched *The CSSM,* a monthly magazine for adults, giving news of the work, brief notes on the daily readings, and an outline for a children's talk based on the reading for each Sunday. The same year he published *CSSM Choruses* and started a major revision of the hymnbook *Golden Bells*. In 1926 the first of a series of *Sunday School Lesson Books* appeared. By the 1930s CSSM was publishing some seventy-five different booklets and had entered the hard-backed publishing field with the 'Wigmore' series of children's story-books.

All this needed more staff and more office space. Reluctantly the committee agreed to Hubbard's plan to buy a valuable site in Wigmore Street, and to put up a substantial building. Part of it was let to help pay the mortgage. The rest, including a first-class ground-floor bookshop, was occupied in 1925. Near the corner of London's famous Harley Street, it served as Mission headquarters for thirty years. Today the only SU presence is the bookshop, but it is still a meeting point for Christians from around the world.

SKI PARTIES AND SAILING CAMPS

The 1920s also saw a rapid growth in the number and variety of camps, which were now an official part of the CSSM programme. By summer 1921 there were five for boys and two for girls. Next winter the first ski party was arranged. Twenty-one boys, with their leaders, travelled overnight by train to Switzerland, and spent two weeks skiing, skating and tobogganing, with prayers morning and evening. It was judged 'a great success from every point of view'. The following year a girls' party was arranged as well, safely housed in a separate hotel nearby. 'I found, as the officers said we would', wrote one of the boys afterwards, 'that all the joys of Camp were not to be found in the

The CSSM monogram was widely used in publicity in the 1920s and 1930s.

The original SU badge was introduced for the Golden Jubilee in 1929.

snow or on the ice, but in the evening meetings. I believe many found themselves face to face with God as they had never done before; and those of us who had believed on Jesus as Saviour before were strengthened.' By 1924, numbers had risen to 230 and the winter-sports parties had become an annual event.

Another new initiative, in 1924, was the sailing camps on the Norfolk Broads. They were the idea of Joe Church, a Cambridge medical student, who had been converted at the CSSM beach mission at Whitby a few years earlier, and was later to be at the centre of the East African Revival. Four or five boys and their two leaders, who formed the crew of each boat, shared rough weather and calm, sunshine and rain, at close quarters throughout the week. It was a good test of character and an excellent background for the evening meetings in the camp launch. Sixty years later the Broads at Easter are crowded with Christian groups of various sorts. It was a couple of students, under CSSM auspices, who set the ball rolling.

The growing programme of holiday activities was still almost entirely staffed by volunteers. Some of the seaside missions were led by members of staff, like Hudson Pope or Bryan Green, and the camps were organised from the office. But the majority of leaders, and all their assistants and helpers, were men and women in other full-time occupations who took time off from their holidays and gave it freely to the mission. It meant that a great deal could be done at very little cost, for the leaders and helpers paid their own expenses. It was also first-class training for the younger workers. From time to time however, the amateur approach led to a lowering of standards and follow-up was difficult. When the children met at seaside missions and the teenagers converted at camp came from live churches or good Christian families, lack of follow-up did not matter so much. When they came from homes where they had no encouragement, or were away at boarding school for most of the year, it was more serious.

THE TOP THIRTY SCHOOLS

All this began to change in 1932 when Eric Nash joined the staff. 'Bash', as he was usually called, had first applied three years earlier but the Council had decided that 'there was no vacancy where his gifts could be well used'. In that decision they nearly missed one of the most influential appointments in the history of the Mission.

Bash concentrated on the thirty leading public schools, the fee-paying boarding schools where most of the sons of the wealthier sections of society were educated. It used to be said that 'public school religion is that which fits you for life and ruins you for eternity', and in Bash's early years there was probably some truth in the saying. Certainly many school authorities were suspicious of evangelical Christianity. So Bash worked quietly, inviting boys to his summer camps, visiting the schools, holding informal meetings in the houses of friendly members of staff, and writing innumerable letters. The camps were the prime focus of his method. He used them both as a means of evangelism, and as a training ground for young Christians.

John Stott recalls 'a memorable day in February 1938, on which, it was announced, there would be a visiting speaker named the Reverend E J H Nash,' at the informal Christian group in his school.

> He was nothing much to look at, and certainly no ambassador for muscular Christianity. Yet as he spoke I was riveted. His text was Pilate's question: 'What then shall I do with Jesus, who is called the Christ?' When the meeting was over, I went up to ask our speaker some questions, the nature of which I do not now recall. What I do remember is that he had the spiritual discernment to recognise in me a seeking soul. So he took me for a drive in his car, answered my questions, and explained to me the way of salvation. To my astonishment his presentation of Christ crucified and risen exactly corresponded with the needs of which I was aware. But he exerted no pressure upon me. He had the sensitivity and wisdom to let me go, so that I could 'open the door' to Christ by myself, which I did that very night by my bedside in the dormitory, while the other boys were in bed and asleep. (*Bash, A Study in Spiritual Power*, p.57f)

Over the years hundreds of boys took a similar step of faith. Many of them went on to positions of leadership in British society and exerted a firm Christian witness there. Many others, like John Stott, went into the Anglican ministry, for Bash took every opportunity of encouraging them to do so, or to take a teaching post in one of the schools he was concerned with. Over the years more and more schools had evangelical chaplains and schoolmasters, who backed up the camps, often giving a large share of their holidays to them.

The camps themselves were meticulously organised. From 1940 onwards they were always held at the little Dorset village of Iwerne Minster, in an old country house that had been turned into a school. Though Bash was not at all athletic himself, there was an emphasis on games in the early years, which had a strong appeal to most public school boys at the time. Bash insisted on a high ratio of officers to boys, so that every activity could be properly organised and every boy given suitable pastoral care. The officers were carefully recruited and thoroughly trained. Most of them had come through the camps as boys, others had been converted at university and first arrived as 'senior campers'. Those who did not reach his high standards or were not prepared to make Iwerne Minster their top priority were advised to use their talents elsewhere. Every part of the camp operation was finely tuned to achieve its purpose of attracting the boys and winning them for Christ. But the style was relaxed and informal. Bash had a horror of intensity, believing that spiritual commitments made in a highly-charged atmosphere, by teenagers at any rate, were unlikely to last. He knew the value of well-timed humour, and used it to help boys to relax and think through issues calmly. Perhaps that is one of the reasons why so many of them continued as Christians into adult life.

Another reason was without doubt the care Bash took for the boys who were converted. John Stott recalls 'the extraordinary devotion with which he nurtured me in the early years of my Christian life. He wrote to me every week for, I think, seven years. He also prayed for me every day. I can only begin to guess what I owe, under God, to such a faithful friend and pastor.' (*Guard the Gospel*, IVP, p.29). This patient nurture continued after a boy left school and was part of a clear long-term strategy. If he showed leadership potential, a boy was invited back to camp as a 'senior camper' or junior officer, and was gradually given more responsibility. Those who went on to university were encouraged not only to join the Christian Union but to attend a weekly camp prayer meeting. Bash himself visited Oxford and Cambridge nearly every term. Like Arrowsmith fifty years before, he realised the strategic importance of the universities and regularly recruited new helpers there. Oliver Barclay describes his influence on the Christian Union at Cambridge:

> A succession of people connected with camps for public schoolboys, especially the 'Bash Camps', sent up to Cambridge a remarkable group of students who already had some skill in evangelism. They emphasised the 'simple gospel' and, being trained in work with schoolboys, were sometimes anti-intellectual and anti-theological. That gradually righted itself, however, for most of them as they gained experience. Their ablest men became intellectually and theologically some of the more adventurous and effective evangelists and teachers of the next generation. They were also excellent personal evangelists. At one time it was a joke that to be a member of the University Hockey team it was necessary either to be a

CICCU member or to attend CICCU sermons. The reason was that a 'Bash camper' was the Captain of Hockey and brought all the members of the team along to the Sunday night sermons – often trailing in a little late because he (and the Secretary, also a Christian) had been rounding up a straggler. (*Whatever happened to the Jesus Lane Lot?* p.105)

Bash had a remarkable gift, for such a quiet man, of commanding the loyalty of his colleagues. 'That single-minded dedication to the Lord, which I saw so clearly in Bash, has been the greatest single influence on my own life', writes Michael Green, the well-known preacher and author (*Bash,* p.93). Some of the younger men even followed him to excess, unconsciously copying his mannerisms and characteristic expressions. This brought a certain amount of criticism. Some Christians who supported his general aims considered that he had too strong an influence on his younger helpers, in such matters as their choice of career, and that he demanded too exclusive a loyalty. Certainly he was a man with a single vision. Like Paul he could say, 'This one thing I do.' He believed God had called him to serve him in a particular sphere, the leading public schools. He gave himself totally and wholeheartedly to that particular task, and wanted those who were helping him to be equally committed to it.

In his later years, in the more egalitarian climate that followed World War II, Bash was frequently criticised for concentrating on the leading public schools. To quote John Stott again: 'It was easy to dismiss him as an élitist or a snob. But people who thought and taught that way simply did not understand Bash. What motivated him was not snobbery, but strategy. He believed that God had called him to work in these schools, and that the reason for this divine call was that the future leadership of church and state was to be found there.' (*Bash,* p.62)

When Bash died in 1982 *the Times* described him as 'a quiet, unassuming clergyman who never sought the lime-light, hit the head-lines or wanted preferment; and yet whose influence within the Church of England during the last 50 years was probably greater than any of his contemporaries, for there must be many hundreds of men today, many in positions of responsibility, who thank God for him, because it was through his ministry that they were led to a Christian commitment.' The revival of Evangelical Anglicanism in Britain in the last twenty-five years has had a number of tributaries, but Bash's camps were one of the most significant.

13

New Pattern in New Zealand

Meanwhile events were taking place on the other side of the world which were to have a remarkable influence on Christian life there, and set a new pattern for CSSM and SU worldwide.

Before 1930 the movement had made little impression in New Zealand. Henry Hankinson had visited the islands in 1886, and 'walked many miles' in search of someone to take responsibility for Scripture Union. Just before returning to England he met S C Farr, of Christchurch, who took on the task with enthusiasm, and distributed the cards and magazines efficiently for many years. He was succeeded by an energetic widow, Mrs Taylor, who had run a branch for the Maoris at Wanganui since about 1880. On her death in 1914 her son, the Rev Basil Taylor, took over. According to J H Hubbard, Basil Taylor had 'distinct gifts for work amongst boys and girls, and was also musical'. But he was 'not precisely a business man and the SU did not flourish greatly under his leadership.' Martyn Gooch and Bob Drury paid lengthy visits in 1902 and 1903; and Edmund Clark in 1914 and 1923. But though numbers of individual lives were touched, no regular children's work developed.

A NEW START

A new start was made when Alec Binnie arrived from England. He was a young business man who had attended CSSM Camps and beach missions as a boy. In January 1930 he got a group of young people together to run a beach mission at Brown's Bay, near Auckland. They were very conscious of their inexperience but reported that 'the Lord walked "in the midst". It was really a wonderful mission from beginning to end, in point of numbers, power and definite conversions.' They had over 300 children at the morning beach services and 1,000 adults at their open-air meetings. The following summer the same group ran two beach missions, at Takapuna and Brown's Bay, and also a small camp attended by just half a dozen boys.

Cartoons from New Zealand camp brochures in the 50s.

Meanwhile Athol Donnell, a young teacher at Auckland Grammar School, started a Bible study group for the boys in a church near the school. Donnell, with Dr W H Pettit and others, had founded the Evangelical Union at Auckland University three years before.

Hearing about Howard Guinness's dynamic tour of Australia, they invited him to come on to New Zealand. He arrived in September 1930 and in his typical fashion travelled all over the country 'like a whirlwind', speaking in schools and colleges. In many of the schools he started small groups of boys or girls for prayer and Bible study. Without consulting the Crusaders Union in England, he decided to call them 'Crusader' groups.

THE IRISH DOCTOR

Guinness's vigorous spiritual challenge made a deep impression. At Auckland Grammar School, where Donnell was teaching, he spoke at the morning assembly, and invited boys who wanted to form a group to meet him after lunch. Because of the pressure of his programme he forgot to turn up himself, but the group still started and soon became a recognised school society. The headmaster would only allow boys to attend if they brought written permission from their parents, and he banned 'controversial subjects such as justification by faith'. However, weekly Bible studies were held, and a daily prayer meeting in Donnell's room before school. Guinness wrote later:

> The New Zealand school campaign was the most strenuous piece of work that it had ever been my lot to do. I never spoke less than twice a day and sometimes three or four times. In order to reach all the schools which had asked for me I had to spend seven nights sleeping on various trains. My normal practice was to address the school at morning assembly, meet in the lunch hour those boys or girls whose hearts God had moved, and at night organise a Crusader Group to function within the school. Such a lightning approach to such a vital and difficult question carried with it enormous risks. In some schools as a result the Crusaders found themselves with unsuitable leaders, and would have collapsed entirely but for Dr John Laird whom God raised up at this very time to follow up my beginning and to lay permanent foundations for a lasting work throughout the country. (Howard Guinness, *Journey among Students,* Anglican Information Office, Sydney, p.71)

THE SCOTTISH DOCTOR

John Laird, who was twenty-five at the time, had been involved both as a boy and a leader at CSSM camps and seaside missions in Scotland. He was hoping to go to China as a medical missionary, but meantime had signed on as a ship's surgeon on the training ship 'Northumberland'. He arrived in Auckland a few weeks after Guinness had left the country. He recalls that he found a 'rejoicing but slightly bewildered committee with a new organization on their hands and very little knowledge and experience to guide them what to do next. They had given themselves much to prayer for guidance and particularly that the Lord would send someone with experience of this kind of work to follow up the splendid initiative which Dr Guinness's visit had created.'

An apparently chance meeting in a bookshop put Laird in touch with the Auckland committee as soon as he arrived. Dr Pettit sensed that here was a potential helper, and immediately asked him to leave his ship, either to take over his medical practice for a time so that he himself could be free to visit the schools, or to visit the schools himself. As the ship worked round the coast, loading and unloading, Laird had time to think over the proposal. Whenever possible he went ashore to meet Crusader leaders and hear more of the opportunities. Eventually, after a day spent in prayer high on the hills behind

Wellington, Laird agreed, provided a doctor could be found to take his place on the return journey. He offered to stay for six months. In the event he stayed for fourteen years.

One of the ship's ports of call was Napier, on the east coast of North Island. As they were lying off shore, a violent earthquake shook the town, the worst in New Zealand's history. 'Looking ashore we saw the whole of a big cliff face rolling down into the sea, sending billows of yellow dust in front of it and high up into the air. Some large buildings were blazing and a great volume of smoke went up.'

Laird immediately went ashore to join the rescue team, and spent a day and a half with the wounded. The experience was a tragic one, but Laird's involvement helped him in his new work. 'Later I found that my name was already well known through newspaper reports,' he recalled, 'and headmasters were invariably willing to let me give a talk to the boys about the earthquake. This opened many schools to the message, and became a valuable introduction wherever I went.' It was particularly helpful where school authorities had been put off by Howard Guinness's aggressive methods.

There is no doubt that John Laird was God's man for this particular moment in New Zealand. Writing of 1931, when he reckoned that he 'addressed something like 10,000 schoolboys – a never to be forgotten experience', he points out how he and Howard Guinness complemented one another. 'He, the Irishman, had led the cavalry charge, I, the Scotsman had now to follow, and build the bridges.' Like Josiah Spiers, John Laird was described by one of his colleagues as 'the prince of children's speakers. I can remember his merry laugh, his kind, sometimes merry, at other times serious, eyes, as he spoke to the children of their need and the Saviour's love. I can remember his interest in particular children, and the way he would give himself to them.'

THE LAIRD STRATEGY

Unlike Spiers, Laird proved to be a strategist and an able administrator. A few months after he arrived he drew up 'a memorandum sketching out the principles on which the future work in New Zealand should be built. Looking back on it now', he wrote in 1957, 'it is interesting to see the way in which things did in fact develop along the lines then forecast.'

Laird laid down the principle that 'the work should be begun and carried on quietly, without undue publicity even among the general Christian public. One of the surest ways of stunting and destroying spiritual work is to talk too much about it, and to publish it abroad, particularly at its inception. It will not be long before the right kind of people get to know about the work and pray for it. We must make haste slowly, for only so can an enduring work be built up. Each step must be taken in prayer and faith, and must be planted deep on a sure and solid foundation.'

An important feature of his plan was a systematic attempt to form Christian groups in every secondary school in the country. 'If we are to gain access to the young people of school age it will be necessary to win the respect and confidence of the clergy, ministers, headmasters and parents. For this reason we feel that the movement should not associate itself with any one denomination.' 'Right from the beginning', Laird recalled in 1957, 'there was a strong emphasis on conservative, strongly ethical, evangelism. We always tried to avoid short cuts and spurious emotionalism. Emphasis in the schools has been on the importance of witnessing by the quality of their scholarship, sportmanship and school citizenship, rather than fervent evangelism. The reaping in the spiritual sense has mostly been at the camps and not in the schools.'

Another part of the strategy was to develop a parallel and closely related work in the Universities. Laird gave a good deal of time to this, even acting as chairman of the Inter-Varsity Fellowship executive for several years. 'We followed the plan of concentrating on the schools and leaving the students more or less to look after themselves. This concentration on the school field resulted in an increasingly strong IVF. This in turn resulted in a steady stream of Christian men and women going into the teaching profession where in turn they gradually added to the strength of the Crusader witness in schools. The impact on the churches also was considerable and cumulative.'

A further important factor in the growth of the work was that, as in Scotland, work among girls was treated with as much importance as that among boys. 'In the early stages of my visitations to New Zealand schools', he wrote, 'the New Zealand Council assumed that I would visit girls' schools as well as boys. This I emphatically declined to do, urging upon them the need to appoint a lady worker.' In 1931 Margaret McGregor, a former teacher at Nelson Girls' College, started her fourteen years on the staff, taking charge of the girls' work in camps and seaside missions in the summer, and in school groups through the rest of the year. 'The work among the girls', Laird wrote, 'was steady, quiet, effective and far-sighted, and was characterized by spirituality and dignity which must have left its mark on many, many generations of New Zealand schoolgirls. I cannot speak too highly of the outstanding work done by Margaret McGregor.' This healthy balance between the work among girls and boys set an important pattern for the future, but one that has sadly not always been followed by other countries.

A FINE COMBINATION

In New Zealand, as in Australia, the small population made it particularly important that the various strands of evangelical work among young people should co-operate closely. 'One of the important things that happened in the 1930s was the welding together of what had at first been three separate movements, namely Crusaders in the schools, the beach missions started by Alec Binnie in Auckland, and the old established, but rather small, SU branches represented by the Rev Basil Taylor. The process of welding their divergent interests together was not easy, but with patience and care it gradually came about. Each strand strengthened and contributed to the other and together they made a very fine combination.'

One secret of the spiritual impact of these years, when CSSM was touching the life of a nation in a way that it had not done since the 1880s, was that Laird was careful to keep his spiritual lines of communication open. 'What the Council most expects of you', J H Hubbard had said when Laird visited him in England in 1933, 'is that above all else you should become a man of God.' Apart from his regular times of prayer and Bible study, he spent much time in the preparation of his talks, especially for the monthly Crusader rallies which did so much to give young people in Wellington a firm biblical grounding. In addition he recalls that 'from time to time I went into "retreat" in some quiet place for a day or two. This gave an opportunity for the ministry of intercession – there were literally hundreds to be prayed for. It also enabled me to think about current problems, of which there always seemed to be a fair share.'

When Laird and his family left New Zealand in 1945, there were seventy-three Crusader groups in schools, attended by over 2,000 boys and girls; SU Bible reading membership of 29,000; sixteen camps and six beach missions were held each year; and there was a staff of fourteen, including two schools travelling secretaries, a children's evangelist and a general secretary. All this was in a country of at that time only one and a half million people, which had been at war for the past six years.

14

Retrospect 1939

On 15th April 1939 the Royal Albert Hall in London was packed with ten thousand friends and supporters from all over Britain for the sixtieth anniversary celebrations of the Scripture Union. Though few realised it at the time, it was the end of an era. Within five months the world was plunged into war. The British Empire, which had been crumbling at the edges for forty years, was about to break up as first India, and then the other colonies, became independent. Britain itself was on the threshold of a social revolution.

OUTSTANDING ABILITY

The impressive team of speakers at the crowded meetings well illustrated the progress CSSM and Scripture Union had made in the past forty years, and some of its strengths and weaknesses. The Mission had managed to attract men of outstanding ability into its ranks, and to provide a framework in which they could fruitfully exercise their gifts over a number of years. Roddy Archibald, Hudson Pope, W G Ovens, Eric Nash and John Laird, all of whom spoke, were each very different types of men: but each of them was being used in a remarkable way to win young people for Christ and train them in his service. Edmund Clark, Frank Millard and Ernst Aebi were of similar calibre. There can have been few Christian organisations at the time that had a more gifted staff team.

This very strength, however, brought its own problems. For one thing, CSSM in England had become much more of a staff affair than it was in the previous century. There was still a great deal of voluntary help from SU branch secretaries and workers at seaside missions and camps; but the growth of the administration with the passage of years, as well as the sheer calibre of the most able staff members, meant that CSSM depended more and more on its paid staff. Even the Committee (called a Council from 1930) had to battle to retain its proper share of control. 'I give them as much rope as they want', Hubbard once told John Laird, 'and when they are not looking I pull it in again'.

Poster to advertise the Diamond Jubilee meetings.

Secondly, like many strong natural leaders, a number of the gifted and dedicated men on the staff were individualists, who worked best on their own, or running their own team. Hubbard and the Council wisely gave them a great deal of freedom, backing them up financially and letting them get on with their work in their own ways. Diversity, however, could very easily become disunity, with each man's work developing along separate lines. Only in Scotland and far away in New Zealand was there any serious attempt to weave the various strands of CSSM and SU work into a single, harmonious pattern.

SHALLOW IN THEOLOGY

There was a deep theological unity underlying these differences of method. But that in itself was something of a problem, as it reflected the rather shallow, defensive theology of British evangelicalism of the period. Describing the 1930s Oliver Barclay writes:

> The evangelical world was suffering from an intellectual inferiority complex.... Many were frightened of intellectual activity. The evangelical world generally seemed to be in decline. Many of its ablest young men and women were going liberal or losing their faith at university. (*Whatever happened to the Jesus Lane Lot?* p.106)

Rationalistic views about the Bible, which were already on the increase at the turn of the century, as we have noticed, had spread so widely, especially in theological faculties and colleges, that they were taken as a matter of course by most people. To quote Oliver Barclay again, Christian Union members 'were regarded as anti-intellectual, anti-theological and obscurantist, clinging tenaciously to outmoded beliefs simply because they were afraid to face the facts'. Most church leaders would have thought the same about their evangelical members, and about the organisations, such as Crusaders, IVF and CSSM, which they supported.

SOCIAL PROBLEMS IGNORED

In the face of such prevailing attitudes, evangelicals held resolutely to their convictions about the inspiration and authority of the Bible, the necessity of the atonement, the historical nature of the resurrection, and so on. But they tended to shy away from serious theological study, and particularly from any fresh thinking about social or ethical issues. The leadership of the CSSM reflected current evangelical views. The daily notes, for example, were excellent doctrinally and devotionally, but were hardly prophetic. Like so many evangelicals at the time, they had a deep concern for overseas missions, and gave generously for the support of Christian work abroad, particularly the CSSM in India; but they appear to have overlooked the spiritual and social needs in the slums and dole queues on their own doorsteps. Even Roddy Archibald seems to have spent his forty-five years in India without giving serious attention to the vital issue of caste; certainly I have not found reference to it in his voluminous writings.

This detachment from current social trends helps to explain an aspect of CSSM policy which was criticised at the time and which a later generation finds hard to understand, namely the concentration of effort on children from wealthier homes. Vincent Craven, on a visit to England 'was shocked to be told at Cricceith CSSM not to invite the local Welsh children lest the "nice" English holiday children be offended. The snobbishness of the English professional classes was more than he could stomach, and he was thankful that the CSSM at home in Australia ministered to all classes without distinction.' (*Tuned in to Change,* p.117) In defence, leaders like Montague Goodman pointed out that the CSSM held missions for poorer children all through the rest of the year, but for the few weeks at the seaside in the summer they concentrated on the wealthier children who were particularly needy, because they did not go to Sunday School. They were valid points, but not entirely convincing.

Another mark of the evangelical loss of confidence, in the face of persistent liberal attacks, was the conservatism affecting their evangelistic methods, as well as their theology. In the previous century CSSM had been particularly good at finding new methods of sharing the message, and a pioneer, inventive approach to evangelism was an important part of the movement's tradition. But in the forty years 1900–1939, hardly any new ideas were introduced, except the ski and sailing camps soon after Hubbard took over. The beach missions, in fact, were still run in 1939 very much along the lines Arrowsmith had pioneered in the 1880s.

A FAR-FLUNG EMPIRE

The steady growth of the movement overseas, illustrated at the Jubilee meetings by such speakers as Archibald, Laird and Vagar, was also creating a problem. There were now twenty-three CSSM staff workers in India, four in Australia, three each in New Zealand, Switzerland, and South Africa, and isolated workers in Canada, East

Africa, France, Japan and Latvia. The SU cards were circulating in as many as ninety-two languages. All this activity was still ultimately controlled from London, apart from that in Switzerland and France, which London hardly recognised as part of the same movement. 'We cannot support the personal affair of Mr Aebi,' Hubbard told Claire-Lise de Benoit, when she called at his office in 1946, after the war. It was imperative that a way should be found to give the growing number of national movements in other countries responsibility for their own affairs while at the same time preserving the unity of the worldwide family.

THE C.S.S.M. APRIL, 1939

Hungarian
Ituri Kingwana
Jinghpaw Chinyanja
Kanarese Lunyoro
Tahitian Cigogo
Malayalam Alur
Portuguese
Malay Zulu
Ateso Hausa
Greek Oriya
Lwena Hindi
Runyargwanda
Czecho-Slovak
Chiluba-Sanga
Mukuni Lunda
Dinka Urhobo Zande
Silozi Tamil Chila
Chinese Dutch Isoko
Japanese Ibo Lettish
Efik Cree Kaffir Nupe
Norwegian Armenian
Gujarati Kiluba
Urdu Iranian

IN THE YEAR OF OUR
DIAMOND
JUBILEE
SCRIPTURE
UNION
CARDS ARE
PRINTED IN THE
NINETY-TWO
LANGUAGES
SHOWN
HERE

Rarotongan
Singhalese
Chindau
Kisonge
Uchokwe
Bangala
Cebuano
Burmese
Lugbara
Luganda
Umbundu
Lomongo
Swedish
Finnish
Spanish
Italian
Serbian
Russian
Bengali
Swahili
Chibemba Roumanian
Bulgarian English
Chiluba-Kaonde

Ukrainian
Icelandic
Danish
Polish
German
Korean
Telugu
Yoruba
Khassi
Arabic
Gaelic
Eskimo
Mataco
Acholi
Thonga
French
Kikuyu
Sesuto
Marathi
Malagasy

The worldwide spread of SU in 1929.

Part III

Integrated Movements 1945–1960

15

Bringing the Strands Together

The 1939–45 war was a watershed in many ways, not least in CSSM and Scripture Union. It was a very different world that the movement faced when it was all over. It had to make substantial changes, particularly in its structure and organisation, if it still wanted to be effective. In the event it adapted so successfully that the coming years brought unprecedented growth.

More than anyone else, the man responsible was John Laird. As we have seen, he had pioneered a new pattern of work in New Zealand in the 1930s. Towards the end of 1945 he sailed with his young family to England to become one of the joint general secretaries there. For the next fifteen years he was effectively, if not in name, the leader of the worldwide movement. His vision, friendliness and persistence helped to set the work on a new course in numerous countries.

In New Zealand itself, the new pattern led to a remarkable extension of the movement's influence. The 'Crusader' groups in schools, the camps, the beach missions and the promotion of Bible reading in the churches were combined into an integrated programme, in which each part strengthened the others. By the 1950s CSSM/SU, together with Inter-Varsity Fellowship, with which it was closely associated, had become a major focus for evangelical witness in the country.

WARTIME FORWARD MOVE

During the war, when Christian work in most countries was seriously restricted, John Laird launched a three-year 'Forward Move' 'to meet the philosophy of the Bomb with the philosophy of the Bible' by making New Zealand a Bible reading nation. 'Democracy is in danger', he quoted, 'because it is abandoning the spiritual basis of its being. Totalitarianism has no more powerful ally than a despiritualised democracy. It is the enemy within their gates.' Through advertising, letters to ministers, and public meetings the circulation of notes nearly doubled, and it was claimed at the time that 'one in every fifty-six in New Zealand is a Scripture Union member'.

FOUR IN EVERY HUNDRED

John Laird's successor in New Zealand was Colin Becroft. Appropriately, he had been present as a senior schoolboy at the very first meeting Laird spoke at in New Zealand, and at the first camp he led there.

His main gifts were in administration. He had an intensely logical mind and insisted that policy should be clearly defined so that everyone knew exactly what he was supposed to be doing. He was reputed to have had a rather cold personality, but the record shows that first in New Zealand, then later in Australia and in his wider responsibilities in Asia and the Americas, he had a rare gift for choosing men of ability for staff or committees, enthusing them with his vision of Scripture Union, and then persuading them to accept his proposals. He was also very determined. 'If you ever wanted to oppose Colin Becroft,' someone once said, 'you needed a good mind, three hours to spare, fifty-five reasons, and he'd still win.'

Under Becroft's leadership, and that of his successor, Bruce Lumsden, the work in the schools grew from strength to strength. Between 1950 and 1960 the number of pupils doubled in New Zealand's secondary schools, but it was reckoned that nearly four in every hundred attended a Crusader meeting in an average week (school Christian meeetings connected with SU continued to be called 'Crusaders' until 1972). By 1960 there were 180 groups meeting regularly in some 130 secondary schools. Most co-educational schools at the time had separate meetings for boys and girls as the Crusader staff were convinced that 'combined meetings tend to become mostly girls.' With only three travelling secretaries covering the whole country, much depended on voluntary adult leaders. John Laird had always emphasised teaching as an important Christian vocation, and the number of Christian teachers increased steadily. But in the mid 1950s half the groups were still led by volunteers from outside the school. Sometimes even the meeting place was off the school premises, in a nearby home or church hall.

FRESH AIR AND EXERCISE

A wide range of camps backed up the school meetings, and indeed provided the main evangelistic thrust. Camps emphasised a rugged, outdoor life, making the most of New Zealand's magnificent climate and natural beauty. They drew in large numbers of boys and girls who as yet did not come to the meetings. Alongside scores of volunteers, the outstanding camp leader was Vine Martin, who joined for a year in 1947 but continued without a break until 1972. Much of the time he covered the whole country as the only male schools worker. Under his leadership the camping programme became more adventurous, with 'bike hikes', canoeing, mountain and rock climbing, and other vigorous outdoor pursuits.

In the 1950s the number of camps and of campers more than doubled. They were still rigidly divided between boys and girls. The emphasis on the moral value of fresh air and physical exertion would have surprised Christians from another time and other cultures. But it had a long tradition in the CSSM, going back to the first camps in England in the 1890s and before them to the Victorian public schools from which the first campers came. Certainly in New Zealand it attracted both boys and girls in great numbers, and helped to produce a generation of Christian leaders who were notably determined and adventurous.

THE STUDENT CHRISTIAN MOVEMENT

One of the problems that the Scripture Union had to face in its schools work in the 1950s and 1960s, in many countries, was opposition from the Student Christian Movement. It was a serious issue in New Zealand even though SCM had been at a low ebb in the schools there for a number of years. An SCM survey in 1948 admitted that their work in schools was 'almost dead'. Even so they sharply criticised Crusaders as 'a divisive influence'—and aggravated the division a year or two later by appointing their own schools worker!

The conflict was not really a competition between two rival organisations working along similar lines. Although it was evangelical when it started in England in the 1890s, SCM was by this time committed to liberal theology, with a critical approach to the Bible. Its emphasis was on the social application of Christianity rather than a personal relationship with God. In many countries it was closely allied with recently-formed national Christian councils, but its leadership was liberal rather than representative of the whole cross-section of Christian opinion. The majority of church leaders at this period, and many school principals, had been in SCM at university in its hey-day in the 1920s and 1930s, and naturally favoured its approach.

In countries where SCM was already established in the schools, it was difficult for Scripture Union to make a start. But in New Zealand it was Crusaders (SU) that was the established organisation. Moreover the Crusader approach had greater appeal in the long-run. The SCM schools worker herself admitted: 'filmstrips, lavish teas in people's houses, rousing hymn tunes (with appalling theology in the words) and short authoritative talks seem to attract far more (than the SCM programme).' In Peter Lineham's words, 'it was a jaundiced but not totally inaccurate assessment. She failed to mention the all-important contribution made by dedicated Crusader leaders... (who) sometimes made large sacrifices of time and effort to help pupils grow in Christian discipleship.' (*No Ordinary Union*, pp.103, 104).

In New Zealand and other countries, the value of such consistent teaching and friendship over a number of years was more and more recognised. At the same time increasing numbers of men and women who had been in SU at school or IVF at university found their way into positions of leadership in education and the churches. Meanwhile SCM influence declined as its university section concentrated its attention on radical politics. By the mid-1960s SU work in schools in most countries was able to go ahead without the earlier opposition.

A NEW NAME

Another issue the New Zealand Council faced in the early 1950s was how to maintain the unity of the movement as it moved into new types of activity, and what name should be used for its overall operations. The use of the name 'Crusaders' in the schools and camps, of 'CSSM' for missions in churches and on the beaches, and of 'Scripture Union' for the Bible reading system gave the impression to the Christian public that they were three separate, unrelated organisations. In fact they were part of the same movement. In England the CSSM name was still sufficiently well known for it to come first automatically in people's minds, but in New Zealand that position would have been held by Crusaders. Neither really conveyed the right image or was suitable as an overall title.

With his logical mind Colin Becroft saw the need for a name that would unify the movement and describe the central thrust of its varied activities. He decided that essentially it was a Bible reading youth movement, and that 'Scripture Union' was the most appropriate title. After discussing the issue on and off for several years, the New Zealand Council finally adopted the name. It was a good choice in that it emphasised the need for regular, daily Bible reading to boys and girls in school groups and at beach missions and indeed the Bible's central place in all aspects of the movement's work. It was a less happy choice in that the word 'Scripture' already sounded rather old-fashioned and, more seriously, that it gave the impression that the daily Bible reading notes were more important, or a more central part of the movement's mandate, than evangelism.

In his choice of an overall name, Colin Becroft was twenty years behind the Swiss, who had used *Ligue pour la Lecture de la Bible* and *Bibellesebund* for all sides of the work since the 1920s. But he set a course that was eventually followed by the rest of the English-speaking world and finally adopted as the official name of the movement worldwide in 1960.

FROM EMPIRE TO COMMONWEALTH

An important change in the international structure was made in 1947, which made it possible for the movement in a small country like New Zealand to run its own affairs and even change its name if it thought it right to do so. Up to this time the CSSM Council in England had been legally responsible for the movement all over the world except in Switzerland and France. As in the old British Empire, all decisions eventually came back to London. When he reached England, John Laird decided to change all that, and to turn the movement into a commonwealth, a family of independent national movements. He advised the London Council to alter its legal articles and to delegate its power. As we shall see, it was only an interim stage in the development of the international structure. But it was an important one.

By mutual agreement, two categories of national movements were recognised. In the first were those which were financially independent of London, and were autonomous. In 1948 these were New Zealand, New South Wales, Queensland, Victoria and Switzerland. Each was encouraged to become legally incorporated in its own country, and was given formal permission to use the name of the movement so long as it continued 'to conform to the principles and methods of the CSSM, with particular reference to the doctrinal beliefs commonly held in the Mission'. They were responsible for their own staff workers, finance, and policy, but they agreed to recognise the London Council as 'the senior member of the family'.

In the second category were Advisory Councils, still financially dependent on London. In 1948 these were Canada, South Africa, France, East Africa, South Australia and Peru. They agreed not to go into debt or appoint staff without approval from London. But they were encouraged to become financially self-supporting and self-governing as soon as possible. In the next twelve years Canada,

France, South Africa and South Australia all became autonomous, but several new centres had opened up and were included in the second category. To qualify for autonomy they had to have at least one full-time staff worker and be financially self-supporting.

BOOM IN AUSTRALIA

Half the autonomous councils in the world in 1948 were in Australia, where the work was growing fast. A boom in camps during the war led to rapid developments in other sections of the work. In New South Wales five camps were run for girls and six for boys in the summer of 1941–42, and camps were started in Queensland and South Australia. Because family holidays were restricted there was no problem in recruiting campers. But as the war went on, with Vincent Craven and many other men called up, it became increasingly difficult to find leaders for the boys. The girls' work was less affected and numbers reached record levels.

In Victoria beach missions were restarted. In 1942 'a shy young man in army uniform' called Alan Kerr joined the CSSM Council, and soon made his mark. Alan Kerr had been so delicate and sickly as a child, that he had only attended school for about six months. But he had a talent for business. Starting with a piece of scrap plywood, which he painted and sold as a toothbrush holder, he built up a flourishing woodwork business. By the time he was eighteen he had a staff of twenty. Before he retired he had factories all over Australia.

Alan Kerr found the CSSM Council was weak and lacking a driving purpose. A new start was made in 1943. With the help of a South African doctor serving with the Australian Air Force, who had beach mission experience back home, he and his wife led a team at Dromena. Two missions were held the following year, and with the help of men coming back from the forces, the number steadily grew. By 1947–48 there were seven missions and by 1949–50 fourteen, three more than in New South Wales. As John Prince comments: 'Alan Kerr was learning a lesson he was often to pass on – that front-line service on the beach with a CSSM team involves people more deeply and in larger numbers than any other strand of the work. In Victoria now, as in New South Wales twenty-five years earlier, flourishing beach missions set the Scripture Union movement on its feet.' (*Tuned in to Change*, p.135)

ONE MOVEMENT OR FIVE?

Equally significant was the beginning of greater co-operation between the various groups. In Victoria in the mid 1940s Boys' Crusaders, Girls' Crusaders, Boys' ISCF, Girls' ISCF and CSSM – Scripture Union, were all separate bodies and somewhat suspicious of one another. It was a serious weakness, for none of the groups was strong enough on its own to have proper staff or offices. The problem was to know how to put the various pieces of the work together. Some favoured Australia-wide appointments for each section. Indeed, in 1942 New Zealander Thora Jenkins was appointed for Crusaders across the country. Small and dynamic, she travelled ceaselessly for nearly four years, and gave a strong boost to the girls' work particularly in the states where it was weakest, Queensland, Western Australia and South Australia. Others considered that it was unrealistic to expect any staff worker to cover such vast distances, and looked to the closely integrated work in New Zealand as a model. In 1944 the New South Wales council invited John Laird to come over for three months to advise.

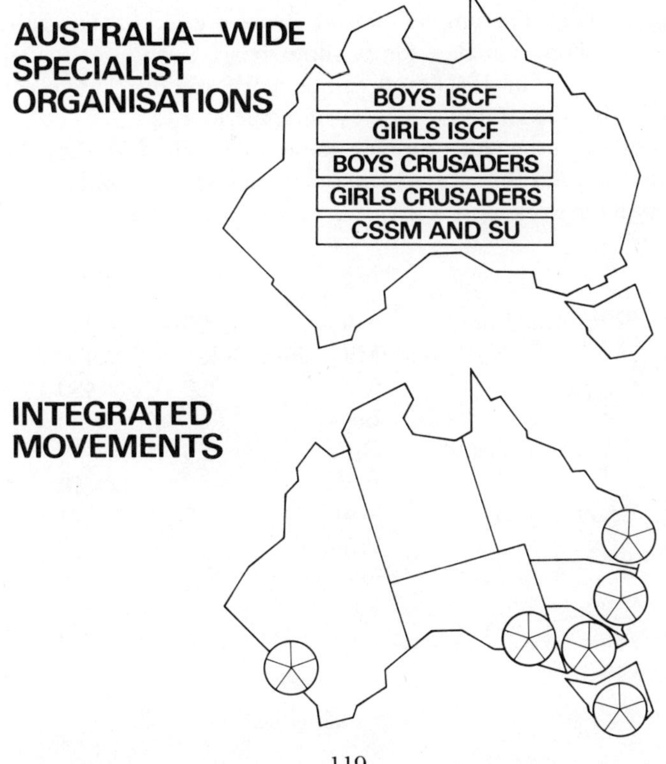

Laird's visit made a lasting impression. After five weeks of patient consultation he spoke at a conference of New South Wales supporters. Instead of separate Australia-wide networks for CSSM, Boys' Crusaders and Girls' Crusaders, he recommended a unified movement, with a suitable leader as general secretary, in each state. As he went on to Queensland and Victoria, he became even more convinced that this was the right way forward. There was a good deal of opposition to his ideas, as each group was afraid of losing its identity in the merger. As it was slowly adopted, however, his plan proved its value.

In New South Wales, the decisive steps were taken in 1947 with the appointment of the Rev Basil Williams, another New Zealander, as general secretary, and the opening of new offices in Elizabeth Street. Williams had pioneered a new type of beach mission, at a camping centre called Palm Beach, based in tents rather than a house. He challenged the CSSM constituency to a strong forward move along these lines. By 1950–51 eleven teams were at work, ten of them following the new pattern. Living in tents on the camp-site reduced costs and brought the team more closely into touch with holidaymakers. The simpler life-style in no way curtailed the spiritual impact: at Toowoon Bay, for example, beach services attracted 400 people a day. The ISCF and camps work was developing equally strongly. By 1953 it had three travelling secretaries.

In other States, integration came more slowly, but was achieved eventually. John Prince gives some statistics which show how the two aspects of the work blossomed in Victoria once they had come together:

		1946–47	1951–52
Scripture Union	Notes	1,900	8,450
	Magazines	1,125	4,450
Campers	Girls	280	450
	Boys	–	150
School Groups	Girls	25	49
	Boys	–	18
Beach Missions	Sites	5	14
	Workers	70	175

INTER-STATE CO-OPERATION

By 1954 four States, New South Wales, Victoria, Queensland and South Australia had autonomous CSSM/SU councils, with staff and offices, and growing work in schools, on the beaches, in camps and with Bible reading notes. Each of them was linked direct to the parent Council in London, which still printed all the notes for the English-speaking world. The time had now come to think seriously about inter-state co-operation. Taking advantage of another visit of John Laird, Alan Kerr and Basil Williams convened a conference over the Easter weekend at the SU camp centre 'The Grange' in the Blue Mountains. It was there agreed to set up a Federal Advisory Council, a simple structure which made it possible for further co-operation to develop. Once again, Laird strongly influenced the pattern that emerged. As he flew over the Australian countryside on his way to the conference, he noticed the scattered farms each clustered around its own little source of water. There was no mutual support or dependence, and each was isolated and vulnerable. He urged the Australians to abandon the 'waterhole mentality' and to work wholeheartedly together.

The decision was made just at the right time. Alan Kerr was appointed chairman, and Colin Becroft, who was moving across from New Zealand to become New South Wales Secretary, Federal Secretary. By the end of the 1955 meeting firm steps had been taken to establish the work in Western Australia and Tasmania, to produce information bulletins and staff handbooks and to support SU missionary work in India. A few weeks later, when Cecil Johnston arrived from India and brought the challenge of East Asia instead of India, the structure was ready for Australia to respond. We shall see in later chapters how far reaching were the results.

The benefits of co-operation were shown in such events as the 'National Scripture Union Week' in 1958. Circulation of notes went up from 58,000 to 104,000 in eighteen months. In Tasmania it increased no less than 231%. Now that they were firmly established in their own territories, the states were finding that together they could do far more than they could ever achieve on their own. Finding the right balance between local initiative and central co-ordination was a problem Scripture Union was to face repeatedly in a variety of circumstances, in the next twenty years. Solutions would vary from time to time and from place to place; but the Australians had found a pattern that suited their situation, and led to remarkable growth and vitality in the coming years.

16

Adapting to Change

John Laird and his family arrived back in Britain in December 1945. They found a country battered and exhausted after six years of war, but on the threshold of massive changes. In the next twenty-five years the economic boom, affecting the whole of the West, brought unprecedented affluence. The technological revolution influenced peoples' attitudes and assumptions as well as their way of life, particularly as television became widespread. New methods of education encouraged children to enquire and experiment rather than to accept without question what the teacher told them. In society as a whole privileges of class and position came under attack, authority and tradition were challenged. Nothing could be taken for granted, no one could escape scrutiny. No one could assume that others would accept his authority simply because of his position.

All this was a tremendous challenge and opportunity for a youth movement like CSSM and Scripture Union. The anti-authority spirit of the age encouraged children and young people to question what they were told. But it also encouraged them to question the materialist assumptions of their parents' generation, and to listen to an older Christian if his life rang true to his message. Moreover university Christian Unions were growing strongly at the time, and this growth was soon reflected in a marked increase in the number of student helpers at the summer activities and of Christian teachers in the schools.

The question was whether the CSSM could change sufficiently to accept the challenge. The pioneers in the nineteenth century had led the way to new methods of approaching children and young people. Would the Mission in the 1950s be as creative? In 1946 it did not seem likely. CSSM was by now very much a part of the 'evangelical establishment'. This gave it the immense advantages of the affection, prayers and financial support of the Christian public. On the other hand it also meant that supporters knew quite clearly what they expected of the CSSM and were worried if changes were made. The long and noble tradition of the Mission had created a great deal of goodwill but hindered innovation.

JOINT LEADERSHIP

The Council was weak and indecisive. J H Hubbard had so dominated it that it did little more than rubber-stamp his proposals. Even the all-important decision about Hubbard's successor was fudged. They appointed Clarence Foster, editorial secretary for the past twenty years, and John Laird as Joint General Secretaries, without even defining individual spheres of responsibility. It was a recipe for chaos, 'the worst known pattern of command', as John Pollock comments. (*The Good Seed,* p.183). But to make matters worse each of them was told privately, by different members of the Council, that, if all went well, he would eventually be in sole charge.

There were ten years of joint leadership before Clarence Foster retired. In his autobiography, *No Mere Chance,* John Laird movingly describes the frustration and confusion that the joint appointment caused. For although they were both patient, godly men, they represented two quite different attitudes. Foster wanted to safeguard the great traditions of the past. Laird, who was described by a member of the Council as 'a young man in a hurry' when he was well over forty, saw the urgent need for change. But in spite of all the problems, the achievements of the ten years of joint leadership were considerable. The decade saw the launch of the Inter School Christian Fellowship in the state schools, a boom in the camp programme and the start of the Sunday School Department. The publishing programme was drastically modernised, and the circulation of SU notes nearly doubled. Abroad, England helped Switzerland to relaunch SU in half-a-dozen countries in Europe, gave autonomy to the established movements in Australia and New Zealand, and took a decisive initiative in West Africa. By the mid-fifties the movement had shown that it had the capacity to change, and that it would play a significant role in the work of God in Britain in the years to come. Years later a well-known Christian leader told John Laird that it was during this time that Scripture Union was brought into the twentieth century.

A NEW START IN SCHOOLS

Technically ISCF was run by a joint committee of four societies. But CSSM found the staff and paid the bills. Quintin Carr, who had worked with Roddy Archibald in India before the war, looked after the new organisation at headquarters, and two travelling secretaries were appointed. One of them, Branse Burbridge, was to give twenty-five years of inspired leadership, first as travelling secretary in the north of England and then as Schools Secretary.

Branse Burbridge had had a remarkable career in World War II. He started the war as a pacifist. Later he felt God was calling him to join the Royal Air Force and he became a very successful night-fighter pilot, winning a string of decorations. His experiences in the war had sharpened his commitment to Christ. 'If God gets me through this', he felt, 'then he must have something for me to do when the war is over.' In the early days his war record helped to get him into some of the schools too. ISCF faced widespread suspicion, and even opposition, from school authorities in the early days, because of its evangelical stand. Over the years, however, its emphasis on 'balanced Christian character and practical Christian living', as one of its early leaflets put it, won it acceptance and respect. Branse Burbridge saw the number of affiliated Christian Unions grow from forty to well over 1,000 with informal contact with as many schools again.

Each group had its own story, but David Winter's account of one of them is fairly typical.

> John was converted to faith in Christ at an evangelistic meeting, and was fired with the idea of personal witness and forming a Christian Union at school. He soon gathered possible members of such a group, but was unable to get the headmaster's permission. The regional ISCF staff member gave the group a large slice of his time, and the head was persuaded to grant permission for a CU to be formed provided this supervision and advice continued.
>
> Eventually the headmaster changed his attitude, but other problems arose – clashes with times of games practices and opposition by some teachers and pupils. But, with ISCF backing, the group grew, John matured, and the situation changed.
>
> Now, eighteen years later, the Christian Union is strong and well-established, and there are four or five teachers who support it. John, after a spell on the ISCF staff, is now in industry and helps the Fellowship locally. (David Winter, *For all the People,* Hodders 1967, p.48)

The emphasis in the school groups was on teaching. It was long-term, low-key evangelism, 'where the exact moment of conversion is not the most important thing, but the end product is men and women mature in Christ, with a faith that is closely related to the whole of their life.' Perhaps at times it was too low-key; but the climate of opinion in schools in the 1950s and 1960s was firmly opposed to an open evangelistic challenge. Too aggressive an approach could have closed the door to further opportunities.

OVER ONE HUNDRED CAMPS

A small programme of farming camps continued through the war. As soon as the war was over, though, the camps blossomed both in numbers and variety. Eric Nash's work at Iwerne Minster (see pages 96–98) flourished. Other series of camps were started for the minor public schools and for the preparatory (junior) schools. By 1960 the Varsities and Public Schools work, as it was called, had four full-time staff. Many old campers were now in influential positions in the schools, and the attitude of headmasters was generally more open to evangelicals than before the war. So Bash and his team found more opportunities for regular meetings in schools and for preaching in school chapels.

In his later years, Bash gave more emphasis to the training aspect of the camps. David Watson, later to be known world-wide as an evangelist and speaker on renewal, was invited to Iwerne Minster soon after his conversion, as a student at Cambridge. In his autobiography he writes about the impact of the camps on his life:

> Undoubtedly the most formative influence on my faith during the five years at Cambridge was my involvement with the boys' houseparties, or 'Bash camps' as they were generally known. Over the five years I went to no less than 35 of these camps: two at Christmas, two at Easter and three in the summer of each year. They were tremendous opportunities for learning the very basics of Christian ministry. Through patient and detailed discipling (although that word was never used) I learned, until it became second nature, how to lead a person to Christ, how to answer common questions, how to follow up a young convert, how to lead a group Bible study, how to give a Bible study to others, how to prepare and give a talk, how to pray, how to teach others to pray, how to write encouraging letters, how to know God's guidance, how to overcome temptation, and also, most important, how to laugh and have fun as a Christian – how not to become too intense, if you like. I also gained excellent grounding in basic Christian doctrines, with strong emphasis being placed on clarity and simplicity. All this was being constantly modelled by those who were much more mature in the faith, and I may never fully realise how much I owe to the amazing, detailed, personal help that I received over those five years. No Christian organisation is perfect, of course; and it would be easy to find fault with a group as powerful and as effective as this one. But if God has given me a useful

ministry in any area today, the roots of it were almost certainly planted during those remarkable five years in the camps. It was the best possible training I could have received. (*You Are My God*, Hodder & Stoughton, p.39)

Meanwhile ISCF developed a flourishing programme of camps and holiday activities for the rest of the schools population. In the summer of 1947, in spite of food rationing and other shortages, thirty camps were held. Eleven years later 115 camps were attended by over 3,000 young people, staffed by over 1100 volunteer leaders or helpers. The traditional programme of swimming and camp games had branched out to include such activities as riding and rock-climbing, conoeing, archery and light-weight camping. For those not attracted by hearty outdoor pursuits there was a 'hobbies camp', building a radio set or taking a 'go-kart' to pieces, and later the 'Come and Make' crafts camp. Whatever the programme it helped to forge the young people and their leaders into a unified group where it was natural to speak of the way Christ could meet man's deepest needs. The activities were not seen as 'bait' to attract young people to camp so that they could hear the gospel, but as an essential part of the process of building relationships, through which Christ could be shared.

One of John Laird's tasks was to try to bring the ISCF and the VPS more closely together. Working in boarding schools, where Christian boys had no help from an evangelical church or Bible Class, the VPS concentrated on a few schools, and spent a great deal of time following up individual boys. ISCF staff were forced by the sheer number of schools to spread themselves much more thinly, to rely on local churches, teachers and even older boys and girls to provide follow-up. The difference in levels of staffing naturally raised questions. The climate of thought was different, too, as the more traditional teaching methods in the public schools meant that boys were more ready to sit and listen. Some VPS staff thought that the 'open-ended' discussion-type Bible study of the ISCF was too vague to be effective. The polarisation between the VPS and ISCF staff teams caused tension at times, and was a particular problem for Branse Burbridge when he became Schools Secretary with responsibility for both sections. But each was working effectively in different ways and God was using them to reach different groups of young people.

CRISIS IN THE SUNDAY SCHOOLS

In its approach to younger boys and girls the Mission was changing too. Hudson Pope, now in his seventies but still active, reported that 'children are less easily moved even by the story of the Cross, because their feelings and emotions are constantly played upon by the cinema, radio and television.' Speakers could assume far less background of belief or Bible knowledge than in the past. It was harder, too, to gain the children's attention. Anything shoddy or ill-prepared showed up badly when unconsciously it was compared with the professional standards of radio and television. Sunday School teachers as well as children's evangelists had to become more professional themselves if they were to hold the children.

An illustration from a do-it-yourself training course for Sunday School teachers. Teachers were asked to say how many things were wrong with this Sunday School room.

Not surprisingly numbers at Sunday Schools all over the country were falling rapidly. The CSSM Council decided that it must do something to help churches cope with the problem. In 1946 it appointed Reginald Hill, an experienced teacher from the north of England, to launch the Sunday School Department. In an article published at the time, he explained what he would try to do 'to meet the crisis in our Sunday Schools'. When most children knew little about the Christian faith, 'to teach "the Gospel" in the narrow sense of that term is no longer adequate: it is to build on a non-existent foundation.' So he would produce a comprehensive syllabus covering all aspects of biblical teaching, with notes to help the teachers make each week's lesson interesting and attractive; and run training courses to show the teachers how to use them.

In a surprisingly short time, these plans were put into effect. The first number of the *Sunday School Magazine* appeared in January 1947. It contained outlines for three months' lessons. A year later three magazines were published, for teachers of different age-levels. They were just what many teachers were looking for and circulation rose steadily. Within ten years over 23,000 were being distributed together with 41,000 of the 'take-home leaflets' for the children, and circulation was still going up fast. Sometimes Reginald Hill came under attack as he refused to dodge questions children were bound to ask, such as the relation between Genesis and the theory of evolution. Older evangelicals could be shocked when a passage was interpreted in untraditional ways. But the magazines steadily won their way as people recognised that they were genuinely attempting to be loyal to the Bible, while facing up to the problems it raised.

The training programme for teachers started the following year. Demand increased to such an extent that by 1956 he was running four residential weekend conferences in different parts of the country each year, plus twenty-eight one-day local conferences on Saturdays. All this was on top of editing two of the three Sunday School magazines himself and taking a regular Sunday School class in his home church 'to keep his hand in.'

CHILDREN IN THE VILLAGES

As its influence spread the Sunday School department prepared the ground for the children's evangelists. In the early days, Josiah Spiers and Tom Bishop had recognised that good, regular teaching in home or Sunday School was the best possible preparation for a children's mission. With widespread ignorance of the Bible, such preparation was even more important now. 'Where children have been well-taught in their homes or Sunday Schools', wrote one of the staff evangelists, 'they respond to the gospel as a flower opens to the sun.'

In the 1950s some twenty evangelists were scattered about the country, the majority in the Caravan Mission to Village Children, which continued as a separate entity until it merged fully with the rest of the Mission in the next decade. But their strategy changed. Before the war they took little notice of whether the local village church wanted them to come. In the post-war period however evangelicals began to take the doctrine of the church more seriously. The mission realised, too, that work in isolation would have little long-term effect where children had no background of Bible teaching. A definite change of policy was made, which was slowly and reluctantly accepted by the older evangelists, to go to places where there was a local church ready to issue an invitation for a mission and able to prepare for it and follow it up. The seed would no longer be sown broadcast but as far as possible placed in prepared soil.

An interesting account of a CMVC mission is found in Ronald Blythe's book *Akenfield: Portrait of an English Village*. A deacon at the Baptist Church told him about it:

> I was baptized into the Strict Baptists after the Caravan Mission to Village Children visited Akenfield in 1950. The evangelist travels across Suffolk in the summer time with his tent and caravan, and when he arrives in a village the church parson and the chapel pastor go out to welcome him. He stays for a fortnight and holds two meetings in the tent every evening, one at six for the children and one at seven for the grown-ups. The evangelist is a strict timekeeper and if he says his meeting starts at seven, it starts at seven – and not at five past. So you know where you are. On the last evening, at the end of the meeting, he said, 'I don't want to force anybody but if there are those present who would like to come forward and make a confession of the Lord Jesus, they would be very welcome.' Well, funnily enough there were seven of us went forward. We were nearly all teenagers. I was nineteen, my wife-to-be was seventeen, there were two college girls of sixteen and three lads round about eighteen. One of the college girls became a missionary and went out to Africa, I became a deacon when I was twenty-one, my wife became a Sunday School teacher and not one of us who accepted Christ that night has fallen away from Him. Five of the converted went to the Strict Baptist Church

and two to the Parish Church. And there they are still. This is because the evangelist is a man who is well equipped with the Word and can more or less explain himself to everyday people in church or chapel. He created a wonderful spirit in his tent and all the village felt it. (Robert Blythe, *Akenfield: Portrait of an English Village,* Allen Lane: The Penguin Press, 1969, p.64)

BEACH MISSIONS CONTINUE

The problem of widespread ignorance of the Bible affected holiday missions, though it was less clear what should be done about it. Beach missions continued at much the same level as before the war.[3] The surge in evangelical life at the universities brought many recently converted students onto the mission teams. Some teams were very large, and as in previous years, they provided first-rate training for young Christians. Several of us who later joined the staff first came in contact with the movement in this way.

Roger Pearce recalls the impact on him of the beach mission at Perranporth in North Cornwall, in the 1940s and 1950s. For thirty years, Harold Ling, the accountant and later the Overseas Secretary at headquarters, emerged from behind his desk each summer to lead a large and lively team of students. Roger lived in Perranporth, where his father kept a chemist's shop. 'There wasn't much Christian influence locally that reached children. But each year this extraordinary group of people used to descend on the beach for a month, and it had a tremendous influence on me. I started going when I was four or five, and continued all through, except for a year or two when I was a teenager. It was the friendship, and the tremendous happiness of the whole mission that got through to me. Everyone looked forward to it, it brought colour and enthusiasm to the place.' Along the way, through a slow process rather than a dramatic crisis, he developed a living faith. As a student he helped on the Perranporth team himself. Then, as he was finishing his Bible college training, Harold Ling told him of an urgent need for an SU staff worker in Zambia. After twelve years there, SU was firmly on its feet, and he was able to hand over to a Zambian successor and move on to other work.

As Roger Pearce's story illustrates, the long-term impact was often greatest on local children. This was one reason for the growth of

[3] In 1936 there were 45 beach missions in the British Isles. In 1957 there were 41, but 4 inland missions had been started. It was reckoned that they attracted about 4,000 children each day and were staffed by nearly 1,000 voluntary helpers.

inland holiday missions, which really caught on in the 1960s. They were held in public parks or church halls near where the children lived. Some of them attracted over 1,000 children, their parents only too glad to have them occupied for part of the long summer holiday. They were nearly always arranged in conjunction with a lively church, or group of churches, which made the local arrangements, often provided a proportion of the helpers, and could follow up children through their Sunday Schools. Some churches in fact made the annual holiday mission the focus of their outreach ministry. It opened the door to many homes in the area with which they otherwise had no contact.

NORTH OF THE BORDER

Over the border in Scotland the movement was developing with its own distinctive style. Legal autonomy came some years later, but John Laird encouraged the movement there, as in other parts of the world, to make its own decisions and stand on its own feet financially. As we have seen, Scotland had shown the way, in the 1920s, in reaching out to all types of secondary schools. In thc years after World War II they put most of their resources into schools work. By 1960 there were active Scripture Union groups in 300 of the 350 secondary schools, ten times the penetration ISCF had achieved in England at that stage.

The concentration of population round Glasgow and Edinburgh and the greater proportion of staff meant that staff could maintain closer contact with individual boys and girls through school visits and monthly rallies. A strong programme of camps reinforced the influence of the school groups. An enormous advantage was that, unlike England, the school groups, the rallies and the camps all used the name Scripture Union. This welded the different activities together, as well as making it clear that each of them had a biblical basis. Moreover it gave the movement in Scotland a clear image, which it often lacked in countries which used a variety of names. Without doubt this was a significant factor in the growth of prayer and financial support.

The outstanding personality in Scottish Scripture Union was James Meiklejohn. Converted, as we have seen, at one of Hudson Pope's beach missions, 'the Boss' as he was known, was a camping enthusiast, and led the schools work from the front. For thirty-four years he spent the summer and Easter school holidays running a series of boys' camps, and the rest of the year visiting schools. By the time he retired 3,000 young people were attending camps each year, and on average 10,000 were present at the weekly meetings.

BRINGING THE PUBLISHING UP-TO-DATE

In its literature work, too, the Mission had to change. Morgan Derham recalls that when he joined the staff as Editorial Secretary one of the first things John Laird told him was that the pre-war format for the children's books 'with large type and thick paper and blank pages scattered here and there' was not good enough. An SU literature competition in 1947 helped to improve the style and content. It brought to light Patricia St John, whose prize-winning manuscript *The Tanglewoods' Secret* set a new standard for children's evangelical story books. It quickly became a best-seller in English and several other languages.

Morgan Derham had to battle at times to bring the literature programme up to date. *Our Own Magazine* was a case in point. Started by T B Bishop seventy years before, 'its peak circulation of over 100,000', as Morgan Derham recalls, 'had been built up by making it a kind of magazine that would not only appeal to younger children but also to old ladies who like sentimental stories with a gospel point at the end. I felt that it was no longer really getting to the children for whom it was intended, and that many well-meaning friends who were distributing it were really wasting their money because the thing wasn't being read.' The Business Department opposed any change, because they were afraid that older readers would give up and circulation would drop. But circulation was dropping steadily anyway and 'we had simply to resist the criticisms and objections both from the old ladies outside and the Business Department inside, and stick to our principle which was that the magazine should be styled to appeal to younger children, that they should be made to want to read it, and the contents produced accordingly.'

A weak management structure made decisions more difficult. Like the Mission as a whole, the publishing operation had joint leadership. Morgan Derham as Editorial Secretary and Hubert Smith as Business Manager were both responsible for different aspects of the same publications. No one had overall responsibility. A Christian publisher always has to strike a balance between different factors. For example, the 'missionary' aim of selling at a low price to reach as many people as possible has to be set against the need for a reasonable profit in order to expand. It is almost impossible to avoid friction when these two factors are represented by different people, each of strong convictions, and each with equal authority.

Substantial progress, however, was made. Alongside the children's books and the magazines for children and for Sunday School teachers, the circulation of Scripture Union notes continued to climb rapidly. *Junior Notes,* for children, had been introduced in 1934, and *Daily Bread,* a simpler series for adults, in 1937. When *Bible Study Notes* (for students) and *Key Notes* (for younger teenagers) began in 1947 there were five regular series, with a total circulation of 260,000. Ten years later circulation had nearly doubled, with an increase of 60,000 in both 1954 and 1955, the years of the Billy Graham Crusades.

BUILDINGS AND BUDGETS

By 1955 another big change was necessary as the Mission had outgrown the Wigmore Street building. The staff at headquarters had increased from thirty-five, when it was first built, to 122. The annual output of SU notes and magazines had gone up from 2.6 million to 4.8 million. The purchase of 47 Marylebone Lane, a few hundred yards away, where property was cheaper, provided the extra space required.

With fine new offices, the circulation of SU notes and other literature increasing rapidly, and John Laird at last in sole charge as General Secretary, all seemed set fair at the beginning of 1956. Then disaster struck. For the first time for many years the end of year accounts showed a substantial deficit. It was completely unexpected. The methods of accounting and financial control had not kept up with the rapid growth of the work. So no one had realised the implications of a steep rise in printing costs. There was an urgent appeal for prayer and for gifts, prices were increased and the number of staff reduced. The surplus the following year more than made up for the deficit, but the experience had been an unhappy one. It was clear that the system of accounts and budgets must be brought up to date so that trends could be detected very much earlier. In view of the inflation that was to hit the country in subsequent years, it was just as well that the lesson was learned then.

Personally, however, I have good reason to be grateful that the deficit was not predicted earlier. If the Council had known the true financial position in the middle of 1955, when they considered my application to join the staff, it seems very unlikely that they would have made the appointment. It involved taking on a whole new area of responsibility, the schools work in Tropical Africa. The exciting developments in Africa of the 1960s and 1970s might have been indefinitely delayed.

17

Recovering from Calamity

Throughout World War II and the years that followed, the Scripture Union in Switzerland continued to grow vigorously. Ernst Aebi was in his prime, and had a nationwide ministry through the radio, evangelistic campaigns in the major cities, and large rallies for young people. John Laird described his excitement at attending a campaign in the Bethelkapelle in Zurich in April 1948. Each day there was an adult meeting at 3 p.m. and a children's meeting at 4 p.m. At 7 p.m. two or three hundred young people marched singing through the streets, led by the Scripture Union band and stopping from time to time for open-air preaching. Then they crowded into the town hall for the evening rally, 1000 young people in the main area, older people in the galleries. 'They rose to sing with all their hearts, in robust, masculine German, under the magnetic and inspirational leadership of Ernst Aebi, some of the rousing hymns and choruses of the Bibellesebund. Never shall I forget hearing them sing, with all the enthusiasm of youth, and all the musical talent of the Swiss-German people.'

Music and joy were a marked feature of Scripture Union in French-speaking Switzerland as well. Claire-Lise de Benoit, the granddaughter of Mme van Berchem, was the only staff member there for several years. But her vivacious personality, her considerable musical and writing gifts and her deep spiritual concern for children, made her a worthy Swiss successor to Josiah Spiers. In 1952 a Reformed Church pastor, Maurice Ray, joined her and began a similar work among adults, with great effect. Frequently they conducted simultaneous missions for children and adults in the same village. Claire-Lise de Benoit describes the twenty years after the war as 'the golden age of evangelism in French-speaking Switzerland', and meetings were often crowded.

Alongside this vigorous evangelism, the camps and Bible reading programme grew steadily, based on the headquarters at Vennes, near Lausanne. By 1960 there were 60,000 members in a population of five million, one of the highest proportions of any country in the world.

The Swiss were very conscious too that they were part of an

international family. The SU badge, first introduced in England for the jubilee in 1929, was worn by many of their members, and featured prominently on flags and banners. But they showed their international concern most vividly by the generous and sacrificial way they reached out to help the neighbouring countries, all of which had been ravaged by war.

ELEVEN MILLION REFUGEES

Germany was the most devastated. When the war ended there were, according to one estimate, eleven million refugees in West Germany alone, one person in four was homeless, there were 250,000 orphans, and sixty per cent of all children were undernourished. With characteristic generosity the Swiss churches braced themselves to help, pouring in lorry loads of clothes, food and medical supplies. Ernst Aebi and his friends were equally concerned to help. In 1947 and 1948 he and Armin Hoppler, at that time still in business but chairman of the Swiss Council, made two extensive journeys to see what could be done. John Laird, who went with them on the second trip, describes the devastation in 'the once prosperous but now ruined city of Wuppertal. Its gaunt and tottering walls seem to symbolize the ruins of western civilization.' Three years after the end of the war 'its inhabitants are eeking out a miserable existence in cellars, crowded air-raid shelters and overcrowded houses. Food is desperately scarce and of wretched quality.'

The Swiss SU regularly sent generous supplies of food and clothing, demonstrating, incidentally, that evangelical social concern was not an invention of the 1970s, as has sometimes been suggested. They also arranged to send free of charge as many copies of the German SU notes as could be used. Wherever they went Aebi and his party found an enthusiastic welcome. They were seen as 'ambassadors of the worldwide SU family', he wrote. 'The German Christians were particularly glad to have this assurance of worldwide fellowship, having been cut off for so long.'

A helpful contact was with Ernst Mogk, director of the motherhouse of the Marburg sisters, a Protestant order with some 5,000 members involved in work with children and needy people all over Germany. Mogk urged the sisters to use the notes themselves and distribute them in their churches, and before long the Marburg branch had 15,000 members. When a German commitee was found, Mogk became vice-president.

In 1950 the first German staff member was appointed. Paul

Schmidt had been a missionary in China for ten years, and had suffered hardship and restrictions in the war because he refused to support Hitler. He travelled throughout Germany helping with Bible weeks and holiday missions. 'Every day some souls come to the Lord,' Aebi reported after visiting Schmidt in 1952. 'Germany is an open door for the Scripture Union.'

The first camp was held near Stuttgart in 1950. In 1953, a children's worker was appointed, Eva-Marie Preüsser, converted during Aebi's visit in 1947. After her marriage in 1955, her place was taken by Else Diehl, who is still on the job at the time of writing, over twenty-eight years later. 'We have to be patient, and set out clearly the scope and intention of our work,' she wrote soon after her appointment. 'Where we have done this we have been given admission to many schools and youth groups. People are becoming more and more convinced of the importance of work among children.'

LA LIGUE IN FRANCE

While it gave Germany relief supplies and SU notes, the Swiss movement gave France one of its few workers. Léonard Bréchet was born in Russia, though his family came from France. When he graduated from Emmaus in 1935 he joined the SU staff, running missions and camps, and encouraging Bible reading in Eastern France as well as Switzerland. In 1946 the French committee, which had just been formed, asked him to become their general secretary.

Since 1936 La Ligue pour la lecture de la Bible in France had been based at Sumène, in the Cevennes in the south. Although most holiday camps closed because of shortages, Sumène kept open throughout the war. It was no easy task to feed 300 famished boys and girls in such conditions. André Adoul describes how he had to scour the countryside for up to 200 miles in the preceeding weeks to lay in supplies. During the camp itself he sometimes spent the whole day in the broiling sun leading a donkey to a nearby town to collect vegetables, arriving back in camp exhausted, but in time to speak at the evening meeting. 'But, though food was scarce and bad, God gave us spiritual food abundantly, and many were saved and have since consecrated their lives to the Lord.'

Bréchet made his headquarters at Guebwiller, in Alsace, a Protestant area. With the help of local Christians, and of Brethren Assemblies in Switzerland, a large house was purchased to be used mainly as an orphanage but also as a centre for La Ligue. Some years later, La Ligue bought the adjacent property, an impressive château, for offices, staff accommodation and a camp centre.

The orphanage *Le Bercail,* was not in fact part of SU's work. But they were so closely associated in Bréchet's mind that after his death it was difficult to sort out which part of the joint property belonged to which organisation.

Rows of chalets and a dining hall were built in the grounds, and soon 200 small children and 100 teenagers could be accommodated, for separate camps, at the same time. Sumène was kept on as a camp and conference centre for the south.

Under the leadership of Bréchet and the committee, French SU soon became self-supporting, and began to reach out further. By 1957 there were three staff evangelists, based in different parts of the country, running missions, SU rallies and adult Bible conventions, and leading the summer programme at the two camp centres. It was uphill work, but gradually the suspicion of many of the pastors was overcome and opportunities increased. Bréchet also made several visits to Africa, as a result of which staff were appointed in Algeria in 1953 and Zaire in 1960.

CYCLING AROUND BELGIUM

The years after the war saw the first staff appointments in several other European countries as well. In 1948 Ernst Aebi discovered a young student at the Brussels Bible Institute, Theo Snitselaar, and asked him to start SU in Belgium. As a teenager during the German occupation Snitselaar had been active in the Resistance Movement narrowly escaping death on one occasion. In addition to his speaking and linguistic gifts, he had a natural flair for business, a talent that proved to be a great asset to SU in Europe in the years to come.

It was a slow hard task he had taken on. The Protestant population was small and discouraged, the Catholics forbidden to read the Bible. Snitselaar travelled long distances by bicycle or bus to speak to a few children or to visit a small Protestant church. 'Encouraging Bible reading among the Christians of the land', wrote his Scottish-born wife, 'is especially necessary in a country where for centuries people have not been encouraged to read, and where, as the evangelical church is young, most of its members are humble, simple folk, who on the whole find reading and understanding a difficult task.'

In the early years Snitselaar also helped in Northern France. Soon after his appointment he made a 600 km tour by bicycle, finding much more interest than in Belgium. 'The churches have up to 200 members', he wrote 'and it has been a refreshing experience to work amongst folk who are eager for the Word of God and drink in every word you say.'

Back in Belgium there was no such encouragement. In nine years he only had one letter of thanks after a church visit. It was a matter of going steadily on with the task regardless of the difficulties. 'I was my own Scripture Union office and secretary, despatcher and bookseller,' Snitselaar recalled. From time to time individual lives were changed, such as when a man picked up a Salvation Army paper in a cafe, read about SU, wrote and ordered a Bible and some notes, and found Christ through reading them. Slowly the circulation of notes climbed, to 1,500.

IN CALVINIST HOLLAND

Across the border in Holland there were different problems to be faced. A Dutch committee had been formed as long ago as 1914, and it had published notes from time to time. But its members were now elderly and too busy with other things: Scripture Union was virtually dead. In March 1949 Laird, Bréchet and Snitselaar visited Holland to try to revive it. They found that the committee was uncertain if there was any real need for Scripture Union in a country like Holland, where the Bible was read regularly in almost every Protestant home, and churches were full. However, they agreed that Snitselaar, whose parents were Dutch, could be staff worker for Holland as well as Belgium, and that he could try to restart the Dutch notes.

Snitselaar soon found the key person for the task, a middle-aged lady called Annie Floor. She had hoped to be a missionary in the East Indies but had stayed at home instead to nurse her sick mother. She knew nothing about Scripture Union before Snitselaar came to see her but then, 'I saw my calling: to write for Calvinist Holland in an unseen way a Bible-explanation to concentrate believers on the Lord Jesus Himself'. She was concerned that 'we Dutch have much theological but often little spiritual knowledge. The emphasis is on believing right doctrine but little about being born again. A chapter is read from the big family Bible after the evening meal but no explanation given.'

At first Miss Floor translated notes from English, but she soon realised that this was not satisfactory. 'We in Holland think in a different way.' For nine long years she wrote all the notes herself; only in 1958 could three young pastors be found to help. She also had her problems with the committee. 'The kind old chairman, a Reformed pastor in Amsterdam, got furious that I was in contact with Dr Laird. He said: "Let England stay in its own pagan country. In Holland we are our own masters. There is nothing we have to learn from England." My impression is that he wanted to keep the SU baby in its cradle, to be able to handle it easily, like in the past. Once I asked him: "Does Scripture Union belong to you or to the Lord Jesus?" He got so furious that he left the committee.'

Money on the other hand, was less of a problem because of a generous supporter. John Kessler had been educated in England where he had been converted and became an officer at SU camps, and he was about to leave for missionary work in Peru. His grandfather had helped to found the Royal Dutch Shell Oil Company, and he had inherited a considerable sum of money which he was determined to use for Christian work. When the notes were restarted in 1949 he gave the capital for the first 10,000 copies. Five years later, back on leave, he not only offered to pay the salary of another staff worker, but found the man for the job. In 1955 Jaap Shriek joined the staff and H A Colijn, a prominent businessman of strong evangelical commitment, was elected chairman. Scripture Union in Holland was on its feet at last.

ONE IN SIX

In the years after the war the influence of the Swiss SU made its impact in other parts of Europe too. In 1947 the young manager of a firm of printers in Lisbon came to Vennes for a year's study at the Emmaus Bible Institute. He helped at SU camps on the adjacent site and caught the vision of what SU could be in his own country. Back home in Portugal Abel Rodrigues became a freelance evangelist, living with his young family in one room in extreme poverty. 'We often woke in the morning not knowing where the day's meals would come from. But God continually provided.' In 1949 he ran his first youth camp, almost single-handed. The following year, at the suggestion of an English missionary, he started to publish Portuguese *Daily Notes*.

All this time he had no direct contact with SU elsewhere. Then in 1953 a visitor to London called to see John Laird, and expressed his feelings of disgust at 'the atrocious living conditions of your representative in Lisbon'. John Laird quite rightly protested that SU had no staff worker in Portugal, but immediately wrote to the man concerned to establish contact. Within a few months Abel Rodrigues officially joined the staff. SU England sent a grant to cover his basic salary, and a small committee was formed in Lisbon to take responsibility for the expenses.

In a strongly Roman Catholic country like Portugal it was hard work getting SU established. The Protestants were a tiny minority. Also, as often happens when Christians are under pressure, they were deeply divided among themselves. 'The greatest of all our difficulties', Abel Rodrigues wrote, 'has been the sectarian spirit of so many of the churches; a hindrance to the development, for though each church will gladly receive what emanates from within its own denomination, there is little or no interest in anything without.' However, his energy and persistence slowly broke down barriers. Children's notes were started in 1953, and five years later it was reckoned that one in six of the 9,000 active evangelicals were SU members.

The increasing programme of camps and youth rallies also helped to break down barriers as young people from different churches found they had more in common than they expected. Abel Rodrigues travelled the length and breadth of the country to build up the work, sometimes covering 90,000 kilometres a year on his Vespa motor-scooter. In 1955 the first camp was started in the north of the country, followed up by monthly youth rallies at Oporto. In the south, three camps were held each year, one of them taking children as young as six. In 1959 Abel Rodrigues achieved a longstanding ambition, when he was able to purchase a permanent camp site at Carrascal, about fifteen miles north of Lisbon.

A BIBLE FOR EIGHT POUNDS OF POTATOES

While all this was going on in Portugal, a young civil servant, Miltos Anghelatos, was pioneering a similar work in Greece. Here again evangelicals were in a tiny minority and under pressure from the state church. Again SU in the rest of Europe knew nothing about it.

Miltos Anghelatos had a remarkable story. He was brought up in a Greek Orthodox family on the island of Corfu. 'At a very young age I began to search for God. I used to sit with a friend on the marble steps of our school building. Looking up at the skies we used to ponder "What about God?"' He had no Bible to help him find the answer. In fact, by the time he was a teenager, he still had never even heard that the Bible existed. As he grew older, he gave up his search. 'For eight years I lived a life of base, sensual excess.' At the same time he longed for knowledge. 'I set myself wholeheartedly to study. Day and night I probed into human wisdom, with only a short pause for food and a few hours of sleep.' None of this satisfied him, however. By the winter of 1942, when he was twenty, he was in despair. 'Intellectually I stumbled in darkness and confusion. Morally, I wallowed in passion and lies and sins. Mentally I was wavering and in despair. Like a shapeless rag, I was living because I had not the courage to die.'

One day, when he was reading a novel by the Russian author, Leo Tolstoy, he noticed some words on the title page that puzzled him. 'Unless an ear of wheat falls to the ground and dies, it remains only a single seed. But if it dies it produces many seeds. John 12:24.' He was intrigued by these words, but had no idea who John was or what the numbers 12 and 24 meant. So he asked his English teacher, who told him they came from the Bible. He asked his teacher what the Bible was. The teacher replied that the Bible was a book that people called missionaries had taken to the South Sea Islands, and when they had given this book to cannibals, the cannibals stopped eating people any more.

This made Miltos determined to get a Bible and to read it. He searched the whole town, and at last was able to buy one second-hand. The price was eight pounds of potatoes, a very high price in wartime, when food was scarce.

'It was about midday when I began reading the Bible and it was almost midnight when I put it down. I put my Bible under my pillow so we could sleep together for a while. That night was the first one I had slept in peace, without nightmares and anxieties. I woke up to find myself hugging my new companion tight, this book which promised an answer to all my questions.

'The next day, sitting on the small hill behind our house, I sat there, with the Holy Book of God open in my hands.' For those first months he read for over ten hours a day. 'Nothing could withstand the light of this book of God. Ever clearer I saw how wretched I was. Snapshots showing scenes of hate, deceit, theft, embezzlement, which had so far ornamented my life, were dragged to the surface. In no way could I excuse myself.'

Things came to a crisis the following January. 'At last I came to the end of my tether. That afternoon, like the magicians of old, I brought out the archives of the life I had led before I knew Christ, my books, my pictures, my writings, and threw them all on to the fire. Then I knelt down. I did not say much. It was tears that gave me tongue. In shame and repentance I brought to the foot of the Cross of Christ the whole of my liabilities, all my sins which the Holy Sprit had brought to my memory. I felt in the very depths of my soul the joyful assurance that "the blood of Jesus Christ cleanseth you from all your sin". In my diary I wrote: "I stop keeping this diary, because I am entering, or rather I have been reborn, into a new life. I have discovered the truth I was searching for. I did not find it in human wisdom but in the Gospel of my Lord Jesus Christ."'

When he told his parents what had happened, his father was furious. His Bible was thrown into the fire, and he was forced to leave home. 'The Bible will make you bankrupt', his father told him. He left Corfu for Athens, where an evangelical pastor took him in. He was still young, and had never been away from home before. The first night he had a nightmare, and woke up shouting for his mother. The pastor's wife came into the room: 'I will be your mother', she told him.

The Bible did not make Miltos Anghelatos bankrupt. He became a civil servant, in the Greek Ministry of Foreign Affairs. In his spare time he ran various meetings for children and started a small publishing programme. Some years later Maurice Ray, on holiday with his family in Athens, was introduced to 'someone who is doing exactly the same work in this country as you are doing in Switzerland.' It was Miltos Anghelatos's first contact with the SU family, but he soon became its official representative. In the land where the Apostle Paul had first planted the gospel in Europe, SU was beginning to grow.

18

Planting New Seedlings

Before 1960, only limited progress was made in other parts of the world, though several seeds were planted which were to grow vigorously and fruitfully in the next decade. In India there was even some decline: the team of twenty-five that met for the Staff Conference in 1937 was down to sixteen by 1954.

Cecil Johnston, who took over as leader in India after Roddy Archibald's retirement, had already had nine years' experience in Burma. Another in the long CSSM tradition of gifted children's workers, he travelled ceaselessly, by train, all over the country. Sometimes he left his base in Calcutta in January and did not return until the following December. In a typical year he visited sixty-eight schools, in thirty of which he held a week's mission, and spoke to 10,000 children. Like Archibald, he concentrated, in his personal ministry, on the English-speaking schools, where his vivid stories and energetic games soon won him many friends, and there were frequent professions of conversion.

HAUNTED BY DEVILS

Joe Mullins, who came to help him in 1952, writes about 'a nervous little Hindu boy', one of the hundreds who found help at their missions over the years. '"Sir," he said, "I am haunted by devils; they come flying at me all day long, and in the night I lie awake terrified and cannot sleep. My grandfather gave me some pink powder from the guru and told me to throw the powder in the devils' faces, but it doesn't work, sir." I showed him the verse in 1 John about fear having torment. "Is that true of you?" I asked. "Yes," he said. Then I pointed him to "Perfect love casteth out fear", and told him of the love of Jesus in dying on the Cross for him, and that when His love flooded the heart there was no room for fear. I also showed him Proverbs 3:24–26, "The Lord shall be your confidence...when you sit down, you will not be afraid, when you lie down your sleep will be sweet."

After school he came running over to my room, beaming all over his face. "It works, it works!" he cried.'

The opportunity for missions in many of the English-speaking schools continued even after India's independence. But the school population had changed. In Archibald's day most of the children were Anglo-Indians, nominally Christian. Now the majority were from Hindu or other non-Christian homes. They were still surprisingly willing to come to the mission meetings and frequently the whole school attended, quite voluntarily of course. Some were even prepared to make a private response to the call of Christ. But few, while still children or teenagers, were able to make a public stand as Christians. 'Some of them', said Cecil Johnston, 'find it impossible to tell their parents because they would be thrown out of the school, and that would prevent all further Christian influence. We feel that we cannot press them. We must leave it to the Holy Spirit.'

So while Cecil Johnston and Joe Mullins revelled in the opportunities for sharing the gospel with Hindu, Muslim and other children, the long-term results were comparatively small. The well-known power of Hinduism to suck back individuals who try to break away from the family tradition, and the difficulty of adequate nurture, were formidable problems. There was also a serious lack of voluntary helpers. Joe Mullins wrote:

> The crux of our need in this subcontinent today is for local Scripture Union secretaries, camp officers, keen teachers in the schools to follow up missions...The idea of 'leave it to the missionary', whether national or foreign, dies hard. Too often the staff worker finds himself a 'one-man-band' – general secretary, local secretary, translator, distributor, treasurer, children's missioner – all rolled into one. Perhaps the fault is ours to a great extent, for in a land of crying need it is so easy to cast our nets too wide, to try to cover too great an area, to visit too many schools. The result is that contacts are tenuous, follow-up is inadequate, results are not conserved, and potential leadership is lost or channelled off somewhere else.

The shortage was made worse by the dispersal of the Anglo-Indian community. As soon as they left school, many of them went off to find work in other countries. Very few indeed went back into the schools as teachers and were available for the vital task of leading SU groups and helping young people converted at the missions.

LONELY EVANGELISTS

Alongside this direct work in schools, both Cecil Johnston and Joe Mullins spent much of their time guiding and training their Indian colleagues. 'We aim to spend a month touring with one of our Indian staff once a year, but more often it is once in two years.' The Indian staff too had many opportunities for holding missions in schools and churches, and were also responsible for the SU notes in the language of their part of the country. In Kerala, in the far south, there was a team of four, and each year they took meetings for thousands of children at the great Maramon convention. In West Pakistan, Sadiq Mall had similar opportunities at the Sialkot and other conventions, frequently speaking to 500 or 1000 children. But for him and others it was a lonely and isolated life. When Pastor Morsha was appointed to work in the Naga hills, on the Burma border, it took him eight days' travelling to reach Calcutta for interview. Most language areas had just a single member of staff, and there were no committees and few voluntary workers to support them. It was not surprising if some of them were in danger of losing their originality and freshness, of repeating old talks and of not expecting fresh inspiration. Staff conferences and regular visits from Cecil Johnston and Joe Mullins were important.

This dependence on the two Westerners, and the lack of local committees and voluntary workers, seriously delayed the growth of Indian leadership. A step forward was taken in 1949 when Paul Das was appointed General Secretary. Cecil Johnston continued as leader of the team however, and Paul Das's responsibilities were limited to administration. Most of the financial support still came from London. When a committee was at last formed, in 1957, it only had advisory powers and was composed entirely of members of staff. 'The main object', it was said at the time, 'was to encourage the movement in India to become self-governing, self-supporting and self-propagating', but these objectives were still a long way off.

EATING, SLEEPING AND THINKING SU

In North America, Scripture Union work was at a low ebb in 1945. Robert Richardson, now aged ninety-two, was still in charge. The sole activity was to circulate some 8,000 notes. There was no committee and no plans had been made for a successor. When Richardson died the following year, Stacey Woods, General Secretary of Inter-Varsity Christian Fellowship, kindly stepped in to keep the distribution going until new arrangements could be made.

Gerald Gregson, the first appointment, was an unusually saintly and spiritual man. But his gifts were those of a pastor and evangelist rather than a builder and administrator. Many lives were blessed, as he preached in Canada and USA, but there was little growth in SU activity. After three years he moved on to other work.

Arthur Rouse, who took over from him, had been a businessman in China for many years, where he had worked closely with the China Inland Mission (now OMF). Although over seventy, he still had great energy, and was described at the time as a man who 'eats, sleeps and thinks SU all day and night'. His urgent concern was to help North Americans to enjoy a deeper devotional life. 'Late hours at night are the usual thing', he wrote, 'and Christians tend to rely on fellowship with other Christians rather than on their own personal relationship with God, developed through a daily quiet time, and a devotional reading of the Bible.' In spite of his strenuous efforts, the circulation of notes crept up only slowly. By 1959, it had still only reached 12,000 in the whole of North America.

LAKESIDE MISSIONS

While the main thrust was in Bible reading, Arthur Rouse also started a number of successful lakeside children's missions. When Tony Capon arrived in 1956, the evangelistic side could be developed more quickly. Tony Capon had a degree in modern languages and theology from Cambridge, and was an ordained Anglican minister. With his wife, he had led the seaside mission at Portrush in Northern Ireland for several years. He found many opportunities in Canada for children's missions in churches, where his clear teaching and unemotional call for response were greatly appreciated. Such church-based children's missions, increasingly part of the ministry of CSSM in England, were unknown in Canada. Twenty-five years later they are still a distinctive SU contribution to church life. Tony Capon developed gifts as a writer as well, and for a number of years wrote a major share of the *Daily Bread* notes used throughout the English-speaking world.

Up to 1959, when a separate organisation was set up in USA, Arthur Rouse took responsibility for the whole of North America. The following year he retired and Tony Capon became general secretary. SU was still in a small way in Canada, with a circulation of some 8,000 notes. But with an effective Council, an efficient headquarters building, twelve lakeside missions each year, an increasing number of invitations from churches, and a balanced budget, it was at last established. It had come a long way in the nine years of Arthur Rouse's leadership.

THE FINEST SPORT IMAGINABLE

There was progress in Latin America too in the 1950s, though it was limited. As we have seen, there had been a few scattered SU members there in the last century, with several branches formed in Brazil as early as 1884. From 1939 onwards a retired railway official, R L Clegg, published a Spanish SU magazine in Buenos Aires, *Albores* ('Light of Dawn'). By 1947 it had a circulation of 15,000, and was accepted by all Protestant denominations. But it did not pay its way. 'When hopes began to revive of making ends meet', wrote Clegg, 'some fresh disaster has knocked us all into fits and landed us in a worse hole than before.' Clegg subsidised it from his small savings, returning untouched a gift that SU in England sent to help, and cutting down expenses by living and working in a single room and doing everything himself. 'I have to struggle on alone, I even hammer out the wrappers on the addressograph and cart all the magazines to the post. But it has been the finest sport imaginable.'

As well as an SU magazine, there were CSSM and SU camps in Argentina regularly throughout the 40's and 50's. They were only for English-speaking children, but one of those who professed conversion was a twelve-year old boy called Luis Palau. Years later, at the start of the 1983 'Mission to London', he was interviewed by a correspondent from the 'Church Times' who wrote: 'His camp counsellor, Frank Chandler, took him aside and asked him: "Luis, do you want to go to heaven or hell?" Chandler got him to write in his New Testament, "If you LUIS confess with your lips LUIS that Jesus is your Lord LUIS" – and then, says Palau, "I got it."'

OVER THE ANDES

On the west coast, the Christian radio station 'Voice of the Andes' adopted the Spanish SU notes for its morning devotional programme. But it was in Peru that the SU plant took firmest root. Through the influence of missionaries who had been involved in camps and beach missions in their own countries both camps and Bible reading notes were started. Felix Calle, then a young man just out of seminary, was appointed staff worker. Now he is Latin American Director of Cruzada de Literatura a Cada Hogar, and a member of the SU Council in

Peru. From 1949–57 he moved about the country, travelling over 16,000 foot passes, through river gorges in Amazonia, and into tiny, dusty desert villages along the coast, attempting to introduce Christians to serious Bible reading habits. As someone wrote at the time: 'Frustration, persecution, weariness – and then when things were rock bottom, a break in the clouds, a brilliant ray of warm sunshine – God has won through in the life of a peasant Indian and there is rejoicing in Heaven. Not another member for SU, just another citizen of Heaven, and a smile of joyful satisfaction on the face of a weary SU worker.' At first notes from Argentina were used. But the content was too heavy for the Indian believers in the mountains, and frequently arrived late. So a special Peruvian edition was started.

CAMP KAWAI

It was in Peru too that the camp idea took firmest root. Early in 1953, John Kessler, from Holland, and Sam Will from Scotland were discussing how to do a more effective work among the boys of San Andres College where Sam was teaching. 'As we chatted on the cliff overlooking the Pacific' John Kessler recalls, 'we were soon agreed that a camp was just what was needed.' In January 1954, the first SU boys camp took place. Although the SU banner was torn down in the night, 'probably by an irate Catholic', the camp was a considerable success. The following year, thirty-four boys spent two weeks together at Ruacho. 'The camp was more strenuous than anything I have yet tackled in Peru', one of the leaders reported.

In 1956, they found the beautiful site at Mala, on the coast, ninety kilometres south of Lima, where Camp Kawai was to be built twenty years later. Two camps were held, one of them for girls, which twenty-two attended. Joan French reported that 'five of the older girls from my Sunday School said that during the camp they had started the Christian Race.'

SU work was still small in Peru, but it was beginning to have an influence. An article published the following year in *Standfast*, the New Zealand SU magazine, describes a day in the life of Pedro Arana, then a prefect at San Andres. Fifteen minutes before school he meets with a few friends to read the SU passage and the Spanish notes. Four other groups are meeting at the same time in other parts of the school. At morning assembly the headmaster speaks on the same passage. On Thursday afternoon, Pedro helps to lead the weekly open SU meeting, with about forty present, and the writer of the article as guest speaker. Pedro gives a strong push for the summer camps. Several of the boys had attended the previous year. 'Last summer both boys' and girls' camps were filled.' As the writer comments, 'it is obvious that SU has an important part in Pedro's day.' Twenty-five years later Pedro Arana is one of the leaders of the Evangelical Church of Peru and a staff member of the IFES. He was a member of the National Assembly elected to draw up a new constitution for his country.

NEW START IN ASIA

On the other side of the Pacific, Scripture Union was also on the move. In spite of its sixty years of history, SU work in Japan came to a halt during the war. But the publication of notes resumed in 1955, and by 1960 the circulation had reached 2,600. Also in 1955, the Christian Witness Press in Hong Kong started to publish Chinese notes, and the Far East Broadcasting Company began to use SU notes in their daily programme. But it was further south, in Malaya and Singapore, that the most exciting progress took place.

Once again, John Laird had a hand in it. On his way to Australia in 1954, he spent two days in Singapore and saw an open door for work in schools. At his suggestion, Cecil Johnston, the tireless and enthusiastic leader of the SU team in India, visited Singapore and Malaya the following year. He planned to spend a few days, but found such opportunities that he stayed seven weeks. 'I visited forty-four schools', he reported, 'and spoke to more than 17,000 different boys and girls, all of whom speak English well, though ninety per cent of them are Chinese Buddhists.' Over 1,600 new members joined the Scripture Union, and committees were formed in both Singapore and Malaya, each of them representative of the different churches and races in the area.

Johnston went on to Australia and New Zealand and challenged the SU movements there with the needs and opportunities in East Asia. His enthusiasm was infectious and the timing was right. The Federal Council responded warmly to the challenge and New Zealand was equally enthusiastic.

In May 1956, Lester Pfankuch, from New Zealand, arrived as the first SU staff worker in Singapore and Malaya. He had a mixed reception in the schools and churches, with a warm welcome in places where there was someone in charge who had known SU before, but considerable suspicion elsewhere. A number of school groups were started but plans for a camp were abandoned because only eight boys registered.

However, Pfankuch had formed particularly close relationships with Chinese Christians. When he resigned at the end of 1957, after eighteen months of constant travel, SU in Singapore and Malaya was firmly established as an organisation in which people of all races could work together as equal partners. It was to be an important characteristic of SU in East Asia. Tony McCutcheon, who arrived from Melbourne in 1958 to take Pfankuch's place, was to build effectively along the same lines.

OPPORTUNITIES IN AFRICA

This partnership in the gospel between people of different races was a key factor in Tropical Africa, another part of the world where SU grew strongly in the 1950s and 1960s. As we have seen, Scripture Union cards had circulated in large numbers in several African languages in the latter part of the nineteenth century. SU groups were meeting in Accra, Onitsha and Lesotho by 1892, and a Sierra Leonean, William Smith, had been appointed as 'Colporteur' as early as 1897. The staff appointment had lapsed, but the circulation of SU literature continued all over the continent where British missionaries were at work. By 1939, the SU card was printed in forty African languages, a significant proportion of the worldwide total of ninety-two. But, apart from the vigorous and effective camps and missions run for white children in South Africa, and the missions for all races led for a few years by Fred Crittenden and John Duncan in East Africa, there was no SU youth work on the continent.

All this began to change in the early 1950s. Large numbers of Christians from overseas came to Africa as teachers and in government service. Many of them had been converted through SU or IFES and had helped at camps and beach missions when they were students. Most of them came to Africa with the firm purpose of sharing their faith. They found that the vast majority of young people in the schools and colleges were Christians in name but not in heart. 'Because Christianity has been the way to education and hence to prosperity', wrote Jim Findlay, 'hordes of young Africans have called themselves Christians without knowing or understanding what Christianity really is. So the churches are in danger of becoming vast hollow edifices, bodies without souls, gathering places of people who read the Bible but do not understand its message.' Jim Findlay had helped with SU camps in Scotland. With a number of friends he organised the first camp in Ghana (then the Gold Coast) in January 1953. It was held in the Methodist School at Winneba, on the coast forty miles west of

Accra. There were only thirteen boys, and at the time it seemed something of a failure. But it was a start, and three of the boys were later to become active leaders in the work.

One of those converted was Sam Bortei-Doku. He gave one of the main talks at camp the following year, when sixty-five boys turned up, five more than the planned limit. 'Sam's talk on prayer', wrote Tony Wilmot, the camp leader, 'was a living testimony to the love and power of God and was the turning point in camp.' It was the quality of camp life that made the most profound impression. 'Many campers confessed', Wilmot continues, 'that the first thing which moved their hearts and minds towards the things of God was the wonderful spirit of fellowship in camp – it was something they had never seen before. It cut across all barriers of tribe, race, temperament and age. It was so obviously of God.'

OPEN TO THE GOSPEL

A year later it was my privilege to share in this development. Tony Wilmot wrote to the CSSM Council in London asking for help. 'We have been able to organise an annual camp for secondary school boys and the results have been wonderfully encouraging. A similar camp for girls has also been arranged. But there are limits to what busy people can do. There is a need for a full-time staff worker.' I was appointed by the London Council, as staff worker for the whole of West Africa, and reached Ghana in November 1955, just in time for the two boys' camps after Christmas.

Looking back twenty-eight years later, the strongest impression is of the remarkable openness of young people in Ghana to the challenge of Christ. The churches there were mainly in the 'liberal' tradition, and the Student Christian Movement was well entrenched in the schools and at the university. But almost everywhere I went I was welcomed to speak about Bible reading and the SU notes, to show Fact and Faith (Moody) films, or to talk about the camps. Everywhere there was a big demand for Christian literature. A colleague in England laughed when I told him how much of it I was taking with me. Before long, we were selling that sort of quantity each week. Most important, perhaps because a vital biblical challenge was little known, many responded, deeply and lastingly, to the claims of Christ, and became enthusiastic fellow-workers.

One of them was Florence Yeboah, converted through a talk by Tony Wilmot at the first girls' camp at Abetifi in 1954. She joined the staff in 1962, and had an extraordinarily fruitful ministry until she moved on to other work. Tony Wilmot nearly missed the critical meeting. He drove up from Accra for the evening. When he was nearly there, he remembered that he had promised to bring Jim Findlay with him. A promise is a promise, so he dashed back seventy miles to Akropong on tortuous roads to collect him, and just arrived back in time to speak.

Another person converted in those early years was Gottfried Osei-Mensah, who is now Executive Secretary of the Lausanne Committee for World Evangelisation. His headmaster, Clifford Sims, a former leader of the North of England SU camp, organised weekly SU meetings in his home. The first time Gottfried attended he arrived late and all the chairs were taken. To his astonishment, the headmaster sat on the floor to make room for him. He says he was too embarrassed to take in anything that was said. But the incident led to his conversion. He was a 'junior officer' in my dormitory at the first camp I attended. There were many others converted in those early years who went on to become camp leaders or 'sponsors' of school groups.

While the deepest work was often done at camp, there were also great opportunities in the schools. Often an invitation to speak to the whole school about 'Why should we read the Bible?' could be followed up with a meeting for those more seriously interested on 'How to read it', and the start of a regular voluntary group. After a few years, young men or women converted at school or university went back into the schools as teachers, and were encouraged to take responsibility for leadership as much as they could. It was the way to help them to grow.

A NOISY GREEN LANDROVER

While this was happening in Ghana, SU was moving forward in other parts of Africa. In Nigeria, missionaries had been circulating thousands of the SU cards in several of the main languages for years, so the SU name was well known. A new chapter opened in 1957 when a national Committee was formed. The majority of founder members were expatriates, who knew the movement in their home countries, but the chairman was Dr Ishaya Audu, later to become Nigeria's Minister for Foreign Affairs. In the first year, a camp for boys was held at Oyo, one for girls at Ibadan, and notes were published in Yoruba. In 1958, Hausa notes were started and John Dean was appointed as the first Nigeria-based staff worker.

John Dean was an agriculturalist and had been converted to Christ while a student at Cambridge. He was teaching at the Sudan

United Mission school at Gindiri, in Northern Nigeria, and the mission generously agreed to continue to pay his salary while he did SU work. As soon as he arrived at Ibadan, he threw himself into a strenuous programme of school visits, camps and other activities. 'There must be few secondary schools in the country', records the 1960 Annual Report of SU Nigeria, 'that are not familiar with the sound of a rather noisy green Land Rover, covered with fine red dust and filled with books, Bibles and SU Notes. In six months, John Dean took 223 meetings and covered 10,000 miles. Many new SU groups began during the year. There are now 22 in the West, 11 in the East and 38 in the North (of the Fellowship of Christian Students).' He kept up a programme of this intensity for the next twenty years. No doubt one of the reasons he was able to do so was that, wherever he happened to be, he would take time out almost every evening for a four-mile run. In years to come, 'callisthenics' became a regular feature of staff training conferences.

In South Africa, Frank Millard's extremely effective camps and missions continued right up to his retirement in 1960. 'In a typical year, 1952, we had 25 camps, with 195 officers at work among 1,249 boys and girls; and 17 holiday missions staffed by 157 workers.' Most of the work was still in the Cape, but from 1940 Paul Reed lived in the Transvaal and made regular trips north to what is now Zimbabwe. Paul Reed was a trained lawyer from England. He was so tall and thin that his camp nickname was 'Bamboo'. In 1955, the South African Council made the bold decision to send one of their best young workers, Elizabeth Semple, to be based in Zimbabwe. At first she was only working among white children, but it was a start.

GOD SPOKE THROUGH HIS BOOK

In other parts of the continent, SU work with young people had to wait until the next decade. But the SU cards and notes circulated in their thousands and prepared the ground. In 1954, for example, an American lady missionary gave a copy of *Key Notes* to Amos Lavaly, then in his second year at the Government Secondary School at Bo, in Sierra Leone. Later he wrote:

> I felt that daily Bible reading would disturb my school work. I hoped that the booklet would get lost. I decided to read the Bible until the end of the holidays (in case I was asked whether I was reading it or not) and then stop. But a strange thing started happening to me – I was feeling very unhappy and uncomfortable.

> I had a burning urge to read my Bible and it was only after I had read it that I felt really satisfied. I finally decided to fix a definite time for daily reading, immediately after school in the afternoon. As I continued reading my Bible day after day, I realized for the first time in my life that I was a sinner. God spoke to me through His Book, the Bible. I then asked God to forgive my sins, and I yielded my life completely to Him. (*This Faith Works*, Africa Christian Press, 1967, p.22.)

A few weeks later he was encouraged by a remarkable answer to prayer. He very much wanted the notes for the following quarter, but his missionary friend had gone on leave. He prayed about it but nothing seemed to happen. Then the first day of the next month 'during the lunch hour, I received a letter – and inside were my notes, just in time for my first reading.' They had been sent by a girl in another school, who said he had asked her to send them ('but I am sure I never did'). After that, he prayed for other boys in the school, and before he left he had sixty SU members. Later, he started the Bible Study Union at the university in Freetown, helped at the first SU camp, and was one of the first members of the national committee. He was one of the foundation stones God was laying in preparation for the strong growth of SU in Sierra Leone in the next twenty years.

19

Old Jordans

Late in May 1960, twenty-one leaders from CSSM and Scripture Union around the world arrived in England for an historic conference. They came with a keen spirit of anticipation. It was the first time such a representative group had met and the agenda opened up the possibility of a radical change in the way the movement was organised. Some came with a certain sense of apprehension too. Was London really ready to 'break the mould' and make it possible for a truly democratic international movement to develop? So few Christian organisations seemed to be able to achieve this measure of detachment and trust. Would Scripture Union worldwide be strong enough?

John Laird set the scene at a public meeting in London a few days before the conference. He referred to the fact that SU was already an old society, just seven years short of its centenary. 'Old societies, like old men, can easily become set in their ways, stiff in their movements, and vision and insight can become dim by reason of age.... Can a society be born when it is old?' he asked, 'the answer surely is an emphatic "yes"! Indeed, unless it be reborn, by the power of the Holy Spirit, it can never enter, or play its part in, the Kingdom of God.'

It was with this sense of anticipation in our minds, and with John Laird's call for prayer for 'the wind of the Holy Spirit to blow through the conference', that the meeting took place. The conference centre was Old Jordans, a 400-year old Quaker Hostel a few miles north west of London. The beautiful countryside and perfect summer weather helped to make it an ideal setting for a memorable week of fellowship and discussion.

Most of the twenty-three members of the conference had many years of experience in the movement, either on staff or as members of committee. Only one was a woman, Claire-Lise de Benoit from Switzerland. They came from twelve countries, so were a reasonably representative group. There were only two Asians, however, O C Matthew from India and Akira Hatori from Japan. Two West Africans had been invited, but neither had been free to come; so Africa was represented by Paul Reed and Otto Dose, from South Africa, and myself.

WORLD SURVEY

Under the skilful leadership of Derek Warren, chairman of the London Council, the conference members considered, debated and tested almost every aspect of the movement's activities and relationships. First of all, members reviewed the world situation and listed targets for the years ahead. The survey showed remarkable progress since the end of World War II. Colin Becroft referred to phenomenal growth in Australia which now had thirteen staff workers, 460 school groups, fifty-eight beach missions, 110,000 SU readers and 1,000 voluntary workers. In twenty years the Australian SU scene had totally changed. Other strong movements outside the UK were in New Zealand, with six staff, a well-developed programme of camps and beach missions and 40,000 SU readers; South Africa, also with six staff, all working among the English-speaking section of the community; and Switzerland, where the lively programme of camps and missions continued, and there were 60,000 SU readers. In the UK itself, there were as many as forty-four children's evangelists and schools workers in England, as well as a large headquarters staff. Scotland had eight staff, 300 of the 350 senior secondary schools had SU groups, and there was an extensive programme of camps. Northern Ireland now had its own full-time staff member, and school groups, camps and children's missions were all developing strongly.

In other parts of the world, progress had been slower. India and Pakistan had twenty evangelists, rather less than twenty years earlier, and most of the support still came from England. Elsewhere in Asia, committees were producing notes in Japan and the Philippines, and a good start had been made with schools and camps work in Singapore and Malaya. But the work was still in its infancy. In Africa, the cards or notes were produced in fifty-seven languages, and schools and camps work had begun in a number of countries. But there were only four staff outside South Africa, one each in Algeria, Ghana, Nigeria and what was then Rhodesia. In the Americas, there had been progress in Canada, where the movement was at last established and there were three staff, and Peru with its regular camps and Bible reading notes. An office had been opened the previous year in USA, but all it did was to send notes to some 5,000 subscribers. In Europe, SU was growing in Germany, where there were three staff, but France still only had two, and Holland, Portugal, Austria, and Southern Ireland one staff member each.

INTERNATIONAL STRUCTURE

The conference discussed ways of keeping the growing movement together. All were convinced that from now on SU was to be a family of equal national groups. But how could this loosely-knit family work together, so that the stronger movements could help the weaker ones, without dominating them, and consistent standards be maintained? What was to stop the emerging national movements going off in different directions? How could the true spirit and essence of the movement be preserved when it was planted in different soils? Alan Kerr, from Australia, urged the setting up of a small but strong international secretariat, which would have authority to maintain standards and could take the lead in pressing forward into new areas of opportunity. While some supported this idea, others, such as Léonard Bréchet, from France, were fearful that any type of international structure would interfere with the autonomy already granted to national movements in 1947.

Eventually the answer emerged along four lines. Derek Warren's clear legal mind helped the conference to see that what was needed was not a superstructure, controlling the emerging national movements from above, but an infrastructure, a secure framework within which various national movements could freely co-operate and support one another. The diagram shows the two possibilities:

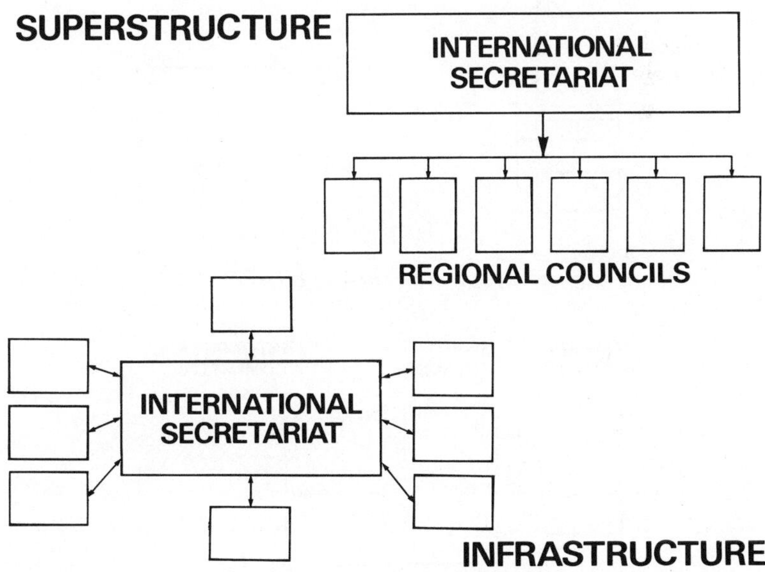

The recently formed ANZEA Regional Council (see p.199) pointed the way, and served as a model for future co-operation. Two councils, Australia and New Zealand, had combined to take responsibility for work in a new area, namely East Asia. They expected two East Asian movements, Japan and Singapore, to be in a position to join them as full members within a year or two. Each national movement retained its autonomy, but co-operated for joint projects and to develop and support new work. The conference agreed that over the next few years similar regional councils would be formed in other parts of the world, and that an international committee would link together the different regions.

The advantage of this arrangement was that it made it possible for the various national movements to work together, while retaining full responsibility for the work in their own country. It did so, moreover, without creating a large international committee on which all national movements would be represented direct. This was rejected as too cumbersome and expensive. It was felt that as the work grew, co-operation would be better achieved at the regional level, with the regions rather than individual countries being represented at the international committee.

DIRECT REPRESENTATION

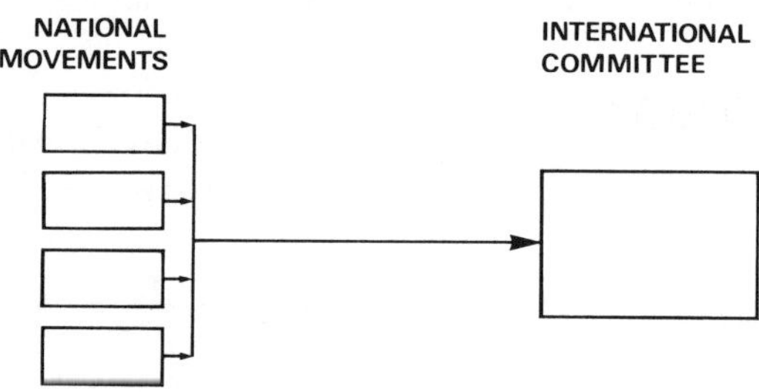

REPRESENTATION THROUGH REGIONS

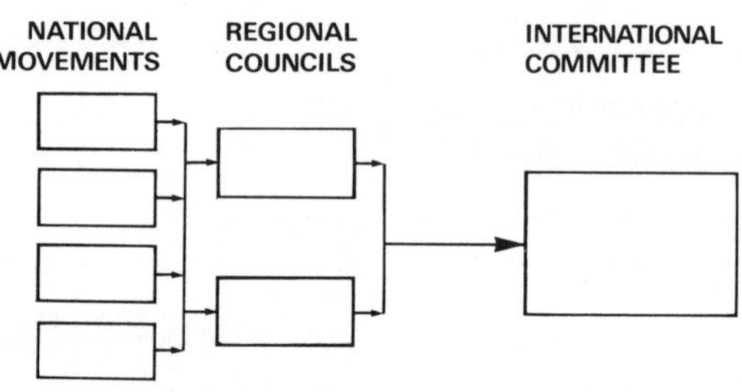

KEEPING THE MOVEMENT TOGETHER

The first part of the answer, then, was to set up an International Committee (later called the International Council) consisting initially of just five members. It was clearly understood that it was not to exercise control over the regional councils but to provide guidance and leadership, and to be a means of liaison between them. It was also agreed that from time to time further international conferences and special meetings were to be arranged to make it possible for more national leaders to take a direct part in council discussions. Such meetings were held at Lausanne in 1967, at Port Dickson, Malaysia, in 1972 and near Edinburgh in 1979.

The second part of the answer was the appointment of an International Secretary, free to travel and to give leadership, encouragement and advice. John Laird refused the appointment because he wanted to concentrate on his work as General Secretary in England. As we shall see in the next chapter, Armin Hoppler proved to be just the man for the task. The developing network of friendships and relationships which he built up around the world and which was fostered by international conferences and committees at different levels were important factors in maintaining SU's unity and common purpose.

Thirdly, the conference laid down clear guidelines to help emerging national movements to understand what Scripture Union stood for. After long hours of sub-committee work, statements were agreed covering the movement's aims, some of its doctrinal convictions, its methods, its basic philosophy, and its relationship to the churches and other Christian bodies. It is worth noting that in a day when there was far less emphasis on racial issues and the perils of nationalism the conference affirmed that 'the aims of the Scripture Union movement had no social, racial or intellectual limits' and places on record its belief in 'the unity of all true believers in Christ without distinction as to race, language, colour or social position, and their equal worth in the sight of God.'

An important point is that those statements were not imposed on the existing national movements by the conference but were 'a banner to which they freely rallied'. Conference members expressed their unity by accepting them, and national councils and committees were glad to adopt them in due course as statements of their own positions.

Fourthly, the conference recommended that 'Scripture Union', or a translation of it, should in future be the movement's official name throughout the world. Other subsidiary names, such as ISCF and CSSM would continue to be used for specialised activities. But it was a unifying factor that the main name in every country was the same; and it was a name that emphasised the central place of the Bible in all its activities.

PRESSING FORWARD IN THE REGIONS

One of the chief objectives in setting up regional councils was to stimulate the development of SU in each country to the point where national movements became autonomous and were then ready to share responsibility for further development within the region. Within the next few years the ANZEA Council took steps to make this happen by appointing a regional secretary who was free to travel regularly to the various countries, by arranging regional conferences and training courses, and by sending financial help to the younger movements. The European Committee still only had advisory powers, so for the time being Switzerland and London looked after the various emerging movements in Europe, while France took responsibility for French-speaking Africa. Until other Regional Councils were formed, the London Council looked after the rest of the world; but within a few years the Africa, Americas and South Asia Regional Councils were formed. The present situation, with six regions covering the whole of the SU world, was completed when the British Isles Regional Council was formed in 1969.

As we shall see, the new arrangements led to rapid growth. At the time of Old Jordans there were autonomous councils in just seven countries, Australia, Britain, Canada, France, New Zealand, South Africa and Switzerland. Twenty-four years later there are thirty-six autonomous SU councils and committees or honorary representatives in another fifty-five

It is generally agreed that despite the inevitable small problems along the way, the international arrangements worked out at Old Jordans have served the movement exceptionally well. Responsibility for worldwide development was effectively transferred from the London Council to the international body over the ensuing decade. The first international office was established at Winterthur in Switzerland. This was partly because it was convenient for Armin Hoppler but particularly because the movement wished to demonstrate to its worldwide membership the truly international character of the Scripture Union as it approached its second century. The rapid advance of the next twenty years and the spiritual harvest that resulted were in large measure made possible by the decisions that were made.

Part IV

Vigorous Regions 1960–1984

20

The Man in the Middle

Old Jordans set the movement free to advance. The decision to decentralise, to encourage national movements and regional councils to press forward in their own parts of the world as strongly as possible with the minimum of outside control, led to unprecedented growth. In fact, SU grew so fast it could easily have disintegrated. The man in the middle, who built up the international structure and made it work, and who more than anyone kept the movement together, was the International Secretary, Armin Hoppler.

Armin Hoppler was from Switzerland where, as a young man, he owned and managed a successful factory, making socks and stockings. After he met Ernst Aebi, he increasingly gave his spare time to Scripture Union, and before long became chairman of the Swiss committee. As John Laird commented: 'The two men complemented each other: Ernst Aebi, ebullient and impulsive, and a born evangelist; Armin Hoppler, calm and wise and an able administrator.' As International Secretary, to quote Laird again, 'he was the ideal man for the job. Fluent in several languages and a good traveller, Armin quickly became established as an international leader.'

There were still some SU leaders around the world who could not see the point of the international structure and thought it was a waste of money. Some even viewed it with suspicion. Armin Hoppler travelled widely in the next few years, encouraging lonely staff, sharing news and ideas, discussing problems, and building up the fellowship of the worldwide SU family. His gift for making friends with a wide range of people, and his careful Christian diplomacy soon allayed suspicion and built up confidence. By 1967, when the second international conference was called, the structure planned at Old Jordans was working smoothly and was everywhere accepted.

It was in Europe itself, however, that he had his deepest influence. All through the fifteen years that he was International Secretary, he was also chairman of the European Council. Since there was no Regional Secretary, he took on the leadership, the travelling and the pastoral care of the staff himself. In 1962, for example, he made no less than fourteen visits to other parts of Europe. Moreover, from the time of Ernst Aebi's death at the end of 1962, he led the movement in German-speaking Switzerland as well. In effect, he was doing three jobs.

The regional arrangements in Europe were a compromise worked out at a critical meeting of the European Advisory Committee at Guebwiller in May 1959. Maurice Ray saw the need for more drive and direction particularly in countries where SU was still small and struggling. He wanted a full-time Regional Secretary with power to direct and co-ordinate the work throughout the continent. Léonard Bréchet and others were afraid that the regional structure would infringe the autonomy of national movements, and stifle initiative. The compromise agreed was that Armin Hoppler, as Chairman of the European Committee, would do the work of a Regional Secretary but with advisory powers only and no budget. Mainly because of his personality, the arrangement worked well and lasted until he retired as chairman in 1982.

EXTRAORDINARY GENEROSITY

However, the lack of a full-time general secretary held back the work in German-speaking Switzerland itself. Until 1968, there was only one other staff worker. The circulation of notes was maintained, and a few camps were held. But the most notable feature was a series of rallies all over the country at which Armin Hoppler spoke about the movement in other countries. The Swiss members responded with extraordinary generosity. At one stage, Bibellesebund in Switzerland was taking financial responsibility for Germany, Austria, Greece, and Spain; and it was sending large annual grants to French-speaking Africa and to other parts of the world. In a typical year, 1977, it gave away more than half its gift income.

When Peter Hoppler joined his father, in 1968, the progress resumed. By 1982, there were twelve staff workers. In the four years since 1978, the staff had doubled, the number of camps for teenagers and young people had increased from four to eighteen, and a whole range of family camps and Bible conferences for adults had been started. The rest of the SU world benefitted as well, for although the extra staff required a larger share of the budget, they were still giving away thirty per cent of their gift income. The grants they sent to other countries were even higher than before.

NEW METHODS OF OUTREACH

In French-speaking Switzerland a major milestone was the opening of additional buildings at the SU Centre at Vennes in 1962. Maurice Ray continued to have many opportunities for missions in the state church. For fourteen years, he also had a ten-minute radio programme every Wednesday evening, reaching a large audience. Each week he dealt with problems raised in letters from his listeners, particularly about marriage and family life. His replies were published in the Radio and TV magazine and were the starting point for some of his many books. In 1975, he was joined by Philippe Decorvet, whose experience with SU in French-speaking Africa helped to prepare him to take over the leadership when Maurice Ray retired.

Meanwhile, Claire-Lise de Benoit and her colleagues in the children's work were experimenting with new methods of outreach. For example, Henri Bacher, a trained pharmacist who joined SU as an evangelist in 1975, used a twenty-year-old bus: 'The main aim is street evangelism, and to bring children into Bible clubs, linked with local churches. We bring the bus right near to the place where the Bible club is held. The bus attracts the children because it is so old. We tell them to come in, and there is music playing inside and puppets to attract their attention. We have enough room for about forty to sit down. Then we have a meeting for them with Bible quizzes, songs and sharing the Gospel.'

Another imaginative Swiss attempt to use new methods was the formation of an audio-visual centre. Centre Evangélique de Productions Audio-Visuelles (CEPA) was independent of SU but affiliated to it. One of Maurice Ray's sons, Jean-Luc, had been converted to Christ while he was in North America training as a TV cameraman. He uses his considerable photographic gifts and secular training to great effect, and CEPA rapidly became widely respected for the quality and effectiveness of its productions.

AN EVANGELIST AT HEART

Across the border in Germany, SU was also growing steadily. When Paul Schmidt retired in 1966, after seventeen years of fruitful service, the movement had five staff workers, and was already well established. Karl Schäfer, who took over as general secretary, had first met SU when he was serving as a pastor in Austria. In 1960 he became SU youth evangelist for Southern Germany and Austria, based near Salzburg. He and Noldi Pfeiffer, the staff worker in

Austria, ran their first ski camp together the following year. Karl Schäfer is an evangelist at heart and all the time he has been general secretary he has continued to run several ski camps and other youth activities each year.

Young people's camps have been one of the most significant aspects of SU's work in Germany. One of those converted through them is Eberhard Baade, now a pastor in Northern Germany. 'The contact with Scripture Union helped me to survive the study of theology without any spiritual damage', he told Karl Schäfer recently. With the encouragement of his parish, he still runs SU children's camps and a Holiday Bible School, and is a member of the SU Council.

Another council member who grew up in the camps is Peter Hahne, editor-in-chief at Saarland Radio. 'I was converted at the age of nine in our church, which is greatly influenced by Scripture Union', he writes. 'My spiritual foundation was laid by SU. First as a participant, and then as a voluntary helper, I attended innumerable camps, conferences and seminars.'

BEACH MISSIONS IN GERMANY

Each summer the German SU also runs a lively programme of beach missions, the only movement outside the English-speaking world to do so. As part of her training when she joined the staff in 1955, Else Diehl helped Quintin Carr at the Bude beach mission in south-west England. Thirteen years later she led the first team on to the beaches of the North Sea. Each summer now over 100 voluntary helpers in fifteen teams contact some 10,000 children. The staff who lead the teams are involved in children's missions in churches, tents and halls all the year round. But they reckon that it is at the beach missions that they have their most effective outreach to non-Christian families.

Moreover the contact sometimes reveals deep need. At a campfire one evening at one of the 1983 missions, a team member noticed a teenager standing on the edge of the circle looking desperately unhappy. He was just sixteen years old, but had problems at school and his girl friend had left him. He told the team member that earlier in the evening he had planned to go down to the sea and take his life. But he had suddenly remembered attending the beach mission a few years before, and decided they were the only people who could help him. Later that evening the team member led him to Christ. He came regularly for the rest of the week and is now linked with a local church back home.

In 1973 a large legacy and generous gifts from supporters made it possible for SU to buy some redundant school buildings in lovely countryside near Marienheide as a camp centre. A year later, the office moved from Wuppertal to a building nearby. Under Karl Schäfer's leadership the literature ministry from Marienheide has grown steadily. A number of books have been published each year in close collaboration with SU Switzerland. But their greatest success has been with their Bible reading notes. Series have been produced for children, teenagers and adults. Good promotion and attractive covers have helped circulation to reach over 100,000. With almost another 50,000 in German-speaking Switzerland, more notes are published in German than in any other language apart from English.

FROM THE CRADLE TO THE GRAVE

In the 50's and 60's Armin Hoppler and John Laird worked together to develop the movement in the rest of Europe. The Swiss took a special interest in Southern Europe, where the small Protestant populations were under considerable pressure from the Roman Catholic or Orthodox authorities.

In Greece, Miltos Anghelatos built up his publishing programme, for children and adults, and soon made SU the leading evangelical publisher in the country. In 1966 he was able to start boys' and girls' camps and an adult Bible conference. Two years later, as a most unusual type of ministry for Scripture Union, he started an old people's home. At the time the Greek government's Social Security scheme made no provision for Protestant old people. Finance was provided by the (American) Eastern European Mission and Miltos Anghelatos ran it as part of his SU responsibilities. Among the residents were his elderly parents, who had thrown him out of home when he was converted, but had since found Christ themselves.

At the other end of the continent a committee based in Barcelona published Spanish notes and other books. With Swiss help they were eventually able to appoint a part-time staff worker, Bernado Sanchez. Then in 1979 Pedro Puigvert joined on a full-time basis. It was over seventy years since the last full-time staff worker, Josiah Spiers' niece Beatrice, had left to get married.

THE KISS OF PEACE

Meanwhile Abel Rodrigues maintained his strenuous programme to reach the young people of Portugal. He 'is a human dynamo' a visitor from England reported. 'Nearly half the Protestant population are SU members.' His work focused on the two camp sites, Carrascal, near Lisbon, and Torreira, near Oporto, both bought with help from Switzerland. Activities were arranged for all ages, from camps for children aged 5–6 to conferences for the 'Over 60's'.

A visitor in 1972 reported: 'Five hundred young people passed through the two camps last summer. About half the campers each year are entirely new to SU work. The young people came from the Baptists, the Brethren, the Pentecostals (the largest readers of the Bible notes) and the Lusitanian Church. A typical day at camp begins with gymnastics in pyjamas at 7 am with the mist still rising from the ground.'

By 1981, numbers at summer camps had risen to over 1,000. 'I am utterly exhausted', Rodrigues wrote, in a personal letter at the end of the summer season, 'we have just had eleven camps at Carrascal, plus a convention and four camps in the north. For the last three months, I have not had a single day off, or a free Sunday, because the camps follow one after the other.'

To interest the younger children, a small zoo containing sheep and goats was installed. Someone noted that 'the building in which the animals are housed is so constructed that it can easily be converted into sleeping quarters for extra children if required.' Another unusual feature was the 'kiss of peace' on the final evening of the camp for the youngest age group. 'The children all sit round the camp fire, huddled in rugs and blankets. After some singing and prize-giving, the children are invited to apologize to one another for any times when they have been unkind during the week. Then came the kiss of reconciliation and gone are all the hard feelings.'

SMALL MINORITIES

Another Emmaus graduate who planted SU in Southern Europe was Guiseppe Barbanotti, from Italy. His link with Vennes was specially close as he married Maurice Ray's secretary. He was appointed his country's first staff worker in 1958, concentrating on literature work and campaigns in the churches. Ten years later, he was able to start a programme of camps, which still continue. Noldi Pfeiffer, from Switzerland, has been staff worker in Austria since

1959. It is another strongly Roman Catholic country, but he is able to run camps and tent missions throughout the summer, and ski camps and meetings in schools and homes in the winter. In January 1984 he was joined by Walter Schmitt, the first Austrian member of staff.

In each of these countries, Protestants were in a small and scattered minority. SU only kept going because of regular grants from England and Switzerland. When it was considering Belgium, the European Council assumed that it too would need financial help from abroad. 'Under present conditions, Belgium will never be self-supporting', the minutes of the first meeting record. However, they had reckoned without the business gifts of the staff-worker, Theo Snitselaar. Only four years later, Belgium was able to balance its budget and was granted autonomy. Frans van Dijk, who took over the leadership in 1964, kept up the momentum. In the next ten years, the circulation of notes more than doubled and donations increased fourfold. When the committee decided that the time had come to buy a house as headquarters, the money was raised in just four years, most of it from the 3,500 members.

THE BIBLE SOCIETY TO THE RESCUE

In Holland, by contrast, progress was disappointing. In spite of the strong Bible reading tradition in the country, SU notes did not sell in large numbers. For a few years, a special series was published in co-operation with a Roman Catholic group, but it only achieved a small circulation. Since SU in Holland did nothing other than publish Bible reading notes, most Dutch Christians saw no need to send any gifts. A large gift of capital kept the movement going for some years, but with inflation its value steadily declined. The crunch came in 1975, when Jaap Shriek resigned from the staff, the offices had to be vacated and the money had almost run out.

At this critical point, the Netherlands Bible Society came to the rescue. One of its staff edited the notes, another handled the distribution. The following year one of them, John Beokhout, gave up his responsible Bible Society job and joined SU full-time. It was a brave decision, in view of SU's precarious financial position; but John and Riet Boekhout had just come to a new experience of Christ through the conversion of their two sons. Three years later the purchase of a former school hostel at Culemborg, as an SU centre, helped to re-establish the work.

THE OLD TESTAMENT COMES ALIVE

While Switzerland looked after most of Southern Europe, England gave its attention to Scandinavia. The best progress was made in Norway. John Laird visited Oslo several times and formed a committee, but the decisive influence came from Ethiopia. A Norwegian missionary, Marie Wilhelmsen (now Mrs Berg), was impressed by the effect of SU notes on the lives of some of her students and on their Christian Union meetings. She had been brought up in a lively Christian atmosphere but did not know the Bible. 'As young people we were always being told to read the Bible. But I did not know how.' When she went to Norway on leave she decided to try using SU notes.

'I was amazed', she later said. 'Before, the Bible had been the old Book of stories – the ten lepers and so on – that we heard at Sunday School. But here it was alive and speaking to me. In particular the Old Testament passages came alive to me. I remember we were going through the books of Kings and Chronicles. I'd read little of the Old Testament before.'

Marie Wilhelmsen offered to return to Ethiopia as an SU worker, but could not get a visa. So in 1964, she became the first SU staff worker in Norway. The circulation of notes had been under 2,000 for several years, but within two years they had 11,700 regular adult subscribers and had introduced series for children and teenagers. Norway had so many Christian activities for young people already that the SU committee decided not to start any more but to limit itself to promoting Bible reading. To avoid any danger of competition, they financed everything from the sale of notes. Any gifts received were used to help the work in Africa.

In other Scandinavian countries, a little progress was made. Through Marie Wilhelmsen's contacts with leaders of IFES notes were started in Swedish (1966) and Danish (1967); but fifteen years later, the circulation was still only about 3,000 in each language. In Finland, the Finnish Missionary Society sponsored the notes until a separate SU organisation could be formed. They appointed a retired missionary, Liina Lindstrom, to look after them, and circulation soon reached 5,000. Every two years from 1969, the four countries have met for the Scandinavian SU conference.

DISAPPEARING STRUCTURES

Meanwhile, Theo Snitselaar had moved from Belgium to France to be administrator at the Guebwiller headquarters. Under Léonard Bréchet's leadership La Ligue had become a significant force on the

French evangelical scene. It had four evangelists in different parts of the country, and two good camp sites, at Guebwiller and Sumène. Two thousand young people attended its camps each summer. As a result of Bréchet's vision, it was also taking a strong lead in French-speaking Africa. But too much depended on Léonard Bréchet personally. After his sudden death, at the European staff conference in 1965, Scripture Union went rapidly downhill. There were four years of confused leadership, during which the chairman of the committee and two of the evangelists resigned, and the finances sharply deteriorated. In 1969, when Theo Snitselaar was eventually appointed general secretary, La Ligue was in a mess.

Theo Snitselaar soon put things right. By 1974, the team of evangelists had increased to six. The finances had been put straight, and a huge bill for the repair of the elaborate roof of the château at Guebwiller had been paid. France continued to send a large annual grant to French-speaking Africa, though the responsibility was now shared with the other autonomous countries in Europe. More than two hundred voluntary workers were running camps, in twelve different places, 'with programmes as varied as sailing, flying, music and singing, discovering Greece, or taking part in evangelistic commandos.'

In a new departure Snitselaar had developed an extensive publishing programme. By carefully choosing the right titles, rigorously controlling costs and ploughing back profits, he built up this side of the work so effectively that in ten years La Ligue had become one of the leading evangelical publishers in the country. Theo Snitselaar's sudden death, in 1979, at the age of fifty-four, caused another set-back. But Scripture Union in France was now firmly rooted, and came through the crisis well. Two years later, when Claude Gaasch was appointed general secretary, progress could continue. A major advance the following year was the purchase of a new camping centre, le Rimlishof, a few kilometres from Guebwiller.

In its publishing and in some of its evangelistic work, La Ligue was beginning to reach outside traditional Christian circles. This was important, because young people in the 1970s in France, as in the rest of Europe, had to a large extent abandoned their Christian heritage and culture. 'All the traditional structures that used to prop people up are disappearing one by one', a leading French doctor pointed out. Even modern structures were questioned. 'We are witnessing, I believe, the crumbling of scientific certainty. The young are violently rejecting that science which, claiming to explain all man's problems, has destroyed the secret and the sacred, the poetic, the intimate, and what cannot be expressed in words, what they call "vibes".'

ARRESTED BY JESUS CHRIST

At least one man on the staff of La Ligue understood the new mood. Gérard Peilhon's father had died when he was a baby. He tells his own story:

> When I was seven my mother sent me to an orphanage. She had seven children and couldn't look after us all. But after a year, I was expelled, because I was so difficult, and went to live with a Christian family in Belgium. They looked after me for a year but after that they could not stand it any longer. But they continued to pray for me.
>
> I went back home and one of my half-brothers arrived from Italy. He was extremely hard, a real fighter, and I followed his example. I became a delinquent. But the Christian family in Belgium took me again in the school holidays and paid for me to go to Bible camp. I was sixteen-and-a-half at the time. I wasn't interested in it as a Bible camp; but it was mixed and I went there to meet the girls.
>
> One evening the speaker spoke about the Crucifixion and it was so real that I saw myself as one of the executioners. Up to that moment I could not have cared less about God. I had even stolen from the offering plate in church. But that evening I understood my guilt. I had tried to control myself on the sexual level, and to stop thieving, but I couldn't. I had often thought of suicide. But that evening, in my room at the camp, I cried to God and knew that it was the start of a new life.

After military service and Bible training, he spent six years as a chaplain in a home for alcoholics, during which time he formed a singing group 'The Lord's Commandos' because he realised that 'music with a message is easier for young delinquents and drinkers to understand'. After he joined the SU staff, the main part of his ministry was with delinquents and other young people right out of touch with the churches.

> My past life helps me to meet them on their own ground. When I sing in prison, I can tell them 'I am no better than you. I have two brothers who have been in prison. If I am not in prison myself, it's because before I was arrested by the police, I was arrested by Jesus Christ.'

21

In West and East

While he was in England for the Old Jordans Conference, Colin Becroft was asked to leave Australia to pioneer SU in USA. The small US committee or board, formed the previous year, was convinced of the need for SU's Bible reading emphasis and wanted a man with proven experience of leadership in the movement to help them to get it going. With his strategic sense, John Laird realised that if SU was well established in USA it could be a strong base for worldwide missionary outreach. Knowing Colin Becroft had been outstandingly effective in New Zealand and Australia, he encouraged him to go.

AN UPHILL TASK

Arriving in July 1961, Becroft threw himself into the task of building up the Bible reading ministry.

> After my arrival I became more aware of how much this ministry was needed. The evangelical Christian community had not escaped the pressure of the compulsive activism which leaves little place for recollection in the presence of God. And among those interested in the practice of Bible reading, there was often a tendency to implement it legalistically rather than as a means of fellowship with Christ. On the one hand, there is prayer and the Word of God as it comes to us in Scripture. On the other hand are the experiences and demands of daily life. How are these to be related in a practical way? Clearly this was an area where Scripture Union should have a contribution.

It was an uphill task. The SU notes looked foreign to American eyes, and for the first few years there was not sufficient circulation to produce a local edition. Moreover, there was a whole range of other publications for daily devotions available in America, many of them backed by the authority of a denomination, some of them given away free. Becroft wrote:

There are uncounted numbers of devotional booklets published by denominations and independent bodies. But when you look at them closely, you see that even the best of them are fairly complete in themselves, rather than being expositions of Scripture. They lack an urgent sense of the importance of daily, personal worship through Bible reading, meditation and prayer.

In spite of these problems, and an acute shortage of money, the Bible reading ministry slowly grew. Circulation, which had been 4,000 in 1959 when the Philadelphia office took over the US subscriptions from Canada, had risen to 10,400 by 1965, and for the first time the accounts showed a small surplus. The following year, they appointed their first children's evangelist. Roger Green had grown up with CSSM and SU in New Zealand and had been on the Canadian staff for some years. He was an expert with puppets and had an effective ministry to both children and their parents in churches and at summer beach missions along the East coast.

FINANCIAL CRISIS

In the three years 1968–71, however, the situation took a disastrous turn. Colin Becroft and the board believed that SU would never take root unless there were North American editions of the notes and a sufficiently extensive programme to command national recognition. They employed a firm of Christian consultants, who drew up a plan for rapid development over the next five years, which in its early stages would be financed by borrowed money.

Although the movement was already financed to some extent by loans, the board rejected the proposal for further borrowing, deciding instead to launch an appeal for the funds to pay for the new developments. The North American notes were published in January 1969, and were well received. Unfortunately the board's efforts to raise funds were unsuccessful, while the heavy cost of the development programme continued. The crunch came in 1971 when, in spite of a huge overdraft from the bank and other loans, a printer's bill of $30,000 could not be paid. Total debts amounted to some $207,000.

In this crisis the board had to take drastic steps. It decided to cut out all SU activity except the publication of a single series of adult notes. Russell Hitt, an SU board member and Editor of the Christian magazine *Eternity*, generously offered free office space and the assistance of his staff with several office functions. SU's own staff was cut from over twenty to just three. Roger Green was asked to leave, and, with financial help from SU in the early stages, founded a new organisation, 'Children's Ministries Inc.' to carry on his work. (Rather confusingly, he still used the old initials CSSM for his beach ministry, standing now for 'Children's Sand and Surf Mission'). To find the cash to pay outstanding bills and keep the reduced operation going the board appealed to the Christian public for a large sum of money in loans. The US movement did not own a building or similar asset as security for the loans, so the appeal was strongly criticised in several quarters, particularly by some SU leaders in other countries. However, there was a big response and $228,000 were received within a few weeks. It solved the immediate problem, but left the SU with high annual interest charges, and the need to repay the loans in years to come.

Colin Becroft fought hard with great loyalty to overcome the difficulties of adapting SU to American conditions. But the pressures had become too great and a year later he resigned. His place was taken by Clifford Swanson, a Wheaton College graduate, who had joined the staff as editor the previous year. Partly because of the interest on the loans, the financial position continued to deteriorate, reaching its lowest point in 1978, when total debts were over $337,000. But Clifford Swanson worked hard to make the Bible reading notes more attractive and to find new outlets for them, such as their complementary subscriptions for hospitals and prisons. Circulation steadily increased, and with it the flow of gifts. From 1980, when it topped 40,000, the accounts began to show regular surpluses. A major milestone was passed in 1981 when $104,000 of the loans were repaid on time. A major appeal the following year cleared the greater part of the remaining debt. It had been ten years of hard struggle but SU in USA was at last free to consider moving forward into other types of work.

FOUR VENTRILOQUISTS

Meanwhile, over the border in Canada, SU's dual ministry of children's missions and Bible reading promotion went forward more quietly. Tony Capon led the small staff team throughout the 1960s, but in 1970 he agreed to give his time and energies to Latin America. His place was taken first by Maurice Eastwick, who had joined the staff as a children's missioner two years earlier, and in 1975 by William Tyler.

The pace quickened in the 1970s. A critical decision was taken in 1971, when USA suddenly stopped printing the North American notes. Instead of returning to the English editions, Maurice Eastwick bravely printed all four series in Canada. To produce them in the few weeks available with attractive full colour covers and at a reasonable price was a considerable achievement. Over the next few years, the circulation of notes climbed steadily. Canada was one of the few countries in the Western World to achieve a steady increase in note circulation throughout the 1970s. The secret seems to have been their strategy of appointing SU secretaries in churches, and spending a great deal of time encouraging and helping them.

The number of field staff also increased significantly. In such a vast country, the key to advance was to decentralise. By the end of the decade, there was a vigorous French-speaking committee and staff worker in Montreal, a man working full-time in the Chinese churches, and four children's missioners located at strategic points between Vancouver and Toronto. A curious feature was that all four children's missioners were ventriloquists. The lively conversations they held with their 'dummies' gripped the children's attention, and could be used as an effective method of teaching. However, it was a difficult skill for younger helpers to copy; perhaps that was one of the reasons why the number of missions run by teams of voluntary helpers declined sharply, and with it a valuable feature of the CSSM tradition.

The other English-speaking country in the region with an active SU presence was Jamaica. The SU committee, formed in 1954, ran an annual children's mission in a poor part of Kingston, but otherwise concentrated on distributing Bible reading notes and Sunday School teaching aids. By 1971, when they became an autonomous SU movement, circulation of notes was the highest per head in the region. Over the years, SU co-operated increasingly closely with the Inter School Christian Fellowship, which in Jamaica was affiliated to the IFES. After sharing the same office for some years, the two movements formally merged in 1980. The new joint organisation affiliated to both IFES and Scripture Union International. In the circumstances it was a wise development. It was more economical to have one organisation than two, and Las Newman, the General Secretary, could use his gifts of leadership more widely. Even more important, it strengthened the schools work to be anchored to SU's Bible reading emphasis, and gave SU a wider outlet for its notes. The plan to produce *Daily Power* notes for high school students was a direct result.

BIBLE READING ONLY

The events in USA cast their shadow over the rest of the Americas. The strategy agreed at Old Jordans was for North and South America to work together as a region, with Canada and USA providing most of the financial support. The plan relied on having strong supporting movements in the North. Canada did its best, but its membership was still comparatively small. USA was fighting for its life financially and could do little.

A start, however, was made. Colin Becroft undertook several lengthy tours of Latin America in the 1960s to assess the need and stimulate interest. When the Regional Council was formed he became its Executive Secretary.

In 1970, Tony Capon became the first full-time Regional Secretary. He travelled widely and quickly became fluent in Spanish. He found considerable interest, and twelve countries were represented at the first Regional Conference, held at Huampani in Peru in June 1970.

Reflecting current SU thinking in USA, the Regional Council decided to concentrate its efforts on Bible reading. Following a visit to Mexico in 1970 Tony Capon wrote:

> I talked with every mission and denominational leader I could get to see. Every single one of them, without exception, urged me to get a full range of Spanish SU materials available for Latin America. But one man after another impressed on me the fact that they must be written by Latin Americans, not translated from English.

For some years small editions of notes translated into Spanish had been published in Argentina, Mexico and, at a simpler level, in Peru. It was decided that the only way to produce original Latin American notes was to have an editorial centre for the whole continent. There was already a good circulation in Argentina, and René Padilla, the committee Chairman, was an experienced publisher. So the centre would be there.

The first issue of the new notes, *Encuentro con Dios* ('Encounter with God'), appeared in 1971. It was well received, but financial problems dogged the project from the start. Tony Capon had anticipated distribution difficulties, but they were much worse than he expected. Parcels to some countries were refused import licences; to others they were seriously delayed. A consignment by air freight to Mexico took seven months. One to Paraguay, the country next door, took over a year. As the notes were dated, delays caused serious loss. Even in Argentina, where circulation reached some 6,000 at one time, there was soon a mountain of unsold stock. Rapid inflation drained the publishing capital away. When printers' bills were going up seventy-five per cent in three months it was almost impossible to bring in enough money from the sales of one edition to pay for the next. With thousands of dollars of subsidy, the programme staggered on for several years, but by August 1979 the circulation had dropped to 3,000 and debts were so high that publication ceased.

By contrast, there was a happier story from Brazil, where Portuguese is spoken and half the population of Latin America is found. After Colin Becroft's visit in 1963 a committee was formed. The first notes appeared two years later. James Cook, an experienced missionary from Scotland, translated and distributed them for the first five years. He suffered from Parkinson's disease so was unable to travel or take public meetings, but found the SU notes an ideal outlet for his gifts during the last few years of his life. Over the years, translated notes were gradually replaced by those written by Brazilians, and the circulation climbed steadily to about 10,000.

TWENTY-SIX CAMPS IN PERU

Meanwhile the camps in Peru forged ahead. A report in 1966 said that 'seven camps were held, four for boys and three for girls, with a total of some 220 campers. Two of them were organized for children from Lima's extensive shanty towns staffed entirely by leaders who had been boys at camp themselves.' For fifteen years the programme was run entirely by voluntary helpers, but in 1969 Paul Clark was appointed as SU's first general secretary. Born in Peru of missionary parents, Paul Clark was completely at home in the two cultures, Latin and North American. He had taught geography for several years at one of the top schools in Lima, had directed numerous SU camps and excelled at taking groups of boys on tough walking tours through mountains and jungles.

SU Peru had gained official government recognition in 1967 and, after years of negotiations, it was able to buy the coastal camp site, Camp Kawai, where camps had been held since 1954. Under Paul Clark's leadership a second site, Camp Kimo, was established in the beautiful Chancamayo valley beyond the Andes. More and more ex-campers offered to come back as leaders, the programme grew rapidly and each year there was fresh evidence of the Holy Spirit's work in young people's lives. In 1978 no fewer than twenty-six camps were arranged. Paul Clark gives us some vivid snapshots of the sort of things that happened.

JUNGLE SOUNDS

Camp Kimo. The sounds of the jungle at night – nothing under you but a hammock, nothing over you but a mosquito net to keep out the vampire bats. A Camp Director lies awake thinking of those around her. Girls who have travelled over the Andes for the sake of adventure. Girls who have come because they assumed drugs would be available. Girls who acted tough and yet were soft and gentle. Girls who said they did not want to hear but were longing to be told. Troubled girls. Happy girls. Gentle, soft-spoken girls. Rebellious ones – defiant, arrogant, base. One thing in common – their best Friend they did not know. Long hours of night, the never-ending rasping sounds of the "chicharra", sleep-talk, that new sound that makes one revert to a frightened child; but at a deeper level than all this the lack of sleepiness because you are not "getting through" to them and there is only one day left. And then the jungle sounds continue, perhaps even louder now, but there is a strange calm inside – you have just remembered the little book tucked in the muddy duffle bag and the verse that assures: "My Word will not return unto me void".

ABANDONED AT THE AGE OF FIVE

Camp Kawai. A camp for boys from a Reformatory who have been allowed 'out' as a prize for 'good behaviour'. A long chat on the way to the beach after several days of trying to break into the young life, and the discovery of a world unknown. A counsellor who would never have dreamed that this twelve year old, as thousands of others, was abandoned by his parents at the age of five, 'lost' by them in a large city market. A counsellor who could hardly believe that lying, cheating, thieving, and the foulest of sins could be the mainstay of so young a life. Crime, capture, school, and the dream of escape – an escape back into the underworld where older and hardened criminals hold sway. The absolute frustration of not knowing how to communicate the Good News and the better life; then the realization: 'Lord, I cannot. Lord you can' and a testimony at a campfire from a transformed lad, born into the Kingdom for such a time as this.

NIGHT LIFE AT VILLA GESSEL

While the camp programme was developing strongly in Peru, it was going on more slowly in Argentina. In 1972, John Ellison, on secondment to SU from the South American Missionary Society, started to take groups of young people to the seaside resort of Villa Gessel for an 'Encounter, an experiment in community living'.

> Most of the first day is spent studying how to use the Bible in personal conversation. Then around 9.30 pm they go out to mingle with the holiday crowds for street evangelism. That first night they usually come back bewildered but rejoicing. They have taken the first jump. After that there's a daily programme of Bible study, prayer, worship and workshop sessions, punctuated by volley ball, swimming and sleep. Then at nine thirty out on the streets again – till one or two in the morning.

Back in Buenos Aires after the holiday, the programme of late night street evangelism continued.

NEW INITIATIVES

In the rest of Latin American, Union Biblica (Scripture Union) meant Bible reading notes, and nothing more. It was inevitable that progress was slow. As some of the visitors at the 1970 Regional Conference pointed out, the genius of SU is that the two sides of its work, evangelism and Bible reading, fit together and help one another. A Bible reading movement on its own can easily look as if it is just a commercial operation. If SU is to become a national movement it must have a strong group of enthusiastic workers and supporters. Experience in other countries had shown that most of such people are first involved with SU at a camp, a beach mission or similar activity. To try to run SU as a Bible reading movement alone was like trying to run a race hopping on one leg.

In 1976, when Paul Clark became Regional Secretary, direct work with young people received a new impetus. His experience in Peru had made him an enthusiast for camps, and he quickly shared his vision with key people in several other countries. Events moved quickly. In 1977 Maurice Eastwick rejoined the staff and became SU's first full-time representative in Mexico. Within three years, camps had been started, a national committee had been formed, a local edition of *Encuentro con Dios* published, and Eliud Gutierrez appointed as the first Mexican staff worker.

In 1979, the first SU camp was held in Chile, led by a group of young people who had gone to Peru for training the year before. The same year Pauline Hoggarth was appointed to establish all aspects of SU in Bolivia. Brought up in the high Andes, where her mother had helped to produce the Peruvian version of the Spanish SU notes, Pauline Hoggarth spoke Spanish, English and Quechua, and quickly gathered round her a group of Bolivian friends who shared her vision for what SU could do.

The same year, too, SU Argentina got away to a new start with the appointment of Eduardo Ramirez. A few months later they were almost drowned in a sea of debts, arising from the publishing programme. The car had to be sold and the office closed but, mercifully, the camping property at Villa Gessel was spared. Eduardo slowly built up a programme of evangelism and training for young people at secondary school. When I visited them early in 1984 I found that they had just completed a series of five camps attracting over 200 young people.

The decisive year was 1981. In April the first SU camps were held in both Brazil and Mexico. The same month Leonor Acosta, from Peru, became the first camps and schools worker in Chile. She had had several years' experience as a camp leader at home, and had given up a well-paid teaching job for this pioneer task. Towards the end of the year, Gustavo Oropeza became the first national staff member in Bolivia. It should have been the year of the first Bolivian camp too, but a military coup a few days before it was due to start meant it was postponed till the following January.

In February 1982, when the third Regional Conference met at Camp Kawai, near Lima, there was a strong feeling that SU in the Americas Region had at last turned the corner. None of the nine national movements represented was large but each of them was established. Each of them could send a group of staff and voluntary helpers who shared a vision of SU's potential in their own country. SU in the Americas had come a long way in the last five years. But there was still a long way to go.

CONTRAST IN INDIA

In contrast to Latin America, Scripture Union in India was already sixty years old by the time of Old Jordans; and with a team of twenty-one Indian staff evangelists, and SU members in fourteen languages, it was well established. A survey published in 1976 gives a helpful picture of the progress in the intervening years. In many parts of the country the schools were still open for missions even though India had now been independent for twenty-five years. 'During the past year 270 missions were conducted for a week or more.' Most of them were church schools but 'ninety per cent of the students, perhaps ninety-eight per cent in some cases, are non-Christians.' In over 150 of the schools there were regular SU meetings.

In other parts of the country, the churches ran hostels for children attending the local state secondary schools. Another 105 missions were held in such hostels, and over 300 in the churches themselves.

> They are shorter, usually just three or four days. Storytelling, visual aids, object lessons, slides, filmstrips and flash-cards are all used to make the truth meaningful to young minds. Many children express their response by writing a note and posting it in the special letter box the evangelist sets up. One of the important functions of Scripture Union is to help these children in Christian communities to come to a personal experience of the Lord, so they don't grow up as one more generation of nominal Christians. (*Light of Life*, September 1976, p.4).

On the Bible reading front there had been modest progress with SU notes in eight languages and cards in eleven, and a total distribution of over 100,000. Following Africa's example, the notes were printed as annual books, which kept down the cost and made distribution easier.

SCATTERED GROUPS OF CHILDREN

A new development has been the Vacation Bible Schools, India's equivalent of the beach missions and holiday clubs which have proved such a valuable training ground for Christian workers in other parts of the world. The Indian VBS movement provides teaching materials, but SU staff train the teachers and often lead the teams. Steven Das describes a VBS at Gandhinagar: 'There are only a few Christian families there. Children from various denominations came and a few non-Christians. The daily programme included a Bible class, handwork and a chapel time.' During 1976 SU staff were associated with 121 such Bible Schools attracting some 40,000 children, and the numbers have increased since that time.

But while the total figures are impressive, the distribution is very uneven. By 1976 there were twenty-nine evangelists on the staff. But ten of them were in the two southern states of Kerala and Tamilnadu. The vast Hindi-speaking area in the north with 200 million people, only had five staff (and at the time of writing that number had been reduced to two). The Christian population in that part of India is small and scattered, so the staff have to be away from home for weeks at a time, travelling long distances in slow and crowded trains to meet small groups of children at church or hostel. Each member of staff is expected to be on tour for two or three weeks each month. It is a hard and lonely life in the Hindi area, perhaps too hard. Not many have been prepared to face it.

A PIECE OF PAPER IN THE ROAD

Further south it is a different picture. Several states have made good progress but Tamilnadu is the shining example. N Gnanaraja, the leader of the team there, was converted at the age of seventeen through a piece of paper he found lying in the road. It was a page torn from an English Bible. He had been brought up in a Christian home but failure and frustration had caused him to deny the existence of God. He took the page home and said to his family, 'If God was alive, he wouldn't allow this page to be torn from the Bible!' But his sister read out the verse at the top of the page: 'His boastings have wrought nothing.' 'This verse was a shock to me', Gnanaraja said later. 'I became restless and saw that unless I changed, I could not have peace.' So he knelt beside his bed and committed his life to Christ.

In 1968, Gnanaraja resigned his position as a headmaster and joined SU as a children's evangelist. When he was interviewed, Cecil Johnston advised him to shave off his large moustache 'as it would frighten the children'. A few months later he saw John Jacob, who had taken over as General Secretary in the meantime. 'Why have you shaved off your moustache?' John asked him. 'Grow it again. It will attract the children.' With or without moustache, he found many opportunities for school missions. But he was concerned at the lack of follow-up. So in January 1973, he arranged a boys' camp at Velachery near Madras. A few days before the camp started a group of teachers went with him to pray at the camp site. 'There the Lord gave them a vision to do something for teachers also. After much prayer and preparation, the first Teachers Retreat was arranged. To our surprise 125 teachers came.'

The Scripture Union Teachers Fellowship, which arose out of this retreat, was a key to the advance in Tamilnadu in the next few years. Gnanaraja formed branches in various parts of the state, and encouraged the members to follow up the children converted at his missions, to help at the camps, and to give towards the support of additional workers. By 1976, they were running eight camps a year, and had increased the staff from two to four. Five years later SU in Tamilnadu had become fully self supporting, with a staff of five, and was even financing an evangelist pioneering SU work in Bihar, one of the Hindi-speaking states in the north.

DECENTRALISATION

The growth of self-support within a state was a result of an important decision made in 1965. Up to that time efforts to establish committees in India had had little success, mainly because of the size of the country and slow communications. As we have seen, an All-India Council had been formed in 1957. But it was composed entirely of staff and only had advisory status. The real decisions were still made by Cecil Johnston, the general secretary, or, sometimes, by the London Council which supplied most of the money. SU was still a foreign mission, not a national Indian organisation. A structure that had been normal and acceptable when R T Archibald arrived, however, was quite unsuitable in independent India.

Cecil Johnston saw that the way forward was to decentralise. He decided to form a committee in each state or language area, and to encourage the states to move towards self-support and a measure of self-government. The state committees could meet regularly without wasting too much time on travel, and soon began to take responsibility. In some states, events moved quite fast. In 1971, for example, the Kerala committee decided to raise money for a house, as a base for their own work and as an All-India headquarters. When the house was opened three years later, eighty per cent of the cost had been raised locally. I was privileged to speak at the opening ceremony. The programme had sixteen items, including six addresses, two of them by bishops who as young men had been involved in CSSM in Archibald's day. The formation of state committees breathed new life into the All-India Council. As representatives of their states, members were prepared to travel, sometimes for two or three days, to the annual meeting, and were in a better position to contribute to discussion. By the time Cecil Johnston retired, in 1972, the Council had found its feet.

(Left) Abel Rodriges speaking at a camp in Portugal (1955).

(Right) SU member in France (1965).

Maurice Ray speaking at the centenary rally at Vennes (1967).

(a)

(b)

(c)

(d)

(e)

(f)

(g)

Some SU leaders in the 60's and 70's.
(a) Derek Warren, England, in 1961 when he was chairman of the International Council. (b) John Laird, General Secretary in England; and Armin Hoppler, International Secretary (1963). (c) Alan Kerr, Australia, who became chairman of the International Council in 1972. (d) Philemon Quaye in 1972, when he was chairman of the Ghana committee. (e) Professor Khoo Oon Teik, for many years chairman of the Singapore and then the Anzea Councils. (f) Colin Becroft, originally from New Zealand, pioneered SU in the USA. (g) Claire-Lise de Benoit, children's evangelist in Switzerland (1967).

Boys playing puddox during one of John Jacob's school missions in India.

CSSM/SU evangelists speak to thousands of children at the great Maramon convention in South India each year.

Selling books in Ghana (1963).

Bible study at Aburi Girls' Secondary School SU group in Ghana (1983).

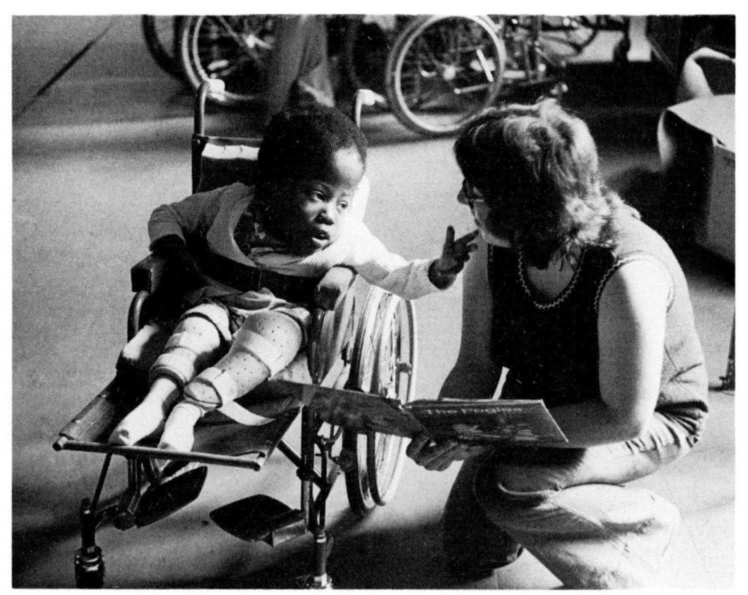

An ISCF member reads to a handicapped child at a work party at Cheyne Hospital in England (1973).

Sailing at an ISCF camp in Australia (1981).

ISCF leaders in Fiji (1981).

Junior ISCF in Singapore (1983).

Junior camp at Carraty Wood, England (1983).

'Peter and John running to the empty tomb', from the prize-winning soundstrip, 'The Champion' (1978).

Breakfast time at Camp Kawai, Peru (1984).

Tony Berry in action at the Southwold beach mission (1983).

SETBACKS THROUGH SICKNESS

Cecil Johnston's efforts to find Indian leadership at top staff level were less successful. First he selected O C Matthew, the saintly and efficient leader of the Kerala staff, who had given up a well paid job as a bank manager ten years earlier to become a CSSM evangelist. Just before he was appointed, however, his doctor said he was not fit enough for the strenuous travelling involved. He was made secretary/treasurer instead and looked after the office and finances until failing eyesight forced him to retire. In 1965, Rev Sam Sanjeeva Rao became general secretary; but only four years later he suffered a heart attack and died. Cecil Johnston, who had become Regional Secretary, had to take over again. When he left India, his place was taken by John Jacob.

John Jacob had been born in India, but his parents were Armenian. When John was aged twelve, Roddy Archibald took a mission at his school in Darjeeling. He recalls that, in a personal conversation, 'God spoke to me and a change Christward began. There came into my boyish imagination a longing to serve the young as Mr Archibald had done.' After teaching for some years in South India, he went to Scotland on holiday, and while he was there joined the SU staff as Camps Secretary. He returned to India in 1962 as an evangelist and soon showed exceptional gifts with children and young people. Like Cecil Johnston, he is unmarried and has travelled constantly, taking missions on his own in English-medium schools, and working alongside younger colleagues in the Indian language. 'The best (and hardest) training of the staff', he wrote 'is in the actual working out of our SU philosophy in the field. Living, praying, criticising, struggling together over a prolonged period is most revealing.'

Almost every year Cecil Johnston or John Jacob spent a few weeks in Sri Lanka (Ceylon) where they were warmly welcomed to take missions in many of the leading schools, including those run by Roman Catholics. In 1979 Manel Dhamakiriti joined the staff, the first national worker for forty years. But after three years she resigned, and so far it has not been possible to find a replacement.

A NEW LEASE OF LIFE

In Pakistan, Sadiq Mall carried on his lonely ministry. Another gifted children's worker, for over twenty years he was constantly travelling and speaking. Most of the time he was on his own: when a second worker was appointed, he was a thousand miles away and they never met. In 1975, however, SU in Pakistan took on a new lease of life. David Bainbridge, was generously seconded by the Church Missionary Society to be Organising Secretary and, a young graduate, Johnson Charles joined the staff as well. With these reinforcements it was possible to start some camps and a Teachers Christian Fellowship. Efforts to establish school SU groups made only slow progress, but the programme of missions and Vacation Bible Schools developed well and local giving picked up. Although a fair slice of the budget still comes as a grant from England, SU in Pakistan became autonomous in 1982, as it had in India fifteen years ealier.

CSSM and Scripture Union has a long history in India and Pakistan. In some ways its early years during R T Archibald's ministry were the most fruitful. But in the years after Old Jordans, SU as a movement began to take root in a new way in the soil of the sub-continent. If it had not done so it could not have survived in a changed climate. But now that it has done so, it has the potential to become even more fruitful.

English children's SU notes, 1984.

22

The Anzea Story
(Australia/New Zealand/East Asia)

One of the most exciting countries for Scripture Union development in the 1960s was Australia. The careful reorganisation of the 1950s had laid the foundations for spectacular advance. Each state now had its own autonomous council, bringing together the different aspects of SU activity. Through the Federal Council the different states helped one another to find staff, shared ideas and planned joint projects. In each state the number of camps, beach missions, ISCF groups and readers of SU notes grew rapidly. By 1980 it could be claimed that 'Scripture Union touches on the lives of one in every seven people in Australia'.

Moreover, the movement was thinking deeply about its methods. David Claydon, who became leader of the New South Wales staff in 1961 at the age of twenty-four, and Federal Secretary in 1972, put it like this:

> At the end of the 1950s, SU was seen to be a stable, conservative, but perhaps somewhat out-of-date, movement. Yet it had within it the seeds for new growth, and these started to blossom during the '60s. The movement was rethinking its rationale for all it was doing, and in the process it attracted new, creative talent. This thoughtful, prayerful planning blossomed out in all directions in the '70s.

BURSTING FORTH

It was only just in time, for Australian young people were caught up in the 'youth revolution' just as strongly as their contemporaries in Europe. As David Claydon continues,

> In the mid-70s, most religious activity within the life of the government secondary schools had all but died out, and attendance at ISCF voluntary lunchtime activities had been almost halved. After much prayer and thought, and a great deal of effort, SU was again able to burst forth with new leadership in the schools work, with the application of new ideas.

In two states there was a revival of the traditional ISCF pattern. By 1978, New South Wales had active groups in ninety per cent of the state high schools. In Queensland, the number of groups had grown from sixty to 143, and the number of campers had increased fivefold. In the other four states new methods were being tried, with varied success.

One example was the 'Christian Option Programme' which Ron Buckland pioneered in Tasmania. A team of staff and voluntary helpers would spend a week in a particular school, taking several classroom periods with each class, presenting Christianity 'as a valid option for life'. In both 1977 and 1978, 7,000 young people heard of the claims of Christ in this way.

Another new initiative was the Coolamatong Farm Camp in Victoria, the only SU sheep farm in the world! The local education department sends whole classes for a week's study of farming life, during which the SU staff have the opportunity of presenting Christian truth. Life at Coolamatong can be exciting. When I was there for a staff conference in 1977, I had to help fight a bush fire and watch a sheep being slaughtered. The following year, a group of teenage girls had to stand for severals hours in the lake up to their necks in water and with wet blankets over their heads, to escape another fire.

In most of its schools and camps programmes, however, ISCF, according to John Prince, 'had not reached beyond respectable middle-class and largely church-related youth.' In 1967, one of the beach mission leaders in Victoria, John U'Ren, decided to break new ground with a coffee shop, 'The Loft'. It was such a success in attracting teenagers with no church background that the following year a separate team was formed to run it. Thousands of teenagers flock to the Australian beaches each summer, and within a few years, Victoria had seven teams running youth missions at different resorts, and was producing a monthly paper 'Theo's Sun' to follow them up. As John Prince recalls: 'A new type of worker, formerly regarded as "long-haired dropouts", has helped the movement to take the gospel to some of the foot-loose youth it has never reached before.'

Meanwhile, beach missions for children continued to be an important part of the programme. In 1979, there were 129 teams in action, and it was reckoned that total attendance was over 40,000. This aspect of the work became the centre of a lively debate in the Scripture Union world in the 1970s. Some of those involved in children's evangelism began to question its whole philosophical basis. Australia played a central part in the debate. Bill Andersen, chairman of the Federal Council, chaired the International Council's 'Commission on Children's Evangelism' and Ron Buckland, from Tasmania, and John Prince, from Perth, produced important books (*Children and the King*, 1979; *Whose is the Kingdom?*, 1979).

ISSUES IN CHILDREN'S WORK

There were several issues in debate. Some of them arose out of modern studies of the way children learn. To what extent should modern teaching methods be used in helping children to come to know Christ? There were no simple answers as modern methods are based partly on genuine insights, partly on secular assumptions. So modern methods could be helpful, but only up to a point. But to which point? And how much, at any particular age, could children understand of what it meant to respond to Christ? Did children respond in the same way as adults? If not, how should it affect SU's methods? How urgent was it that they should make a commitment? When Jesus said that 'the Kingdom of God belongs to such as these', did he mean that they were in the Kingdom until they chose to reject him, or what?

Other issues arose out of the increasing secularisation of society. In an earlier age, in Western society, most children attending SU activities had some knowledge of the Bible. Many of them now knew almost nothing about it, and had been brought up with secular assumptions which were totally in conflict with its teaching. How could they learn enough in a week's mission to make a meaningful commitment? Most parents in the past would have allowed their children to attend Sunday School, even if they did not go to church themselves. Now this was often not the case. Yet the Bible stressed obedience to parents. How could such children be asked to respond to Christ without being subject to intolerable conflict? Mission leaders tried to make more room in their programmes for the whole family, but the questions still needed answering. After widespread consultation, a small group of those deeply involved in the debate met at the Enlarged International Council meeting near Edinburgh in 1979. Working late into the night on several occasions, there was a real 'meeting of minds' and the group produced a unanimous statement which the Council later adopted. It did not answer all the questions, but it set useful guidelines for SU's ministry with children and helped staff and voluntary workers to feel confident that it had a sound theological and intellectual base.

It was an indication of the extent to which Scripture Union in Australia had come of age that it had given a lead to the movement worldwide in the debate. For it was not about some side issues that were small and unimportant, but about one of SU's main thrusts, the area of activity where the work started. SU in Australia saw the need for clear thinking and did something about it.

A FESTIVAL AND THINK-SHOP

Across the Tasman, in New Zealand, SU was grappling with the same issues. New Zealand's special contribution was to arrange a 'Congress on Children and Families' in January 1978. They assembled a strong team of speakers representing several parts of the SU world and differing points of view, and managed to combine serious theological debate with practical training and lively worship. 'Typically for New Zealand', Peter Lineham reports, 'it was a combination of festival and think-shop.' (*No Ordinary Union,* p.150).

New Zealand's regular ministry to children focused on some twenty 'Scripture Union Holiday Programmes' as beach missions came to be called. SU's main thrust in the country was still in its schools and camps programme. In the 1960s and 70s SU New Zealand felt the winds of change in the youth culture as strongly as other parts of the world, and in some ways seemed less able to adapt. Teenage coffee bars were run successfully by several of the beach mission teams, but groups in schools began to decline. There were many more Christian teachers in the schools than twenty years earlier, but they seemed to have less influence. 'In spite of all the hard work of its able and devoted field staff', Peter Lineham reports, 'Christian pupils still complain that their school Christian fellowship is boring, even though they run it themselves.' One has to remember however that the decline was from the very high level of effectiveness of the '50s and early '60s when 'four per cent of secondary school pupils attended one of the school group meetings in an average week'. (*No Ordinary Union,* p.148). In 1980 ISCF was still one of New Zealand's largest youth movements.

A NEW START IN EAST ASIA

One of the most significant developments in SU worldwide in the 1960s was its firm planting in East Asia. We have seen in chapter 18 how Cecil Johnston, from India, urged Australia and New Zealand to take up the immense opportunities he had seen in the schools of Singapore and Malaysia, and how they responded enthusiastically and sent first a New Zealander, Lester Pfankuch, and then an Australian, Tony McCutcheon, to take up the challenge.

In 1958 Colin Becroft, then Federal Secretary in Australia, made an extensive tour of East Asia to see what other opportunities he could find. He was amazed at the potential. Five or six countries were ripe for SU development. John Laird, from London, urged Australia and New Zealand to press forward together, and a joint committee was formed. It was known as the ANZEA Council, as it was to link together the national movements in Australia, New Zealand and East Asia. Australia and New Zealand were the foundation members, but Japan and Singapore became full members in 1962, Hong Kong in 1964 and West Malaysia in 1966. It quickly became an effective partnership between people of different races, cultures and backgrounds in the cause of Christ.

In 1961, Tony McCutcheon became Regional Secretary for East Asia. Two years later, now that national staff had been appointed in Singapore and Malaysia, he moved his base to Hong Kong. The same year, he organised the first Regional Conference, at Port Dickson in Malaya. It made such a deep impression on those who were there that it has been repeated every five years since. Until he had to return to Australia for family reasons in 1965, he made regular visits to most of the countries of East Asia, looking for key people and sharing the SU vision with them, stirring up interest, and preparing the ground for later advance.

ROOF-TOP SUNDAY SCHOOLS

As always, the key to establishing SU in any country was to find the right leader. In Hong Kong, the man for the hour was Wong Cheung Ho, who joined the staff for Bible reading promotion in 1962. For ten years, the Christian Witness Press had been publishing a Chinese translation of *Daily Bread*, and a small committee had recently been formed. Backed by Wong Cheung Ho's vigour and enthusiasm, circulation trebled in three months, to 1,200, and it doubled again the following year. Chinese junior notes were started in 1964. But the real breakthrough came in 1972 when SU Hong Kong decided to stop translating from English and to produce original notes by Chinese writers. Dr Philip Teng, a well-known pastor and speaker, who had been the first chairman of the committee, agreed to write the first four-year cycle single-handed. Circulation rose to 10,000, within a year.

Alongside the Bible reading thrust, SU Hong Kong developed an imaginative programme of outreach to children. Tony McCutcheon showed the way, with a series of five evangelistic meetings for those who could speak English. Wong Cheung Ho caught the vision and, when he became general secretary in 1965, he formed a separate CSSM committee to take it further. Evangelistic rallies were held in the crowded refugee camps, sometimes with as many as 1,000 children and 100 voluntary workers involved. An unusual feature were the roof-top Sunday Schools for children living in the many high-rise apartment blocks. Like Josiah Spiers, Wong Cheung Ho believed in training others to share the work. In the 1970s, four teams of accredited CSSM volunteers were formed, each of which was expected to lead one mission and conduct six evangelistic meetings during the year. When Wong Cheung Ho left in 1976, to work for SU in the Chinese churches of Canada, one of the team members, Virginia Chan, took over the leadership of the CSSM department.

A QUIET BOY STANDS UP

Another country where the SU plant was growing in the 1960s was Japan. *Seisho no Tomo*, the old Japanese Scripture Union started in 1883, had been closed down during World War II. When a new start was made in 1955, the key person was Junichi Funaki. Brought up in a Christian home, he had taken a bold stand for Christ at high school. 'One day the teacher was ridiculing Christianity, comparing it unfavourably with Shintoism and saying that no true Japanese could be a Christian. Suddenly he stopped; he asked could there possibly be anyone so foolish in that class as to be a Christian? One quiet boy, Junichi Funaki, stood to his feet. Teacher and boys alike made fun of him. But it made a deep impression on one of them.' Akira Hatori, a sixteen-year-old boy from a Buddhist family, was converted through the incident. He later became a well known evangelist and radio pastor and, for a time, was chairman of the SU Committee.

In 1953, Junichi Funaki was asked to take charge of the translation of the notes. Although he was soon to be principal of the Japan Bible Seminary, he agreed, and *Seisho Domei*, the Japanese SU, revolved around him for the next thirty years. A quiet scholarly man, he has an immense capacity for work. In addition to his many other responsibilities, he was editor-in-chief for the new Japanese translation of the Bible and for the New Bible Commentary.

Alongside its Bible reading and publishing programme, *Seisho Domei* joined with two other organisations to form CSK, an association of Bible clubs for junior high school students. There are now some 500 clubs. They are attached to churches and use a variety of names, but CSK runs annual youth camps and training courses for them, and provides them with Bible reading notes and other literature. Since 1970 Hiroshi Inagaki has been their senior staff worker, but he will soon take over from Junichi Funaki as general secretary of *Seisho Domei*.

HIGH SCHOOLS IN MALAYSIA

Meanwhile, SU in Singapore and Malaysia was developing ISCF groups in high schools on the pattern familiar in other parts of the world. In Malaya (West Malaysia from 1963 onwards), James Phoa was the first staff worker. His constant travelling, from 1962–1965, increased the number of groups from five to seventeen. Over the years, growth steadily continued and more staff could be appointed. By 1982, there were four ISCF staff and 200 school groups, and seventeen camps were being run each year.

The appointment of Peter Young as general secretary, in 1970, was the start of a new period of advance. An English missionary who became a Malaysian citizen, Peter Young had been attracted to SU when he was teaching in Kuala Lumpur, because of its evangelistic thrust. Under his eleven years of leadership, a start was made with children's missions, the training of Sunday School teachers, and a publications programme in the Malaysian language. A chain of five bookshops was also established. The most unusual move, however, was the merger of SU with the Fellowship of Evangelical Students, which took place in 1975. SUFES, as the new joint movement was called, had separate departments for schools and universities, and retained its link with both IFES and SU internationally. But the funds were shared, Peter Young served as joint general secretary, and considerable economies were achieved. In the next few years, the merger proved itself to have been a helpful and far-sighted development.

REVIVAL IN THE CHURCHES

In Singapore itself, where the Anzea story started, SU was forging ahead equally strongly. Parallel ISCF movements, with separate staff, were formed in Chinese-speaking and English-speaking schools. The twenty or more Chinese-speaking groups met a special need, as most of the children were forbidden to attend church on Sundays and had no other Christian contact. The English-speaking ISCF was led for ten years by Freddie Ho. He had been converted to Christ as a schoolboy, and helped to start a Bible study in his school. According to John Prince 'thousands of young people found Christ during his time on the staff', and he is now pastor of a church 'full of the fruits of the schools work of SU', and remains chairman of the ISCF Secondary Schools Committee.

Though SU was growing strongly, for most of its first twenty years it was without a general secretary. Laurence Chia, brought to personal faith and given a vision for SU while in Australia, was appointed in 1962. But only two years later he moved on to university teaching, becoming an active member of the SU Council. Not till 1979, when Alfred Yeo was appointed, could anyone be found to take his place. Leadership was provided by the Council itself which happened to be formed of a group of men of exceptional ability. Indeed it was sometimes said that the reason they could not find a general secretary was that no one felt adequate to work with such a high-powered committee!

Until 1973 the chairman was Professor Khoo Oon Teik, head of the Department of Medicine at the University of Singapore. He had been on the committee since it was formed, and his senior position in his profession and his standing in the Methodist Church helped SU to be widely recognised. His strong leadership was constantly pushing the movement forward. His successor as chairman was another medical professor, Phoon Wai On. Introduced to SU notes by his mother, when he was a teenager, Professor Phoon had been chairman of the Bible Reading Promotion committee when it was running a series of successful SU weeks. The opening of a splendid camping centre on Sentosa Island has been a notable milestone in recent years.

The literature side of the ministry developed strongly when SU took over the Christian Book Room, which had been run for many years by a couple of lady missionaries. The Overseas Missionary Fellowship provided staff to manage the shop for a few years. Then, in 1975, the secretary of the Council, Winston Yap, resigned from business to take over. SU now has three flourishing retail shops and two wholesale warehouses, and is about to open a fourth branch.

When Laurence Chia returned from Australia, his vision for SU was that it would be a means of evangelical revival in the churches. 'Looking back', he writes, 'I believe, along with IFES and other groups, SU has been used to bring this about.'

THE ANZEA COUNCIL

It was East Asian leaders like Professor Khoo, David Boler from Malaysia, Junichi Funaki and Professor Phoon Wai On that helped to make the Anzea Council an effective partnership between different races and cultures. Alan Kerr from Australia was the first chairman and timed some of his regular business trips to Singapore to coincide with Council meetings. Professor Khoo joined him as co-chairman in 1971. At the annual Council meetings, they prayed and planned together for advance through the rest of the region. Moreover, each movement contributed to the regional budget. It was a good arrangement as it not only increased the money available to assist the new national movements emerging in other parts of the region, but helped these movements not to feel they were dependent on Western aid. Such grants as they received came from a budget to which Asian as well as Australasian countries had contributed.

When Tony McCutcheon returned to Australia, no one could be immediately found to take his place. However, the Australian Federal Secretary, John Robinson, knew Asia well. He had been a missionary in the Philippines for a number of years, and had helped to launch SU there. He became secretary of the Anzea Council, and for a time the regional office was located in Sydney. An important development during those years was the decision to publish an Anzea edition of the English notes and the formation of Anzea Publishers to handle them and other materials. It was planned as a publishing house for the whole region, but because of differences in culture and the Sydney location it inevitably concentrated on the Australian market.

In 1969, however, the Anzea Council appointed David Chan as General Secretary in East Asia and the focus of the region moved back to Singapore. Speaking five languages fluently and with an excellent theological education, David Chan was exceptionally well qualified for the job. He soon showed himself to have the personal qualities needed as well: the capacity for hard word and constant travel; the ability to relate quickly to a wide range of people; and a gift for finding suitable men and women for the staff.

OPENING NEW COUNTRIES

In the next few years, there was rapid progress in several other countries. In 1967 Professor Khoo was visiting a Bible College in England and spoke of the need for young Asians to work with SU back home. At one meeting he found staff for two new countries. Pham Thi Son, a shy and delicate girl student, returned to Vietnam the following year. For six years, until the Communist takeover, she faithfully wrote, edited, promoted and distributed the Vietnamese notes.

Mitsuru Iwai, the other to respond, was from Japan, where his brother had been on the SU staff. But he felt called to work in Indonesia, and had already prepared himself by learning the language.

Because of his family's health, he could only spend three years in Indonesia; but his appointment was a superb example of regional co-operation, and helped to lay the foundations of another national movement. PPA, the Indonesian SU, concentrated on promoting Bible reading. They did it so effectively that within ten years they had a notes circulation of 44,000.

In Taiwan the key person was Paul Chang, who left his job as a shipping executive in 1970 to become SU general secretary. A council had been formed nine years earlier, during one of Tony McCutcheon's visits, but progress had been slow. Wherever possible, Paul Chang appointed and trained 'branch secretaries' to promote and distribute the notes, and circulation tripled, to 4,500, within a year. By 1973 SU Taiwan was fully self-supporting and was accepted as a full member of the Anzea Council.

AN SU-SHAPED GAP

Like Taiwan, Korea had a small and struggling SU movement in the 1960s. A brief visit from David Chan in 1972, and the active support of the Overseas Missionary Fellowship changed all that. Although the church in Korea was growing very rapidly, Peter Pattisson, the leader of the OMF team, was deeply concerned about its spiritual state. 'For all its growth and vigour and activity', he wrote 'it was as though Scripture had been plucked out of the life of the church, both at the personal and corporate level.' After much thought and prayer he and his colleagues came to the conclusion that the most urgent need was an emphasis on daily meeting with God through prayer and Bible study. 'Gradually the impression formed that there was what we termed "a Scripture-Union-shaped gap in the Korean church life."'

The problem was that the existing SU notes were scarcely known in the churches. They were published by a group called the University Bible Fellowship, were well written and were widely used in UBF circles. But church leaders suspected them because of their UBF origins. The Anzea Council decided that a fresh start was needed.

David Chan's historic visit in June 1972 made it happen. Within a week he had rented an office, formed a committee and attended the first meeting, and found a staff worker. Yune Zong-Ha was introduced to him by Peter Pattisson as a suitable person. 'When will you be able to start?' David Chan asked him. 'Next week,' was the reply. Notes were published regularly from the following January with Korean writers from the start. Ten years later, two series were being published as well as other books, and a beginning had been made with camps and high school work. With a staff of thirteen, SU Korea was firmly planted, though so far it was only having a limited impact on church life.

AN EXCELLENT YEAR: 1975

Three years later, visits from David Chan helped to bring new life to two other struggling national movements. SU had been started in the Philippines in the late 1950s by enthusiastic OMF missionaries and a small national movement emerged in 1961. It had a series of staff workers, but none of them stayed more than a few years, and the notes only achieved a small circulation. When David Chan visited Manila in 1975, the latest staff worker had just resigned. After making enquiries, he visited a vivacious young newsreader with the Far East Broadcasting Company, Dulce Ison. Although he had not met her before, he invited her to join the SU staff, and gave her a week to make up her mind. Under her leadership SU at last got on its feet. Circulation of the notes in English and Tagalog steadily improved, more staff were appointed, and in 1982 a start was made with children's work in primary schools. A unique feature, which makes use of Dulce Ison's previous experience, is a daily SU radio programme.

In Thailand too David Chan found a woman staff member to revive SU's fortunes. SU had been started by OMF missionaries in 1961, but by 1975, circulation of notes was down to 250, and publication was to cease. A number of missionaries were unhappy with the decision, however. One of them, Arnold Clarke offered to form a new committee, and told David Chan of a possible staff worker. Yawanit Kasaetwatananond was in a good government teaching post, which she did not want to leave. However she knew the value of SU notes as she had found them a spiritual lifeline when she had been cut off from Christian fellowship at university, and saw the invitation as a call from God. She was impressed too by David Chan's willingness to leave his family over Chinese New Year to come to see her. Her vitality and creative energy soon made their mark. It was hard and lonely work as she had to edit and promote the notes almost single-handed. But in two years, circulation of the notes was up to 1,200 and an ideal 'shop-house' had been leased as a base in the centre of Bangkok. Children's notes followed in 1980. By 1982, there was a staff of four and they were looking for Thai writers who could produce relevant Sunday School material.

1975 was a particularly good year for the Anzea Region. Not only did SU find Dulce Ison and Yawanit Kasaetwananond, but also John Kadiba, the first national staff worker in Papua New Guinea. SU was already ten years old in that country. It had been developed by a number of enthusiastic Australians, most of whom were in short-term government teaching jobs. There were SU groups in seventy-five per cent of the high schools in the country; and several thousand people read the Bible using a locally-written series of SU notes in 'controlled English', *Light for Today*, or its equivalent in Pidgin, *Kaikai Bilong Tude*. John Kadiba was only able to stay a year on the staff, on secondment from the United Church, but his appointment was an important milestone on the way to SU becoming a national movement in that country.

GROWTH IN THE PACIFIC

The last few years of the 1970s saw a remarkable spurt of growth in several of the small island nations east of New Guinea. In 1977, David Claydon became Associate Regional Secretary with special responsibility for the Pacific, and made the first of an intense series of visits to the area. In most of the islands, the majority of the population call themselves Christians but there was little Christian activity apart from traditional church programmes. David Claydon found a wide open door both for SU's Bible reading ministry and for its work in schools.

The potential and the dangers were well illustrated in Tonga. On his first visit in 1977 David Claydon found that there were four staff for a population of 90,000, an SU secretary in every town or village, 1,000 attended the August camp and the circulation of SU notes was said to be greater than the daily newspaper! But within two years, the dynamic Tongan committee chairman Rev Senituli Koloi, had shifted his theological position. He launched an attack on the Wesleyan church and even on the government, and tried to organise SU into a separate church. Church leaders lost confidence, and SU as an organisation collapsed. It has slowly struggled back, under new leadership, but still has a long way to go.

In the other islands, progress was less dramatic but more solid. Within a few years in Fiji, the Solomon Islands and Vanuatu, regular camps were held and the majority of high schools had SU groups. SU notes were circulating in significant numbers in English and the national language and national staff had been appointed. The spiritual response to SU's straightforward and relevant presentation of the gospel was enthusiastic, and it was mainly young people converted through the camps and schools groups who were taking the lead in extending the work to other parts of the country. Outstanding among the new members of staff was Mesulame Nainoca in Fiji. Since he had come to Christ twenty-five years earlier, he had read *Daily Bread* notes and they had had a deep influence on his life. He had been a headmaster and then a school inspector, and was known all over the country as, for many years, he had been the leading figure on Radio Fiji's current affairs programme. In 1980 at the age of fifty-two, he became SU general secretary. Within a year, circulation of *Daily Bread* had risen from 400 to 2,400. Active SU groups in schools had increased from four to twenty. Two years later progress was still continuing and the Fiji committee was urgently looking for an extra schools worker.

In five years, SU's position in the Pacific Islands had totally changed. Its very success, however, caused a minor problem. The name of the Region, ANZEA, was not only impossible for those who did not speak English to understand; it made no reference to the Pacific. So the Council decided that from 1983 it would be called the East Asia and Pacific Region. The Anzea story had lasted twenty-five years. It had been an exciting story of effective evangelism, of steady Christian nurture, of fruitful partnership between different cultures and races. But much remained to be done, and the East Asia and Pacific story would follow.

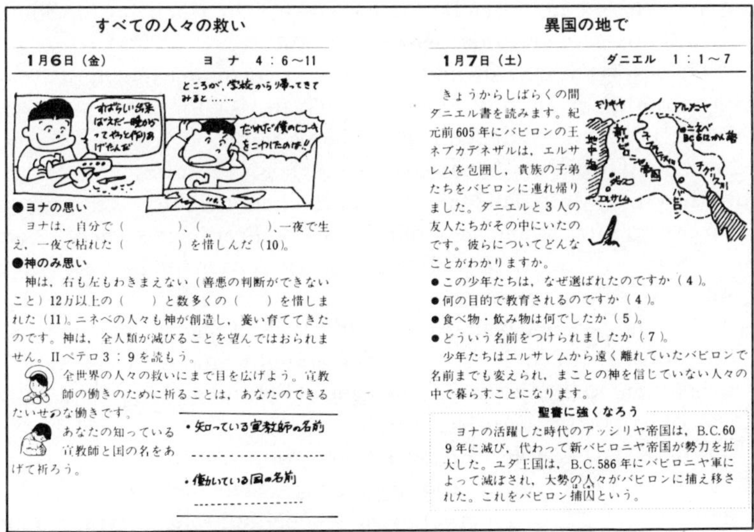

すべての人々の救い

1月6日（金）　ヨナ　4：6〜11

●ヨナの思い

ヨナは、自分で（　　　）、（　　　）、一夜で生え、一夜で枯れた（　　　）を惜しんだ（10）。

●神のみ思い

神は、右も左もわきまえない（善悪の判断ができないこと）12万以上の（　）と数多くの（　）を惜しまれた（11）。ニネベの人々も神が創造し、養い育ててきたのです。神は、全人類が滅びることを望んではおられません。IIペテロ3：9を読もう。

全世界の人々の救いにまで目を広げよう。宣教師の働きのために祈ることは、あなたのできるたいせつな働きです。

あなたの知っている宣教師と国の名をあげて祈ろう。

・知っている宣教師の名前

・働いている国の名前

異国の地で

1月7日（土）　ダニエル　1：1〜7

きょうからしばらくの間ダニエル書を読みます。紀元前605年にバビロンの王ネブカデネザルは、エルサレムを包囲し、貴族の子弟たちをバビロンに連れ帰りました。ダニエルと3人の友人たちがその中にいたのです。彼らについてどんなことがわかりますか。

- この少年たちは、なぜ選ばれたのですか（4）。
- 何の目的で教育されるのですか（4）。
- 食べ物・飲み物は何でしたか（5）。
- どういう名前をつけられましたか（7）。

少年たちはエルサレムから遠く離れていたバビロンで名前までも変えられ、まことの神を信じていない人々の中で暮らすことになります。

聖書に強くなろう

ヨナの活躍した時代のアッシリヤ帝国は、B.C.609年に滅び、代わって新バビロニヤ帝国が勢力を拡大した。ユダ王国は、B.C.586年にバビロニヤ軍によって滅ぼされ、大勢の人々がバビロンに捕え移された。これをバビロン捕囚という。

SU notes for Japanese children.

23

To Train and Trust

In Africa the twenty years after Old Jordans saw dramatic growth, both in the churches and Scripture Union, and in the problems facing the continent. 'We belong to a continent that is aching and bleeding, and is everywhere in turmoil', wrote Emmanuel Oladipo in 1982, a few months before taking over as SU's Regional Secretary for the Africa Region. 'At every level, confidence, direction and clarity of purpose are in short supply. If one chain is broken, half-a-dozen stronger chains are waiting to replace it. How are people to handle them? We do not know the answers. Fortunately, though, we do know the questions. We are right there where they are being asked.'

With ninety-one staff members at work in twenty-five African countries, SU was certainly 'right there' by 1982. In the previous twenty-five years, twenty-five countries had had SU staff appointments for the first time. In some parts of the continent the national SU movement was still small and had limited influence. But in ten or twelve countries it was well established and was making a substantial impact. There had been a big change since 1960, when outside South Africa there were just four members of staff.

The intervening years had seen very rapid change in almost every aspect of African life. In the ten years 1956 to 1966 thirty-five countries became politically independent. Millions of people left the villages, where the pattern of life has changed little for centuries, and flocked into the cities. With half of the population under eighteen years of age in many countries, and new schools and colleges everywhere, there have been enormous opportunities for a movement like Scripture Union. Moreover, young people have been remarkably open to the gospel. 'The political changes and upheavals of the last fifteen years', wrote John Dean in 1972, 'have not brought fulfilment. There is a reawakening to the spiritual dimension of life and to the fact that man does not live by bread alone.'

Where it was able to form school groups SU made the fastest progress and has had the widest influence. 'The idea', I wrote from Ghana in 1960, 'is to honeycomb the schools and colleges with groups of active and witnessing Christians. This is more practical nowadays than the traditional method of reaching young people by running "mission" schools staffed entirely by Christians. The demand for education is too great for Christians to meet it in this way. In any case governments want to run their own schools. Also it is often more effective. Boys and girls in secular schools have to fight for their faith, so they develop spiritual muscles.'

Over the next twenty years, in Ghana, Nigeria and half-a-dozen other countries, that vision became a reality. But it was not always easy. In the early years there was a good deal of prejudice to be overcome. SU youth work was unknown when we started, so the first staff worker in almost every country was an expatriate. Right from the beginning, the plan was to foster national leadership. 'What you should aim at,' John Laird told me before I first went to Ghana, 'is that after ten years you will be able to move on, leaving a national movement with a Ghanaian Council and staff.' This took time however and, inevitably in the post-colonial years, people questioned our motives and intentions. The appointment of the first African staff members, Florence Yeboah in Ghana (1962), Philip Mpunzwana in Zimbabwe (1962) and Reuben Ariko, with the Fellowship of Christian Students in Northern Nigeria (1963), helped to allay suspicion and to demonstrate that SU was becoming a genuinely African movement.

AFRICAN LEADERSHIP

After a few years strong national leadership began to emerge. Boys and girls converted as teenagers were trained through taking responsibilities at camp or their Christian groups at school and university. They went out into professional adult life determined to share their faith with the next generation. Some of them became teachers. Many others were able to visit schools groups regularly or help at camps. They soon took over from the expatriates the leadership of SU in local or national committees. Some of them joined the staff. It was a pattern familiar from other parts of the SU world.

One of them who became a staff worker was Folu Soyannwo. He was converted at an early Nigerian camp. Later he recalled: 'The gospel messages were simple and well-illustrated, the talks were short and meaningful.' But it was the life of the camp leaders that most impressed him. 'It was unheard of for a "white" man to wash plates for a "black" man, how much more for one of his own students. My teacher, who invited me to camp, did such things, and I felt there must be something more to this gospel. There were also very highly placed Nigerians who joined campers in sweeping the floor and cleaning the dormitories. At another camp a bank official helped to wash the toilet!' Sixteen years later, after taking a degree in Agriculture and teaching for some years, Folu Soyannwo became SU General Secretary in Nigeria. Today he is ordained and is an active member of the SU Council.

Another to join the staff was Michael Oye. Brought up a Roman Catholic, he was preparing for the priesthood in Ghana when he came under the influence of Jehovah's Witnesses. He was finally converted to Christ through a Ghanaian schoolgirl, who challenged him about his low moral standards. At Ibadan University, where he studied agriculture for four years, he received assurance of salvation and later became leader of the Christian Union. From 1966–1973 he was an SU travelling secretary, helping to look after the hundreds of SU groups that had sprung up in his part of Nigeria. Today he is in the Methodist ministry.

STUDENT CHRISTIAN MOVEMENT

A major problem in the early years was SU's relationship with the Student Christian Movement. In Southern Nigeria and Ghana, for example, SCM groups existed in many of the schools and colleges. Few of them were active, and many of those that were had programmes that were more social than spiritual. School authorities were suspicious of what appeared to be a rival organisation, particularly one that was evangelical. But it was a help that the groups used the name 'Scripture Union', rather than 'Christian Union' as in England and elsewhere. By making it clear that the main purpose of the group was to study the Bible, it attracted young people who were serious about their faith. But it did not imply that those who did not join were not Christians. So SU and SCM groups were sometimes allowed side by side. Gradually, over the years, the value of SU's approach became more widely recognised, as school authorities saw the effect it had in the lives of the boys and girls. With enthusiastic SU members leaving university or teacher training college each year, the number of groups increased rapidly. Before long the problem facing the staff was no longer how to find a way into the schools, but how to cope with all the opportunities. Hundreds of groups were springing up, using the Scripture Union name. They desperately needed guidance and help, and SU felt responsible for them. But it was impossible for staff to visit them more than once or twice a year at the most.

TRAINING THE LEADERS

Camps, residential leaders' courses and rallies provided part of the answer. In 1959 John Dean could write: 'To date there are fifteen SU groups in the Western Region of Nigeria. Of these, twelve are led by either a committed Christian teacher or a boy converted at one of the camps. Of the other three groups, two are very unsatisfactory.' As the number of groups multiplied, the finding, motivation and training of such leaders became increasingly important. John Dean took as his motto 'to train and to trust'.

> Whether it is in school groups or camps, the older Christian communicates some aspect of Christian service and then leaves the younger Christian to get on with it. At the next opportunity, he communicates something else and the process is repeated. It is important to keep this step by step 'training and trusting' in balance. One without the other kills initiative and builds resentment.

DAILY POWER AND DAILY GUIDE

Another way for the staff to supplement their visits was through literature, particularly Bible reading notes. At camps, conferences and school visits, they constantly taught the 'why' and the 'how' of daily Bible reading and distributed daily reading notes. At first SU notes were imported from Europe but in 1963 Nigeria took the bold step of publishing their own. *Daily Power*, for the younger forms in secondary schools, were brief, to keep down the price, written in the Nigerian context, printed as an annual booklet to simplify distribution and shaped to fit into a schoolboy's shirt pocket. *Daily Power* was an immediate success. In the first year, they were reprinted twice, and the circulation of teenage notes in Nigeria went up six times. The change to an annual booklet opened the way for rapid advance on the Bible reading front. In 1963, Ghana produced *Daily Guide*, an equivalent annual booklet for adults. By 1968, both booklets were being reprinted in East Africa, and the total circulation of the two topped 70,000. The African lanaguage editions which were introduced in increasing numbers generally used the same format. By 1983, circulation of English notes across the continent had passed 200,000, printed in six centres, while the total circulation of all notes in Africa, in twenty-two languages, was over 400,000.

While priority was given to the SU notes, the staff also distributed large quantities of other Christian literature. The demand was remarkable. Staff loaded their cars to the roof as they travelled from school to school, set up large bookstalls at rallies and conferences and appointed scores of enthusiastic voluntary book agents. This informal network proved to be an extremely effective channel of distribution. Until 1971, SU in Ghana, for example, operated out of a borrowed garage.

It was difficult at first to obtain the right sort of books. 'Literature sold by Christian agencies is usually designed for British and American markets and is quite unsuitable for Ghana,' an SU Committee member commented in 1968. To fill the gap, SU helped to launch Africa Christian Press, to publish books 'written in Africa for Africa'. In 1967, Tony Harlow, who had helped to start SU in Zimbabwe and Zambia, was seconded to be its first general secretary. Here at last was a source of books that were on the right wavelength.

FRENCH-SPEAKING AFRICA

In French-speaking Africa, government policy restricted Christian meetings on school premises. So the emphasis from the start was on Bible reading promotion and literature. In 1958, Léonard Bréchet, the general secretary in France, made an extensive tour. He returned to Europe fired with a vision of the opportunity, and determined to challenge his colleagues to do something about it. A special edition for Africa of *La Lecteur de la Bible* was started in 1962. By 1970, most of the writers were Africans, and circulation had reached 6,000. Philippe Decorvet, Swiss staff worker in the Ivory Coast wrote:

> The church has come to Africa in European clothes. It could not have been different. But now most of them have become independent, the churches want to find their own African shape. They want African clothing for the Gospel. This is one of our biggest problems for the church nowadays. She will only survive and grow if she is both really African and really Christian. It is only possible if she has become rooted in the Bible. In Africa as well as in Europe, we have to confront our customs, our ideas, our ways with those of the Word of God. This is why the ministry of SU is so important today.

It was not easy to establish SU in the French-speaking countries. Because of the Catholic background the Bible was very little known.

Unlike the English-speaking areas, there were few expatriate SU members, and the churches were suspicious of an agency they did not control. With little possiblility of school groups the support of at least some of the churches in an area was essential. An attempt to start the movement in Cameroun, for example, had to be abandoned because of church opposition. In other countries, foundations were slowly and patiently laid. In Rwanda, the first SU camp was held in 1959, and Kinyarwanda notes were published the same year. In Ivory Coast, Philippe Decorvet arrived as a staff worker in 1960, the first camp was held in 1962, and in 1964 Lucy Schwarzenbach began her eighteen faithful years as staff worker.

HONESTY CHAIN

But Zaire was the first French-speaking country in Africa where SU became a major force. As early as 1959 it was given official government recognition — by royal decree! Pastor Mavumilusa Makanzu, a dynamic evangelist and widely respected church leader, was very active as chairman until his death in 1980, and did much to set the movement on its feet. With the appointment of Danilo Gay, from Switzerland, as staff worker in 1972, the movement was able to move forward strongly. At one point, the government asked SU to take responsibility for training young people in all the churches. The offer had to be declined for lack of resources, but opportunities for camps, young people's meetings and Sunday School training courses in churches, Bible reading promotion and literature distribution were unlimited.

As time went on, SU leaders in Kinshasa found themselves increasingly forced to face some of the social problems that Christian young people were up against. One response was the 'honesty chain' to resist corruption. Those who join the chain pledge themselves not to give a bribe in any circumstance, and to help one another not to need to do so. Joining the chain is a hard decision for a bribe may be necessary to get a driving licence, or even an interview for a job. When another member of the chain works in the office concerned, however, he can often arrange that the young Christian applicant is treated properly without recourse to bribery.

Another social problem has been in the increasing number of 'second offices', as they are called, where well-to-do men install their mistresses. Most of the young women concerned were driven to this way of life as their only means of livelihood. Calling it 'a new sort of polygamy', Charles-Daniel Maire points out that in contrast to traditional African marriage, the woman has no legal status and no security. He continues, '1,700 of them have already come to the evangelistic conferences dealing with this burning issue. Many have been touched and wish to change their way of life. But to break with these men, many of whom are influential, is not easy. Two of the women themselves, formerly mistresses of senior officials, are the driving force of the movement.'

IN BIBLE SCHOOL UNDER FALSE NAME

In the 1970s SU became firmly established in several other French-speaking countries. In Rwanda, Peter Guillebaud, a mathematics teacher who had been closely associated with the East African Revival Movement for many years, was generously seconded to SU by the Ruanda Mission. Large numbers of young people found Christ in the camps and at meetings in schools in the next few years, and the circulation of SU notes rose steadily. Nathan Umazekabiri, who had given up a good job in a government health centre a few years earlier to take Bible training, took over the leadership in 1980.

Christian youth camps were arranged regularly by friends of SU in Burundi in the 1960s, and the Kirundi notes began in 1969. SU suffered a serious set-back in the 1972 civil war, when a number of committee members were killed. A new committee was formed in 1975, after a visit from Charles-Daniel Maire, now Co-ordinator for French-speaking Africa. Dorothée de Benoit (now Mme Bonnal) who became staff worker the following year, is yet another member of the family which has been at the centre of SU in Switzerland since it started. 'God has done great things in the lives of young people who attended a Christian training camp at Kivoga at Easter', she wrote in 1978. One of those who professed conversion was a Bible school student called Prosper. 'Back from camp, Prosper and his friends gave their testimonies to the rest of the students in the Bible School. As a result, many students admitted thefts and lies and brought back stolen books. One of them even confessed that he was admitted into Bible School under a false name and with a diploma he had stolen.' When Dorothée de Benoit left Burundi to get married in 1983, she handed over to Siméon Havyarimana.

FIVE LOAVES AND TWO FISHES

In the late 70s SU also had a strong impact in the beautiful island of Madagascar. Back in the last century there had at one time been as many as 12,000 SU members; but by 1970 it had almost died out. Then a young mathematics teacher, Gérard Kuntz, arrived from France. Within a short time he had formed a committee, Malagasy cards were being published, and a programme of children's evangelism was under way. In 1976 the chairman of the committee, Emilien Razafiarison, resigned from the civil service, where he was head of a department; after four years of theological training in France he became SU general secretary.

Emilien Razafiarison is a dymanic evangelist, with great energy and vision, and progress has been rapid under his leadership. In 1982, after a visit to Tananarive, Frank Horton, Head of the Emmaus Bible School wrote:

> It would be difficult to exaggerate the importance and the potential of the ministry of Emilien and Lilie Razafiarison. Their influence is growing all the time. Both of them are booked up to preach in different churches several months in advance. A visit to the SU centre in the Rue de Russie gives a thrilling picture of their activities. The bookshop is nearly always full. In a room on the left Lilie and a team of helpers are preparing for a children's mission. In the next room, two friends are quietly at prayer. In a tiny office on the right, Emilien is discussing a relief programme. In an odd moment of calm he types a stencil announcing a series of Bible studies.

In 1983, with generous help from a Christian contractor, they completed the first phase of an SU centre, on the outskirts of Tananarive. Some of the money came from Europe, but, in spite of the economic problems facing the country, over sixty per cent was raised on the island. Within a few months they had embarked on the second phase, and agreed to buy the adjacent property. When complete it will provide accommodation for nearly 100 people for camps and conferences. By September they had already started to use it and could report that 'several of the young people at the camp were converted'. 'We have only five loaves and two fishes', they wrote to their supporters, 'but we believe God is calling us to press forward.'

Charles-Daniel Maire's appointment as Co-ordinator for French-speaking Africa, in 1975, was an important factor in the progress that has been made in the last few years. From his base in Abidjan he has travelled widely through the nineteen countries in his care, encouraging staff and committees where they exist and looking for new opportunities. He and his wife Evelyn have developed a special interest in building up family life. 'One of the most profound causes of misery (in Africa)', he writes, 'is the disintegration of the family, which should be the foundation stone of society and church.' At the time of writing both Zaire and Madagascar are considering the appointment of staff specially for this ministry.

PARALLEL GROUPS

In Sierra Leone, Zambia, Zimbabwe, Uganda and most of the other English-speaking countries, SU developed along the lines I have described in Ghana and Southern Nigeria, with the main thrust being in the schools. In some countries however the circumstances made an SU schools work inappropriate. In Northern Nigeria, for example, the autonomous Fellowship of Christian Students had been formed in 1957. With first John Dean, then Reuben Ariko and Emmanuel Oladipo as successive general secretaries, it was thoroughly evangelical, and had branches in most of the possible schools throughout the northern states. So there was no point in forming SU groups there.

In Kenya, a nationally-based Kenya Students Christian Fellowship was formed in 1958. Its leaders wrote to SU in England to ask for help. When Harry Cotter arrived as SU staff worker, he spent most of his time as KSCF's travelling secretary. It met the immediate need, but was not a satisfactory long-term arrangement, as KSCF got used to having a staff worker without having to pay for him. When eventually it reached the stage where it could appoint its own staff, SU was left without a role. It was some years before an effective Bible reading ministry developed. In Tanzania, a similar organisation was formed called TSCF. It was sponsored by the churches in each area, and SU acted as its literature arm.

A similar arrangement applied in the schools in Malawi. Here, however, as well as in Zambia and several other countries, SU developed an important ministry for young people working in the towns. Many of those who had moved in from the villages were lonely and rootless, desperately in need of friendship and support. Informal Bible studies, usually held on Sunday afternoons so as not to clash with church services, were a helpful way of following up those who had been active Christians at school, and provided them with the fellowship and teaching that was sometimes lacking in the churches. In Ghana, similar groups were organised in the lunch-hour in offices and other places of work. 'There are now twenty-three such meetings held regularly in different parts of Accra, and there were over fifty people present at the one I attended', I wrote after a visit there in 1969.

A number of leading Ghanaians were active SU supporters. One example was William Ofori-Atta, Chairman of the Council of State in Ghana from 1979–1982. He was converted through reading the Bible during solitary confinement as a political prisoner under Kwame Nkrumah. On one occasion, when he was Minister of Education and Sport, he refused to attend an official celebration football match, where he was supposed to welcome the Prime Minister, because it was held on a Sunday. Instead he sat at a child's desk in a hot classroom in a poor part of Accra listening to me speaking at an SU meeting.

MULTI-RACIAL CAMPS IN SOUTH AFRICA

In South Africa, Frank Millard's retirement in 1960 marked the end of an era. But he left behind so many enthusiastic SU supporters, converted at his camps and missions, that the movement continued to go forward. Paul Reed and his chairman Otto Dose returned from Old Jordans with a new vision for the future. Under their wise leadership, the staff doubled in five years. An important factor in this advance was the decision to decentralise. Regional committees were formed, first in the Transvaal and later in other areas, with responsibility to develop the work in their part of the country. It was the Australian debate in reverse. Australia started with autonomous State Councils which joined together to form a Federal structure with limited, but increasing authority. South Africa started in Cape Town but gradually gave more responsibility to the regions. In each case the older centres had to give up some of their power; but because they were willing to do so they eventually achieved a healthy balance between local initiative and overall co-ordination.

When Paul Reed retired, Eddie Prest moved from Johannesburg to take his place. When he was twelve Eddie had attended a mission Frank Millard led near his home in Rondebosch. As he put it 'one very naughty little boy who persisted beyond reasonableness in pulling down the CSSM banner, was brought under conviction of sin and led to Christ at a camp a few months later.' His future wife, June, took her first steps towards Christ at the same mission. Eddie Prest's energy and enthusiasm carried the work forward strongly. A particularly important advance was made in 1973 when SU was asked to look after the school groups of the Student Christian Association, till then a separate organisation.

An exciting development came in 1970 when Nat Nkosi was appointed as the first black member of staff in South Africa. 'Though I grew up in a Christian home, I still developed a hatred for whites', he wrote later. 'I was especially bitter about missionaries who were the whites who lived closest to us. But it was a white missionary – one of my number one enemies – who led me to Christ!' After teacher training and Bible College, he spent two years in a Baptist church in Johannesburg as Christian Education Organiser. 'Then in 1970, I was invited to join the Scripture Union staff. I was very careful to read the constitution first, and it was only when I saw that the aims of Scripture Union had no social, racial or intellectual limits that I was happy to join.'

At first Nat Nkosi was working mainly in Botswana and Swaziland. Neither country had SU staff of their own at that stage, but the evangelistic teams that he brought by bus from the Transvaal met with a warm response. In 1973 he was seconded to lead the schools work in the black schools throughout South Africa. When he came to England in 1979, to undertake a speaking tour as part of the Bible Reading Centenary, he reported that there were 'Christian groups meeting every week in 500 of the 2,000 or so black secondary schools', and that a flourishing programme of multi-racial camps was under way.

RADIANT IN SUFFERING

The economic and political strains which affected Africa so strongly in these years by no means halted the spread of the gospel. 'The spiritual life of the churches and of SU', wrote John Dean in 1980, 'seems to be directly proportional to the degree of hardship being experienced.' In Uganda, for example, SU might well have been expected to collapse in July 1973, when General Amin deported Ron White, the only staff worker, at twenty-four hours' notice. The committee rose to the occasion and took over his responsibilities. Camps and schools groups continued, throughout the Amin years. There was a serious shortage of food and transport, but the work flourished. Writing after a visit, John Dean could say, 'It is a humbling privilege to meet so many with so little in material terms, radiating the joy of the Lord and testifying to his salvation and faithfulness during the Amin regime...Reports indicated that a vital spiritual work is going on, with great potential for SU ministry, but immense practical problems.'

SU RELIEF

A similar burst of spiritual life occurred in Eastern Nigeria at the time of the civil war (1967–70). When the war broke out Bill Roberts was a schools travelling secretary in the heart of the East region. He carried on an extensive evangelistic and teaching ministry all through the troubles, holding 'camp-like activities' at the SU house for young people living in the area. 'It seemed that God used the situation to bring many people into a new experience of Himself', he wrote after it was all over. 'Many of the Christians were revitalised spiritually, while very many other people were converted.'

But Bill Roberts was not just interested in saving souls. As the war went on, food became more and more scarce, and 'we began to hear rumours of people dying of starvation'. He went with one of the medical teams to visit a nearby refugee camp and saw 'two children lying on the floor in the process of dying from hunger. We had no food to give them. The thought haunted me for days.' (*Life and death among the Ibos*, p.55). Quite soon he began to organise a small but useful 'SU Relief' scheme.

> Every day at SU House, there will be many visitors beseeching us for help. There is a woman who has recently had twins, one of whom died from malnutrition, and whose husband was recently killed in the Army. Then there is the family we found in a shack in some hidden part of Umuahia. Most of them were suffering from kwashiokor, a deadly disease due to lack of protein, which causes the swelling up of the legs, hands and face. We were too late to save the father. It was touch and go with one daughter, but she is now recovering well. The eldest son, Efiok, regularly comes to our Bible studies. The mother is a living testimony to the power of Christ in adverse circumstances.' (*Life and death among the Ibos*, p.77).

In October 1968, after he returned from a short leave, Bill Roberts became a Field Officer in the Protestant Relief team and later took charge of all their work in the province. While making every effort to see that his evangelistic and pastoral activities were not swamped by relief work, he used to travel out to the refugee camps and feeding centres in his area, supervising the distribution of the money and relief food sent from overseas. 'From the two stores we supplied food to thirty hospitals, twenty outpatient clinics, eighty-two feeding centres each feeding 400 under-nourished children, and sixty refugee camps each with an average population of 1,000.'

RESISTING CORRUPTION

It was soon apparent that there was a close connection between effective relief work and a genuine experience of Christ. 'There were enormous temptations which came to every relief worker. Just imagine the strength of the temptation if you were working in a relief store, and you knew your mother and three brothers or sisters were starving in a refugee camp a few miles away. I eventually came to the conclusion that, almost without exception, it was only the born-again Christians who had grown strong in their faith who could be completely trusted in this kind of situation. Not only did these young men keep themselves free from corruption, but they prevented those who were working around them from trying it.' (p.82).

In April 1969 Bill Roberts and his team of Nigerian fellow-workers, themselves became refugees. Umuahia was overrun, and the small SU car, 'six of us sitting along the front seat somehow, beds and furniture on the roof,' took them thirty miles, across the River Imo, to safety. Two weeks later they found a small three-room upstairs flat, which became the new SU house, and continued to care for those in need.

> Sometimes we had as many as twenty people staying with us. We had only three beds, which Raymond Nwosu, Nnamdi and I slept on in one small bedroom. The other bedroom – which was Isaac's office by day – had three air mattresses on the floor by night. The rest slept on the floor in the sitting room, sharing a blanket or sheet if there was enough to go round... Many people came to know Christ through Raymond as a result of staying in our house. (p.88)

Even the evacuation of Umuahia led to spiritual progress:

> Just as in New Testament times, the committed Christians were forcibly scattered. But those who had the burning urge to tell other people about Christ took the good news with them. Within six months, the twenty-five SU groups at the time of our evacuation increased to eighty-five. Groups were to be found here, there and everywhere, in villages, churches of all denominations, ammunition factories, hospitals, army camps and refugee camps. The new groups had come to know Christ, and been helped to grow as Christians, through the fellowship at Umuahia.

Nor did it all fade out when the war ended. When I visited Nigeria early in 1983, I was told that nobody knew how many school groups there were in the country, but it must be well over 1,000. There are another 1,000 in the north under the auspices of the Fellowship of Christian Students. There has also been a very rapid growth in the SU Pilgrims groups. They were originally started for those who had been members at school, but were now at work. Today they attract people of all ages, from infants to grandmothers. They are careful to meet at times when there are no church services, and relations with the churches have distinctly improved in recent years. They reckoned there were 300 such groups, some of them very large: 1,000 attend the Enugu meeting, for example, and 600 the one at Aba.

Numbers at camps have also increased dramatically. For the Imo State SU camp in 1980, they expected 200, but 500 turned up. The following year they planned for 500 and had 1,500. When John Dean went there as the main speaker in 1983, there were 3,600 people present, from all age groups. 1,500 of them were accommodated at SU's own Okigwe camp site, and the rest in neighbouring schools. 400 came each morning for training sessions for group leaders and committee members. Circulation of SU notes in Nigeria had also increased dramatically. In 1983 it was 325,000, up 70,000 in two years.

PROBLEMS OF LIFE

Not surprisingly, the rapid growth of SU in recent years, in Nigeria and a dozen other African countries, has brought its problems. Strenuous efforts are made to guide the groups, through training courses, literature and pastoral visits; but the young people's enthusiasm sometimes leads them into conflict with the school or church authorities. All-night prayer meetings have been held when boys should have been asleep in their dormitories. One meeting in Ghana became so excited that school furniture was broken. False teachers from some of the thousands of sects and splinter groups that have sprung up all over Africa are sometimes invited to speak.

While I was writing this chapter, a prayer letter arrived from Joe Kapolyo in Zambia, in which he says:

> Most of the (school SU) groups are large and enthusiastic. Unfortunately, therein lies the chief weakness. Although the conversions are often real, there is an appalling lack of follow-up and discipleship. The potential for abuses and excesses is frightening. On one occasion recently, a boy, a chairman of an SU group,

commandeered and unlawfully drove a coach with a punctured wheel. He was locked up the next day. His justification was that he was on his way to an SU conference and would not accept any hindrances. Other SU members in the bus, including a Christian teacher, were similarly persuaded. One boy added that, after all, 'the earth is the Lord's and the fullness thereof'.

However, these are the problems of life rather than the problems of death. With the speed with which SU has grown and the acute shortage of staff, they are probably inevitable. Relations with the churches have been badly strained at times in some areas. But in course of time, with a number of young men with an SU background offering for training for the ministry and SU notes being widely used in the churches, relations have steadily improved. When I visited Ghana in 1972, the principal of the main theological college told me that sixty per cent of his students had an SU background. On the same trip, the head of the Methodist Church in Sierra Leone told me that all the candidates for the ministry and all those becoming lay preachers in the past three years had come through SU. When the first Pan African Christian Leadership Assembly met in Nairobi in 1976, about two-thirds of the delegates were found to have grown up with SU or were involved in it in some way.

REGULAR DAILY TEACHING

In many parts of Africa the churches have grown very rapidly in the last twenty-five years. In some areas they have doubled in size every three or four years. One well researched survey recently claimed that there had been 'a net gain of 6,052,800 new Christians in the past year (in Africa) or 16,600 new believers a day.'

With millions coming into church membership each year, the need for leadership is desperately urgent, and SU has been making a vital contribution by training young people for it. But it has also helped the churches to provide the teaching that is essential if the new Christians are to become established. Colin Sinclair, a travelling secretary in Zambia from 1974–77, describes a visit to a church near Lake Bangweulu:

> It was still dark when we reached the church at 5.50 am, as people came from the village, men first and then the women. A hymn was followed by the reading of the Daily Power Bible reading notes. Someone explained the Bible passage for 15–20 minutes, which

everyone understood but me – I don't speak Ehibemba! A prayer, a hymn, and by 6.30 am everyone was off on the day's business. 'How long have you been doing this?' I asked over breakfast. 'About twenty years', was the reply. Steadily and systematically that church and others in the province had worked through and opened up the Bible.

So one set of notes or the reading card sometimes reaches fifty or one hundred people, many of whom cannot read for themselves, and helps to give them the teaching they so urgently need. With notes or cards available in fifty-seven languages, this regular daily teaching is having its effect all over the continent.

REASONS FOR GROWTH

Why has SU grown so fast in Africa in recent years? One reason of course has been the rapid growth of the churches. As they have grown SU has grown with them. Then there has been the expatriate factor: the large number of Christians who knew SU in Britain or elsewhere and came to Africa to share their faith. Then SU's emphasis on literature has had a strong appeal in a continent where millions have recently learned to read, and are keen to use their new skill. But there was more to it than that.

A vital factor in the early days was the importance placed on close personal relationships between expatriates and Africans. Bill Roberts tells how he kept 'open house'. People 'felt so free with me that after a while they would come and stay without asking, just as they would with a fellow-African. I felt too that it was equally important that I should go out and receive hospitality from them. Perhaps that is why I was able to get so close to people, and the young people were prepared to discuss their deepest problems with me – because I was "one of them".'

Phineas Dube, describes the impact that this sort of identification made on him as a schoolboy in Rhodesia, (now Zimbabwe). It was when the country was bitterly divided between black and white, heading for the Unilateral Declaration of Independence and civil war, that he attended the first inter-racial SU camp. 'A number of boys had arrived without enough blankets. So one of the leaders gave up his blankets to the boys. And he was white. That was powerful to me. I said to myself, "there may be something big in this." So I went away from camp determined to read the Bible. I bought a little card of SU readings and tried to stick to that... somehow and at some point, the light dawned and I came to know the Way.' Seven years later Phineas joined the staff as a travelling secretary. In 1981 he was appointed SU Field Director in his country.

Phineas Dube was just one of a number of able young people converted through SU in Rhodesia in the early 1960s. The policy of running inter-racial camps was bitterly criticised by some of their supporters. In fact one man who had been generous enough to give them a car the year before vowed he would never make another gift. But the Council and staff believed it was the right way forward, and God honoured their courage and faith. Under the leadership first of Tony Harlow and then of David Cunningham, the schools and camps work grew strongly.

During the bitter civil war the close fellowship between black and white on the staff team was a powerful testimony to the power of the gospel. But it could be dangerous. Timothy Tavaziva, one of the travelling secretaries, had his beard pulled and was called 'traitor' by an angry crowd on one occasion. He well knew that men had died in similar circumstances not long before. On another occasion he was speaking in a school when a group of armed men rushed into the room, shouting 'There is no God'. The spontaneous response of the children was a burst of song, in Shona, 'God is so good; He's so good to me.' Apparently the singing was fantastic, and was too much for the intruders, for they quickly retreated in discomfort. After that, according to Timothy, they had a very good meeting!

Today SU Zimbabwe has one of the strongest SU staff teams in Africa, with what Emmanuel Oladipo describes as 'a beautiful partnership between black and white.' In addition they have sent out several SU missionaries. At the time of writing the neighbouring countries of Botswana, Lesotho and Swaziland all have Zimbabweans as their sole SU staff members. SU is making progress in each country, but they have not yet reached the stage where they can appoint national staff. Zimbabwe is helping them in the mean time.

TRUSTING THE YOUNG

Another vital factor in the growth of SU was that staff were ready to trust the young people who had come to know Christ and to give them responsibility. 'I would trust large sums of (relief) money into Raymond Nwosu's hands', wrote Bill Roberts. 'Our landlord was not a committed Christian so found this very difficult to understand.' Similarly the leadership of school groups was often left to the students, or to a teacher who had only recently been converted himself. Sometimes there were problems but usually the young people responded to the trust placed in them and matured in the process. When I was in Ghana, it was almost a pattern in several schools that the senior prefect and the leader of the SU group was the same person. 'Out of fifteen prefects this year I know that five are Christians', wrote Ron White, when he was teaching in a leading school in Lagos. 'The Senior Prefect last year was so concerned that boys should be given an opportunity to accept Christ that he went round the House meetings giving evangelistic appeals. Nobody objected!'

If people were to be trusted, they also needed to be shown what to do. As Regional Secretary, John Dean adapted his policy of 'to train and trust' from the school group to the national level. Week-long orientation courses for new members of staff and development courses for those more experienced helped people to learn what the movement stood for, and how it could become more effective. In most countries there was even an annual training weekend for members of council or committees, a practice that might well be followed with advantage in other parts of the world!

NATIONAL AUTONOMY

Another key to SU's growth in Africa in these years was its firm policy of national autonomy. In other words, each SU movement was encouraged to run its own affairs. At the earliest opportunity, national committees were formed to guide the work and to raise as much local support as possible. Among other advantages, the arrangement meant that each year more of the budget in each country came from local supporters. The grants from overseas could then be used to start new work elsewhere. In 1965, at a special Service of Dedication at Cape Coast, Armin Hoppler formally presented SU Ghana with its autonomy. In future it would stand on its own feet and be independent of any outside control. In South Africa SU has been autonomous since 1954 and SU Nigeria reached this stage in 1966. The following year, the Regional Council for Africa and Madagascar was formed to take final responsibility for SU work throughout the continent. The movements in Britain and Europe continued to send financial support, but it was the Regional Council that shared out the money and decided which developments should have priority.

Philemon Quaye, chairman of the Council for its first fourteen years, used his wide experience to give strong and constructive leadership. Brought up in a Christian home in Lomé, Philemon Quaye's faith had blossomed while studying at the military academy in Ghana.

When he was a young army officer, he helped regularly at SU camps and conferences, and he was for many years chairman of the Ghana Council. He had a distinguished career in the Armed Forces, serving for some years as a colonel, when he took part in the coup that toppled Kwame Nkrumah, and later as head of the Ghana Navy. In 1974 he became Ghana's ambassador to Liberia. While he was there he gave a great deal of support to the local SU committee and staff worker. A few years later he was transferred to Egypt, where he helped to form an SU committee and to launch the Arabic SU notes.

This chapter ends at a meeting of the Regional Council, at Limuru, Kenya, in 1981. Philemon Quaye had been elected International Chairman, and John Dean had decided that the time had come to have an African as Regional Secretary, so both were resigning. It was a moving occasion as we gathered round the fire to pray and to lay hands on the two chosen to take their places; the end of one chapter, and the start of a new one. It is appropriate that both of them had known John Dean since schooldays. Dr Dan Onwukwe, a physics lecturer, was the new chairman. Converted through the SU group at Government College, Umuahia in 1954, he had been a member of the Nigerian Council for nearly twenty years. Emmanuel Oladipo, the new Regional Secretary, had been leader of the FCS in Provincial Secondary School, Ilorin, in 1961, and had served on the FCS staff since 1967. They had both grown up in the movement, they had matured through being trained and trusted, and they were now taking over its leadership in the continent.

Over 400,000 sets of SU notes are published in twenty-two languages in Africa. Here are samples in Yoruba, English, Ibo and Sesotho.

24

A Lost Generation

While the churches have been growing by leaps and bounds in Africa and other parts of the world, back in Britain, where Scripture Union started, they have been shrinking steadily. But it is not all loss. Much of the decline has been in nominal Christianity. Much of what remains is alive and vigorous. As Michael Hews put it in *Outreach*: 'We are seeing in our country at one and the same time the onward march of the Christian Church and the onward march of paganism. There is an upsurge in praise, worship and celebration and a boom in spiritual ignorance, interest in the occult and a feeling of total pointlessness.'

'Emptiness – that's the overwhelming feeling that hits me as I enter many schools', writes Tricia Tanner, one of the ISCF regional staff. '"Why bother to work when there are no jobs?" "My father? I can't stand him!" Words like these express the bitterness that tears many young people apart as they face the instability of the present and the uncertainty of a future without work.'

Early in 1983 five SU teams took part in 'Spring into Life' missions in various parts of the country and experienced this sense of lostness vividly. One of the staff commented: 'Our week in Telford gave me a new understanding of Jesus weeping over Jerusalem'.'We have met young people who are completely and utterly ignorant, with no idea of a spiritual dimension and no concept of God's power', reported another. In one class of twenty-eight teenagers, only two or three knew that there was a commandment about stealing.

> It isn't that they have rejected Jesus. No one is antagonistic towards him. They are just not bothered. They have never thought about him. 'If Christianity is so important, then why has no one ever told us before?' several of them asked. One twelve-year-old was heard to say that she had been given a cross by someone but 'it had a little man on it and I don't know who he is.'

Schools worker Tricia Tanner (now Tricia Williams following her marriage to a fellow schools worker), writing in SU magazine *Outreach* says:

A week's mission in one school recently revealed a community which seemed almost totally devoid of spiritual awareness. As far as the pupils were concerned, the sole reason for coming to school was the hope of an eventual 'good job with lots of money.' 'Isn't there more to life?', I asked. Polite, intelligent sixth-formers tell me. 'If being a Christian helps you, fine.' But for them, it's obvious, everyone must look after No. 1 – and a good job, a car, a house, plenty of money and a husband or wife are the only symbols of success they are looking for.

Values have been turned upside down: no longer is there right or wrong; the teachers don't know – they are lost, too. The new generation looks for direction and leadership, and only finds a world of make-believe.

EVANGELISM IN SCHOOLS

For its 'Spring into Life' missions SU brought together a team of specialists from its different departments and joined with local churches for a concentrated week of outreach. They were just a small part of what SU is doing all the year round to stem the tide of secularism and push forward the frontiers of the Kingdom of God. For the ISCF members of the team, missions such as these give an opportunity for a style of evangelism that was hardly possible until fairly recently.

In its early years, ISCF had to tread carefully. The main emphasis in the schools was on discussion-type Bible studies usually led by the young people. This strategy, pioneered by Branse Burbridge in the 1950s, proved its value, as the number of school groups and of Christian teachers supporting them increased year by year. By 1971, ISCF had 1,000 affiliated groups, and was in unofficial contact with as many more. Evangelical Christian Unions were now an accepted part of the educational scene.

In the mid 70s many schools were prepared to welcome a more public and explicit type of evangelism. There was less suspicion of evangelicals on religious grounds because there was less religion, and ISCF had proved over the years that its approach to evangelism was responsible. Moreover headteachers were genuinely concerned that their pupils should find some firm ground on which to build their lives, and were prepared to let almost anyone have a say if they could offer guidance and hope. In one school at Torbay, the Christian group rigged up a public address system in the playground and broadcast their meeting, so that it was heard by almost the whole school. One member of staff broadcast his testimony. Such a thing would have been unthinkable ten years earlier.

An important step was taken in 1979 as part of the SU Bible Reading Centenary. ISCF teams, accompanied by an expert Christian drama group and some specially-made audio-visuals, found remarkable opportunities for evangelism. David Blair, who had taken over from Branse Burbridge as Schools Secretary, wrote after the first term: 'In the teeth of snow and strikes, the ISCF team battled to "share the Word" in ten different centres throughout the country. During the term we visited over 120 schools and took over 400 lessons. We contacted over ninety school Christian fellowships, many of which had no previous contact with ISCF.' At each opportunity they presented the claims of Christ as clearly as they knew how. Almost every year since, teams have been formed to work along similar lines.

Such special weeks are a great encouragement to the Christians in the school. But through them and other contacts with schools ISCF staff also reach out to the new, lost generation, which never goes near a church.

Tricia Tanner again:

> A young girl comes to me shaking with fear. Usually the sort who means trouble in a lively third-year class, now she is vulnerable and knows that messing with spiritism isn't just for fun. For once the shutters are up, and she looks at me, desperate for help. She agrees to pray with me to God for His help and protection – intuitively sensing that He is good and more powerful than the forces of darkness she has met.

The main thrust of schools work, however, is the support of Christians in their own witness in school. The accent is on helping pupils and teachers to run the groups themselves and to make good use of other opportunities such as school assemblies. The training evenings in all the main centres throughout the country and the New Year residential training courses, held annually since 1950, have helped generations of young people not only to lead their school groups but also to understand their faith and share it with their friends. There has been real growth, particularly since 1981, when Sylvia Griffiths was appointed, in Nottingham, as the first of a number of 'local schools workers'. Supported by local churches and individual Christians in the area, she has been able to work in some depth in the schools in the city. ISCF has been placing more emphasis on the links between the schools work and the life and witness of the local churches.

In one area, David Blair reports, 'new CU's have started up – one of the local churches saw the need and prayed them into existence.'

FROM GO-KARTS TO FINE ARTS

Meanwhile camps and other holiday activities continue to draw good numbers of young people, many of them with little Christian background. In the 60s and early 70s the idealism of older teenagers gave rise to community service projects and work-parties of various sorts. One group decorated the homes of elderly people, another took a group of blind girls on holiday, a third helped to build an outdoor pursuits centre. A context in which young people are helping others is a healthy one in which to hear the gospel. Working at close quarters in a small team develops close relationships, and prepares the ground for the evening Bible discussions. 'I have never enjoyed myself so much in all my life', said a young man to me as we worked together in the cold and pouring rain building the Christian sailing centre at Tanera Mohr. Numbers of activities of this sort were, however, never large and have declined in recent years.

In contrast, the academic courses, another development of the 60s, were regularly over-subscribed. At their peak they helped 750 older teenagers each year to study their chosen subject, in a Christian atmosphere, and to face up to fundamental questions of meaning and purpose and of right and wrong arising out of it. With evolutionary philosophy dominating much of the teaching of science in schools and secular humanism the arts subjects, young people need all the help they can get. Subjects range from marine biology to biblical studies, and from French literature to fine arts. The courses still continue, but numbers have been lower in recent years, partly because of the change in the educational climate, with sixth forms no longer academic strongholds.

Inevitably, SU holiday activities have faced some competition from the big Christian events for young people that have grown up in recent years, such as 'Spring Harvest'. But a camp or houseparty of forty or fifty has several advantages. It is a community in a way a vast conference of several thousands can never be. A fairly typical comment came from one young leader describing her first camp, six years earlier, when she was aged fourteen. 'It was the atmosphere of love. I told a friend afterwards that it was amazing to live in a Christian community where everyone cared for each other.' It was at that camp that she committed her life to Christ.

Moreover, young people can safely invite their uncommitted

friends, knowing that at least they will have a good holiday. There is a bewildering range of interests and activities on offer. At one place young people can build and operate a radio set, drive and repair some go-karts or programme a computer. At another they can go sailing, rock-climbing, canoeing or caveing. They can join a multi-media workshop, a sports camp, or an 'ocean venture' on the English Channel. They can travel to Paris or Switzerland, or explore the canals of Britain in a narrowboat. The camp programme needs constant improvement if it is to continue to attract the uncommitted.

MAGNETIC BOARDS AND OVERHEAD PROJECTORS

While the ISCF members of the 'Spring into Life' team were in the schools, two or three of SU's full-time evangelists were running after-school children's missions in nearby churches. For them it was part of their normal pattern of work. They hold similar missions all through the year, except for a few weeks in the summer when they lead teams at beach missions or all-day holiday clubs in local churches.

The churches they visit vary enormously. One report speaks of two evangelists, Frank Nelsson and John Hattam, struggling with the acoustics in a large and lofty church in a tough part of Middlesbrough. Fifty or sixty children sit in wooden adult pews and find it hard to sit still for any length of time. One girl came in late on roller skates and accompanied by a black and white dog. A mile or two away, 150 children pack a comfortable church hall. Steve Hutchinson, another staff evangelist, is backed up by a full team of helpers from the church, who will visit the children's homes after the mission is over, and encourage them to come to Sunday School. At the family service at the end of the week it is standing room only.

The basic pattern of the Missions Department has remained the same over the past twenty-five years: beach missions and holiday clubs in the summer, and church-based missions during the rest of the year. But there have been some significant changes in the approach. Henry Warde, who led the team of evangelists for twenty-six years, comments: 'The evangelist has to start "further back", particularly when teaching the basic truths about the nature of God, the person of Christ and the meaning of sin. This takes time, so quite frequently SU staff visit the same place for two or more missions in fairly quick succession.'

There is more emphasis too today on the whole family. 'We believe', writes Cathie Smith, a New Zealander who has led the team of evangelists since 1982, 'that the Good News of the Gospel is not only for youngsters but also for their families. Evangelists aim to make their mission family-centred, so that families can enjoy doing things together at Family Fun Nights, and learning about God together at workshops, services and celebrations.'

Another change has been a shift in emphasis from the villages to the towns. During the 1960s the Caravan Mission to Village Children creased to be a separate part of the SU family. All SU evangelists, whether they had been with CSSM or CMVC, were encouraged to work with churches anywhere in their area. Naturally the older men, who had joined CMVC with a strong sense of call to the villages, continued to spend most of their time there. But as they retired, the younger men who replaced them were equally prepared to go to towns or villages. With the spread of cars and televisions, the old isolation of the villages had largely broken down. There is no longer a need for separate teams of evangelists each having different gifts.

Wherever they went, the staff made use of the best modern equipment available. Henry Warde draws a contrast with his early days as a CMVC evangelist in Buckinghamshire, when the only home he could provide for his young family was a caravan, with the nappies drying over the two little calor-gas rings. His only transport was a single-speed bicycle. 'Today, our staff evangelists have to travel in cars that can carry the kind of sophisticated equipment which the boys and girls of the 80s almost take for granted. True, the Apostle Paul did not need soundstrips, magnetic boards or overhead projectors. But I am sure he would have made good use of such things if he had lived today.'

COMMUNICATING IN THE TELEVISION AGE

A whole new branch of the SU family has developed in the last twenty years to provide tools for Christian workers, like the SU evangelists and schools workers, who are trying to share the gospel in the television age. The Sound and Vision Unit (formerly the Modern Communications Unit) was started in the 1960s and quickly set new standards for Christian audio-visuals. Michael Shoesmith, who later joined BBC Television, was the first producer; Gordon Gray, recruited from Independent Television, was the second. The links with professional television were significant because ever since it started SVU's philosophy has been that nothing less than professional technical standards are good enough if they are to communicate Christ to the young people of today. They have shown their level of competence by winning a number of secular awards, two of them in 1982.

In the early days, Michael Shoesmith decided to concentrate on the 'soundstrip' – a filmstrip or set of slides with an integrated tape, in which words, pictures, music and sound-effects work together to tell a fast moving story. They were less expensive than movies to produce, and most schools and churches had the equipment needed to project them.

By the late 70s the vast majority of older teenagers in Britain owned cassette players, and most young people enjoyed listening more than reading. So SVU started to produce cassette programmes. The *Start the Day* cassettes, with a Bible passage, a comment and a prayer, were fairly traditional in content. The *Discipleship* cassettes, for new believers, were more unusual. They combined music, sketches and jingles in the style of a commercial radio station, with great effect. Then in 1982 SVU produced its first video cassettes. To start with they were video versions of some of the more popular soundstrips, but programmes produced specifically for video soon followed.

SVU has been particularly effective in using modern parables and contemporary artwork. Imaginative soundstrips like *No. 1* and *The Stranger* have been widely used in evangelistic meetings. More recently *The Champion* for teenagers and adults, and *Luke Street* for children, powerfully combined up-to-date music and artwork to bring Bible stories to life. Both have been followed by several similar series.

'HAVE-NOT' YOUNG PEOPLE

While one branch of the SU family was breaking new ground in the field of audio-visuals, another was attempting to do the same in the inner cities. The Frontier Youth Trust was formed in the early 60s, by a number of Christians involved in urban youth clubs. They used the word 'frontier' because they were reaching out beyond the frontiers of the church to 'teenagers who just don't want to know, where the church is concerned.' 'The FYT constituency', wrote Michael Eastman, 'is young people who are at odds with themselves, with society and with God. The frontier task is to share with these young people the good news that those whom society has written off as worthless are worthy.'

Michael Eastman had been on the ISCF staff for some years concentrating on the needs of 'less-academic' pupils. When FYT decided it needed the support of an established society and joined the SU family, he became FYT secretary. At first he and his secretary were on their own, but over the years SU has been able to put more resources into urban mission. Today he leads a team of eleven, including seven 'field officers' deployed in the large urban areas across the country.

The recession of recent years has sharpened the needs of 'have-not' young people, and the pressure on youth workers who are trying to help them. FYT operates as a 'service agency' in the sense that it offers training and support for Christians involved in leading youth clubs rather than running clubs itself. Because they are caring for young people in need, the youth leaders often face acute problems themselves. Sadly, traditionally-minded Christians in their churches often do not understand them. FYT has been a source of contact with like-minded people facing similar problems and the demand for training and support has grown rapidly.

A glance at the programme for the FYT 'National Event' early in 1983 shows some of the issues youth leaders were having to cope with. There were teach-ins on the young unemployed, on racial discrimination and on the drug dependent. There were workshops on discipling across cultures, on using the Bible in frontier situations and on coping with pressures on youth workers. The conference theme was 'Good News for the Poor' and 380 youth workers from all over Britain made the time and effort to be there. The numbers, the enthusiasm, and the realism with which the conference was prepared to look at social problems was solid evidence of the growth in recent years of evangelical concern for the social dimensions of the gospel.

A DANGEROUS PROGRAMME

Unlike most SU activities, this particular conference drew people from all over Britain. Twenty-three had come from Northern Ireland, where the problems of unemployment and inner-city deprivation had been aggravated by the bitter division between Catholics and Protestants. SU in Northern Ireland has for years realised the need for the sort of ministry FYT offers and Michael Eastman and Jim Punton, FYT's Training Officer, have made frequent visits. In 1981 they were at last able to appoint their own FYT worker, Maurice Kinkead.

The two main thrusts of SU in Northern Ireland however have been in schools and children's evangelism. David Armstrong, who became Northern Ireland's first full-time staff worker in 1953, quickly established ISCF in eighty per cent of the province's secondary schools. He and the two colleagues who have now joined him keep up a regular programme of school visits, camps and children's missions. On one occasion David's car was stolen and blown up by a terrorist bomb; but he was underterred and, with the rest of the staff, maintains with great courage what must at times be a dangerous programme. Today, with a strong team of voluntary helpers, they are running nineteen holiday missions and sixteen camps each summer. There are 200 school groups which attract around 3,000 young people each week, and are supported by some 600 teachers.

VILLAGE POST OFFICE UPGRADED

Across the border, in the Republic of Ireland, SU activity has until quite recently been very limited. For many years a team mainly from England has led an annual beach mission at Greystones, near Dublin. As early as 1942 annual boys' and girls' camps were started by a part-time staff worker, Bertie Neill, and his wife. Bertie Neill is a Church of Ireland clergyman, and most of the children came from Church of Ireland schools, so attendance was never large. But a striking number who went through the camps later became active Christian workers.

Alec Motyer, later to become principal of Trinity College, Bristol, and a well-known writer and convention speaker recalls how he went to camp as a junior officer soon after his conversion. 'Bertie's influence and friendship meant more to me than I can say. In the Scripture Union tradition he was a great letter writer. As a matter of fact during his days as a curate at Portarlington I understand that the local post office was upgraded because of the vast increase of outgoing and incoming mail.'

When Bertie Neill retired in 1970, SU was looked after by a committee for a few years. Then, in 1976, a member of the committee, Kingsley Prescott, gave up his job in insurance and joined the staff. The camp programme grew rapidly. In 1983 fifteen camps and houseparties attracted over 1,000 young people. They have also made a start with schools work and Sunday School training and opened a small bookshop in Dublin.

A major step forward was the opening of Ovoca Manor, in the Wicklow Mountains some forty miles from Dublin, as an Outdoor Pursuits Centre. A Christian Trust gave Scripture Union the property free, but it required a large sum of money and a great deal of hard work to put it in order. To keep down the cost, Kingsley Prescott himself, with a team of volunteers, worked long hours making the necessary structural repairs, renewing the plumbing and electrical wiring, installing central heating and decorating. In 1982 the first phase was completed, Herbert Harper was appointed as warden, and Ovoca Manor was fully operational.

As they pressed forward in faith the money for the project arrived. Late in 1983 a sponsored SU team of sixteen runners took part, with 10,000 others, in the Dublin City marathon. Both staff workers from the Republic and a colleague from the north completed the course. In the absence of his secretary on holiday, Kingsley Prescott himself typed the leaflet appealing for sponsors for the marathon team. He had just typed out the news that the SU Council had decided that one third of the cost of the second phase, IR£23,000, should be in the bank before the contract for the work was signed, when he took a break from typing to open the day's post. To his great surprise one of the letters contained a gift of IR£30,000 specifically for the new extension.

SEEING THE WORLD IN COLOUR

Meanwhile in Scotland the progress described in chapter 16 has been maintained. 'Our strong emphasis on schools work, allied to a vigorous camping programme, has always been a special characteristic of SU in Scotland', writes John Butler, general secretary since 1965. 'We have over 600 school groups, most of them in secondary schools but with an increasing emphasis on primary schools.... SU holds a unique place in that it is virtually the only Christian movement in the schools of Scotland, and has the confidence of school authorities.' In a typical year, 1983, a massive programme of no less than sixty-six camps and houseparties attracted more than 3,000 young people.

Like Northern and Southern Ireland, SU (Scotland) is now legally autonomous. As well as allowing the work to develop on distinctively Scottish lines, this arrangement has had financial benefits. Supporters can be more easily involved in a smaller movement that is run locally, and are more willing to give. Both Scotland and Northern Ireland now have three times as many field staff as England per head of population.

In the late 70s Scotland decided to decentralise within its own borders. Staff were located in Perth, Inverness and later in other centres, each with a local committee, and a small office and bookshop to support them. 'We established a network of people, shops and offices through which SU can do its work,' to quote John Butler again. 'The results have been good! Our schools staff are now prayed for and supported by the people they work with. And because the staff are nearer the job, they don't just make hurried tours from Glasgow. They have time to be at local events, to visit a school several times if there is a big problem, and to make deeper friendships.'

Of course it is personal friendships with individual young people, and the impact this has on their lives, that SU staff work is all about. 'I never wanted to go to an SU camp', writes Eddie McKenna, at one time the youngest ever back-marker of the Scottish Youth Sprint Team and now training for the Church of Scotland ministry. 'I was forced to go. My parents had recently been divorced and at fourteen I was pretty mixed up. Someone suggested I should go to an SU camp, and my mother said "Yes". So, full of reservations and scorn for "Bible-thumping cranks", I ended up at camp at Scoughall. I had a good time – in a senior tent where the rest of the boys were Christians. I enjoyed fooling about, writing "I am God" all over the beach.

'It wasn't long before I became aware that the leaders and the boys in my tent were "different". Then several things happened to me – I went to a Gospel concert, I was stuck on a sinking boat in the middle of the Firth of Forth, I couldn't get God out of my mind. One morning in the middle of the camp I went down to the beach and asked Jesus to change me totally. I felt an immediate change. It was like seeing the world in colour after living in black-and-white. That was four years ago, and since then, despite my lack of faithfulness, God has proved more than faithful.'

An important strategy conference in 1980 led to further advance. Council and staff realised that the need in the schools of Scotland was urgent. They knew that no other organisation was in a position to do much about it, and came to a firm conviction that God was calling them to move forward. Within a year they had increased the field staff from thirteen to eighteen. Although at times it looked unlikely, their gift income rose to cover the extra costs and in 1983 was three times what it had been three years earlier.

REGIONS IN ENGLAND

In England too SU has been finding the value of decentralisation. The country was divided into five 'regions' and one by one 'regional co-ordinators' were appointed. Their job was to work with staff and local supporters in the region to develop all aspects of SU there. Alan Martin, who moved to Bristol to set up the South-West Region in 1968, showed what could be done. Within a few years he had formed a chain of twenty-two area committees, covering most parts of the region. They were responsible for putting SU on the map locally, organising a Bible reading campaign in the churches, a Sunday School training day, a series of 'book parties' to sell Christian literature, or a coffee evening for supporters. Alan Martin fed them with ideas, audio-visuals and literature, and arranged for the specialist SU staff in the region to give such help as they could.

A CHAIN OF BOOKSHOPS

The expansion of SU's bookshop ministry in the last twenty years has also helped to bring SU in touch with people all over the country. Edward England, who later made a name for himself as religious editor of Hodder and Stoughton, ran the Wigmore Street shop with great skill for nine years in the 60s. He set a high standard of professionalism in bookshop management, and opened SU's second shop, near his home at Croydon. A chain of fifteen shops has since been developed in England, with five more in Scotland. Some established shops were taken over as their owners retired, but half of them were new shops opened in parts of the country where there was a need. So the bookshop expansion made a genuine contribution to the life of the churches up and down the country.

ALIVE TO GOD

Other aspects of SU's literature ministry have had varied success in recent years. The circulation of the four main series of Bible-reading notes dropped significantly towards the end of the 60s and stayed roughly on a plateau through the 70s. The proliferation of modern translations, which make it easier for people to understand the Bible on its own, and competition from other Bible reading schemes have been factors that have hindered growth. But the four regular series of SU notes are still read by over 300,000 people in Britain; and they are supplemented by a rich variety of other Bible reading aids for different groups, such as *Simon and Sarah* for young children and *AM/PM* for young adults. The creation of a separate department for Bible ministries in 1978, with Colin Matthews in charge, brought this aspect of SU work more sharply into focus, as did the Bible Reading Centenary the following year.

In recent years the notes have increasingly offered suggestions for praise and prayer, as well as for Bible reading and meditation. The trend is taken further with the launch of *Alive to God* at the end of 1983. Written in a popular style, it aims, according to Colin Matthews, 'to bring to life all the essentials that make up the time we spend alone in God's presence.'

A CHEQUERED HISTORY

SU's book publishing has had a chequered history in the last twenty years. Some aspects have been quite successful, such as music. *Hymns of Faith* (1964) has been widely used by adults for whom it was far more suitable than *Golden Bells* which was originally produced for children and had become very out-of-date. *Sing to God* (1971) and *Come and Sing* (1971) have been extremely popular in schools and children's groups, and have done much to raise the level of children's worship. In the late 70s the new joy and enthusiasm in worship that swept through the church as a result of the Renewal Movement gave birth to hundreds of new hymns and songs. *Songs of Worship* (1980) and *Jesus Praise* (1982) brought together many of the best of them.

Another area of publishing which was developed with considerable imagination was that of full-colour picture books for children. The *Jonathan Mark* series (1970) set a pattern which was followed more successfully later. The secret was to co-edition: to co-operate with publishers in other parts of the world to build up a long print run of the colour sheets, to keep down the price, and to overprint in the different languages. In the 1970s, SU (England) became involved in picture books for adults as well as children and became a world leader in this sort of evangelical co-operation. It was a very successful policy for increasing sales: one series of booklets sold a million copies, in eight languages, within two years. But it was highly risky financially, and required a great deal of publishing capital. At the end of 1973, over-optimistic expansion and some bad choices of titles coincided with world recession, and caused a serious cash crisis. Seven years later, similar factors led to even more serious trouble, and forced the Council to cut back sharply. In future, SU would take fewer risks, and keep to areas of publishing more directly related to the movement's aims, in other words, books for children and young people, and for those working with them, and books to help people read the Bible.

ONE MILLION EVERY WEEK

One of the most influential sections of SU publishing has been the Education in Churches Department, as the Sunday School Department is now called. 'Every week, some 150,000 leaders and Sunday School teachers use the magazines and leaflets to teach the Word of God to around one million boys and girls', wrote John Tigwell in 1979, the head of the department at the time. By this date, there were seven magazines for leaders of different age levels including *Grow*

Together for adult groups and *In Touch* for Sunday School Superintendents and church leaders.

Over the years the approach has changed as churches have changed the pattern of their children's work. 'More and more churches are rethinking their approach to children', writes Margaret Old, the current head of department. 'Instead of simply asking "How are we to teach more effectively?" (emphasis on us, on teaching), they are asking "How does a child come to have faith? What *leads up to* conscious commitment? And if a child cannot remember a time when he did not love the Lord, what caused this to be so?"

'The child needs to see the gospel *lived* by the Christian community, not just talked about. This is how he is most likely to come to a real faith of his own. Getting instruction is not enough, even when that instruction is thoroughly biblical, fully explained, shown to be relevant, and applied. Children need to *experience* what we mean by love, forgiveness, trust, justice, peace, etc. They need to be "exposed" to real worship – and they will sense whether or not it is vital, filled with a sense of God's presence and power.'

So in an interesting reversal of the trend Josiah Spiers and Tom Bishop did so much to cultivate a century earlier, more and more churches are introducing all-age worship, and restricting the time when children are taught in their own age-group. The changes in the magazines from the autumn of 1984 are planned to cater for this new pattern, particularly by making the material more flexible so that leaders can adapt it to suit their local situation.

TRAINING FOR MISSION

The training programme for Sunday School teachers has grown and developed with the magazines. 'Three hundred people came to our 1978 annual residential weekend training course to learn more about how to make their work among boys and girls effective', to quote John Tigwell again. 'Three hundred more had to be disappointed and asked to come in 1979 instead. About 5,000 people attended day and evening training events during 1978.' By this time a team of five full-time 'training specialists' were deployed across the country, one for each region. In 1981 the team was formed into a separate 'Training Unit' under the leadership of Anton Baumohl. They recruited more voluntary 'associate trainers' all over the country, and widened the range of training to include virtually anything that would help to equip the local church for mission. They now offer courses not only in Sunday School teaching and youth leadership, but also in subjects such as personal relationships in the local church, leadership of adult Bible study groups, and the family in the life of the church. SU's concern to help churches to strengthen family life is shown by the recent appointment of Joan King as full-time Young Families Adviser.

BY ANY AND EVERY MEANS

If Josiah Spiers and Tom Bishop, the founders of the Mission, could come back today they would no doubt be amazed at the range of activities carried out under the Scripture Union banner, and the variety of methods. But once they got to know what was going on they would feel very much at home. One hundred years ago Tom Bishop defined 'the great aim of our Mission' as 'to use any and every means to lead children and young people to know and love the Lord Jesus Christ as their Saviour... to lead them onward in the Christian life, and to point out to them in due time paths of Christian usefulness.' In other words, evangelism, nurture and training. That is still what SU is about. 'Whatever happens during the next hundred years', wrote Alan Martin, the General Director, at the time of the Bible Reading Centenary, 'we must ensure that our evangelistic heart beats as strongly as ever, that we carry out our Lord's commission to make disciples, and that we train those disciples to live and witness effectively wherever God calls them to serve.'

Just as it was 100 years ago, Scripture Union, in partnership with local churches, is helping 'a lost generation' to meet Jesus. The onward march of paganism makes the battle increasingly tough. But the upsurge in praise, worship and celebration that has been a marked feature of many churches in recent years, offers encouragement and hope. 'I have been connected with SU as a staff worker for nearly twenty-five years', writes Alan Martin again, 'and I have never known a time of greater challenge and opportunity.'

25

The Twofold Growth

In 1867 a small group of unknown men in a London suburb planted a tiny seed. It was one of hundreds of evangelical societies started in nineteenth-century England. Most of them have long-since died. Some have struggled on or changed their character. Only a few have taken root around the world, and are growing vigorously today. CSSM and Scripture Union is one of them. When so many other seeds have died, why should this tree be still alive and well?

It is possible to answer such a question simply from a spiritual perspective: 'God chose it that way'; or 'the sole secret of the work is prayer'. Such answers are important because they focus on the need to be in the centre of God's will and dependent on his resources. But they lead on to other questions. Why does God choose one group and not another? What are the distinctive features God has given to it, which have been the secrets of its life and growth? How has it been able to take root in such a rich variety of soils?

THE TWO LEGS

There is no doubt that one of Scripture Union's most important features is its twofold aim, evangelism and the encouragement of Bible reading. In the SU story we have again and again seen how the two aims have complemented and assisted one another. The remarkable growth of both CSSM and SU in the 1880s illustrates the point well. The circulation of SU cards took off because they were distributed enthusiastically by the friends CSSM had made through its children's missions. On the other hand, wherever the cards went, they told people about Josiah Spiers and his missions. On its two legs of direct evangelism and Bible reading literature, CSSM/SU took a great leap forward.

As the movement spread to other countries the same combination made rapid progress possible. Personal contact through a camp, a school group or a beach mission was again and again the starting point for active involvement in other aspects of the work. The dynamic growth in Australia in the 1950s and 1960s and in Nigeria in the 1970s are just two examples. In contrast, where the movement has concentrated solely on Bible reading, it has nearly always had to struggle to make any growth.

BIBLE BASED EVANGELISM

Moreover the link with Bible reading has deeply affected the way the movement has carried out its evangelistic task. First it has helped to keep it biblical. As the winds of theological fashion have changed, CSSM/SU has continued to emphasise the importance of the Bible in the life of a Christian. One critical period was the end of the last century. As we have seen, many church leaders, including some who had been involved in CSSM beach missions in their student days, were influenced by current theological trends which denied the truth and authority of the Bible. Some organisations started by evangelicals, such as the Student Christian Movement, went along with the general current of opinion. CSSM as a movement committed primarily to evangelism among children might well have done the same. Tom Bishop gave a strong personal lead in holding the CSSM loyal to biblical authority; but the fact that the leaders of the movement and most of its voluntary workers were reading the Bible with their SU cards must have made his task a great deal easier. They knew from daily experience that God spoke to them through the Scriptures, and recognised its intrinsic authority.

The link of CSSM/SU's evangelism with a daily Bible reading system has also helped to keep it on a biblical course in more recent years. Some modern evangelism, under the influence of existential philosophy, has placed excessive emphasis on experience at the expense of doctrine. Some evangelistic appeals have invited people to 'come to Jesus' with very little explanation of what it means. SU, on the other hand, has continued to emphasise the need for teaching.

EVANGELISM AND NURTURE

Keeping the balance between teaching the truths of the gospel and calling for a response is never easy. When Josiah Spiers started his ministry the idea of calling children to decide for Christ was almost unknown. Some twentieth-century evangelists have gone too far the other way, asking children to respond to Jesus without explaining who he is or what he expects his followers to do. CSSM/SU has always stood for a middle way: clear teaching leading to a definite challenge, followed by regular nurture in a caring group. The link with a Bible reading movement has helped the movement to live up to this ideal. The care which Josiah Spiers took to follow up the children who responded at his meetings set a pattern which was reinforced by the SU Bible reading system and has been a marked feature of SU evangelism ever since.

FRIENDSHIP EVANGELISM

Scripture Union's emphasis on evangelism through friendship fits in at this point. For if a young person's decision for Christ is seen as a step on the road, a vital step but only part of a process which starts with teaching and leads on to nurture and growth, then friendship is important. The games at a beach mission, the activities at camp, the small groups in schools or church, the food and the fun, all have their place. For they help the Christian worker to win the young person's confidence, to understand his questions, in Frank Millard's words 'to earn the right by friendship to speak to him about Christ.'

RELATING THE BIBLE TO LIFE

But the interaction between the two aims of SU has not only influenced its evangelism. It has affected its Bible reading ministry too. For its writers and editors have not been able to sit in ivory towers, detached from real life. Many of them take part in camps or missions, or lead a Bible class or youth club. All of them, in the larger movements, have colleagues who are out in the front line, meeting people using the notes. All this has helped to keep the notes practical and down to earth. Sometimes they may have dodged important issues, but on the whole interpretation has related to life.

GOSPEL AND CULTURE

It is this conviction that both Bible reading and evangelism must relate to life that underlies SU's policy of finding original writers wherever possible instead of translating from another culture. One of Josiah Spiers' great achievements was to express the gospel in a way which brought it to life for a Victorian child. The word 'contextualise' was not invented for another 100 years, but that was what he was doing. Using language, stories, hymns and prayers the children could understand and enjoy, he made Jesus real for them. The same principle has been applied to Bible reading. 'They may read the Bible by the candlelight of a foreign language', wrote Roddy Archibald, 'but they cannot awaken to a clear understanding except in the morning light of their own language.' It is not always true, of course, but it is an important principle. And it applies to thought-forms as well as to language. Ernst Aebi's decision to write his own German notes in 1930, and the change from translated *Daily Bread* to Dr Philip Teng's original Chinese notes in 1972, were significant SU milestones; and both led to rapid increases in circulation.

The movement of course has never entirely lived up to this ideal, for the effort to express the gospel in current forms needs to be made in each culture and in every age. Sometimes illustrations and methods used by God in one country have been too readily exported to another. One cannot help wondering, for example, what Indian and Chinese children in the 1880s thought of the picture leaflets which Tom Bishop assiduously sent to them, full of stories and pictures straight out of Victorian England. At other times, SU leaders have been too slow to abandon methods that are no longer effective.

Frequently, however, SU has been in the forefront of experiments in new ways of communicating the old message. The beach missions of the 1870s must have shocked many contempories. The first boys' camps of the 1890s and the soundstrips of the English Sound and Vision Unit in the 1970s are the other good examples. John Prince called his history of SU Australia *Tuned in to Change*: the title accurately reflects the way the movement there has adapted to meet new needs, and innovated to create new opportunities. SU is only going to be useful in the future, and continue to grow, if it is open to new ideas, ready for change. Its message must remain the same, faithful to the Scriptures; but its methods, its illustrations, the way it expresses and applies that message will change from time to time and from place to place, as the context changes and as it is open to the leading of the Holy Spirit.

VOLUNTARY WORKERS

There is a link between this flexibility and willingness to change and another distinctive feature of the SU movement, its dependence on voluntary workers. Ever since Tom Bishop launched the Children's Evangelistic Band in 1873, it has relied on unpaid and only partly-trained voluntary workers, many of them still young and inexperienced, to run many of its activities. Another large army of unpaid volunteers has given sacrificial service on its councils and committees. In the best sense of the word, CSSM/SU has been a lay movement. The work has multiplied out of all recognition as a result, and thousands of young men and women set off on a lifetime of Christian service. John Dean summed it up in his motto 'to train and trust'. It has taken courage and faith at times to trust the good name of Scripture Union to young people with little training or experience. Sometimes standards have suffered but by and large the policy has been amply justified. Certainly only a fraction of SU's growth would have been possible if the paid staff had kept everything under their own control.

A LOOSE STRUCTURE

The same principle of contextualising the gospel underlies SU's loose international structure. If it is important that methods and forms of expression need adapting to the culture of each country, then it is clear that, once they understand what SU is all about, it is Christian leaders from the country concerned who are in the best position to plan its policy there. So the decision was taken to decentralise, to give full autonomy to the national movement in each country as it became ready for it, and to trust the Holy Spirit to guide the SU leaders there. Part of the strength of SU is that there is no blueprint which every national movement has to follow. 'I took over from John Dean', writes Emmanuel Oladipo, 'as Regional Secretary of a work that is very firmly rooted in the African soil. One of the factors, under God, responsible for this is the absence of a standard international manual answering all the questions we are not asking. We have therefore been free to experiment, make our own mistakes and learn our lessons, in the full understanding that "SU is us".'

Surprisingly the other factor Emmanuel Oladipo mentions is that 'as an organisation, we have never had enough input of personnel or funds from abroad to keep us from worrying or striving in our own local constituency.' Shortage of staff and shortage of money are usually thought of as hindrances to the spread of the gospel. But 'the weakness of limited means', as it has been called, is an asset if it forces us to rely on God and to help other people to do the same. It has certainly helped SU to become genuinely indigenous, in Africa and other parts of the world.

UNITY IN DIVERSITY

The decision to decentralise was a brave one, for it could easily have caused the movement to disintegrate. Although there have been problems from time to time in a few countries, the overall effect has been to release an enormous fund of creative energy, as men and women have responded to the responsibility given to them. The vigorous growth that we have seen in the years since Old Jordans has been the result.

It has, of course, allowed SU to develop in different ways in different parts of the world. But in spite of this diversity, the movement retains a deep underlying unity, based on its common aims and evangelical convictions. After an extensive tour of the SU world in 1970, John Laird tried to account for it. 'Looking back on our tour one of the things that impressed us was the wise balance that seemed everywhere to be maintained, in matters of doctrine and policy. SU's Councils and staff members throughout the world are not centrally controlled or bound by mandatory rules and regulations. Nevertheless the sense of unity, co-operation and harmony is unbroken worldwide. We have so far, in the mercy of God, been preserved from heresies, strange notions and unbalanced doctrinal excesses or aberrations. I sometimes think that the reason for this may be that as a movement council members, staff members and voluntary workers, we all follow, or are supposed to follow, the practice of daily Bible reading, not of a few favourite passages selected at random, but systematically throughout both Old and New Testaments. It is this balanced reading of the Scriptures day by day which, I believe, keeps our movement on the right lines, following the paths of wisdom and truth, at least in some measure'.

It is a slightly idealised picture perhaps. But a good example of the way this unity has been maintained when conflict might have been expected is seen in Scripture Union's response to the charismatic movement. In many countries some individual council and staff members and some voluntary helpers have had an experience of charismatic renewal which has given them a new joy in worship and a new power in service. Others can testify to no such experience, but their spiritual lives have continued to develop in other ways. In such countries SU has had to face the question whether colleagues with widely different experiences could work and pray together, fully accepting one another in Christ. It was no easy task in some countries in the early days of the renewal movement when a number of churches were split over the issue. Although the International Council issued some guidelines to help them, each national SU has had to work out its response to the situation locally. Not surprisingly there have been stresses and strains in a few countries from time to time, but there has been remarkably little division. In some countries, particularly in Africa, the leadership has at times found it necessary to restrain some of the more exuberant younger SU members, so that they do not equate spiritual life with excessive emotion. Among leaders of SU throughout the world a clear consensus has developed that God works in different ways in different people; and that whatever his past experiences, every Christian needs to be continually open to a fresh touch of the Holy Spirit. On this basis, SU has been able to benefit from the new life and vigour that has come through the renewal movement without finding it divisive.

SCRIPTURE UNION TODAY

In 1984 there is a worldwide staff of over 900 representing more than sixty different nationalities and located in seventy-two different countries. In another nineteen countries there is an SU Committee or Honarary Representative. In thirty-six countries SU is fully autonomous.

The range of activities under the SU banner is extraordinarily varied, as national movements have responded to local needs in different ways. Every movement distributes SU Bible reading notes or cards. Over fifty of them arrange camps or other residential holiday activities. In thirty-five or more there are regular SU meetings for secondary schools students. In twenty-two countries they hold children's missions regularly in churches, in parks or on beaches. More unusual are the SU Bible studies in several prisons in Taiwan; the literacy programme in Vanuatu (New Hebrides) to help people to read the Bible; the 'drop-in' centre for unemployed young people in Honiara in the Solomon Islands; the SU Youth Employment schemes in Chile and in Tasmania; the knitting machines at Camp Kawai in Peru, where women from the nearby village are trained to earn a decent living. At one time SU Tonga even ran a fruit shop in Auckland, New Zealand, sending a weekly consignment of produce by air so that their members could get a fair price.

The underlying aim of these diverse activities is the same. And there is no doubt that the need for SU's imaginative, responsible, biblical evangelism and nurture is as great as ever. Bill Andersen, from Australia, urges the importance of 'showing love in an age of loneliness; giving reasons in an age of questions; giving witness in an age lacking standards; showing what real life is in an age where real life is being sought; speaking simply of a wonderful Lord in an age that lacks a Master.' As long as SU continues to do this, God will be able to use it to bring his word to a young world.

Appendix A

List of Abbreviations

ANZEA	Australia, New Zealand and East Asia, the name used for the East Asia/Pacific Region 1960–1983.
CEPA	Centre Evangélique de Productions Audio-visuelles: affiliated to Scripture Union in Europe. CEPA produces audio-visuals in French, German, Spanish and other languages.
CICCU	Cambridge Inter-Collegiate Christian Union, the Cambridge expression of IFES.
CMS	Church Missionary Society
CMVC	Caravan Mission to Village Children, founded under the auspices of the CSSM in 1893. The two organisations fully merged in the 1960s.
CSK	An association of Bible clubs for junior high schools in Japan, closely associated with the Japanese Scripture Union.
CSSM	Children's Special Service Mission, founded in 1867 in England. This was the original name of the society now known as Scripture Union.
FCS	Fellowship of Christian Students in Northern Nigeria. Founded in 1956, it has branches in universities and secondary schools, and works very closely with Scripture Union Nigeria.
FYT	Frontier Youth Trust, formed in the early 1960s by a number of Christians involved in urban youth clubs in England, has been part of the SU family since 1966.
IFES	International Fellowship of Evangelical Students. Founded in 1947, it links together evangelical student movements throughout the world. In some countries, IFES member movements also look after Christian groups in high schools.
ISCF	Inter-School Christian Fellowship, the name of the organisation which links Christian groups in the high schools in many English-speaking countries.
IVF/ IVCF	Inter-Varsity (Christian) Fellowship, the organisation linking university Christian Unions in many English-speaking countries. In recent years, several national movements, such as the Universities and Colleges Christian Fellowship in Britain, have adopted a new name.
KSCF	Kenya Students Christian Fellowship. Formed in 1954, KSCF links Christian groups in schools and colleges. It has close links with Scripture Union, but is autonomous.
PPA	Persekutuan Pembaca Alkitab, the Indonesian Scripture Union.
SCM	Student Christian Movement. The name of the national movement in Britain, and several other countries, linked with the World Student Christian Federation.
SUFES	The name of the movement in West Malaysia, formed by the merger of Scripture Union and IFES.

SU	Scripture Union. Originally the name of the Bible reading ministry of the CSSM, Scripture Union was adopted as the official name of the movement in 1960.
SVCU	Schools and Varsities Christian Union: an organisation that linked Christian groups in secondary schools in South Africa in the 1940s and 1950s, it merged with Scripture Union in 1962.
SVU	Sound and Vision Unit: the audio visual production centre of SU England.
TSCF	Tanzania Student Christian Fellowship, an autonomous organisation linking Christian groups in schools and colleges of that country.
UCCF	Universities and Colleges Christian Fellowship, since 1974 the name of the British member movement of IFES.
VPSC	Varsities and Public Schools Camps, camps run by Scripture Union for young people at the public schools.

Appendix B

Principal sources

Elisabeth Aebi *Botschafter der Freude – Lebensbild von Ernst Aebi* (Bibellesebund 1964)
Annual Reports of the CSSM (1867–1913)
Anon. *TBB of the CSSM* (CSSM 1923)
O R Barclay *Whatever happened to the Jesus Lane lot?* (IVP 1977)
C K Becroft *Scripture Union USA 1959/1972: A Personal View* (1983)
Sandra Carter *One Book, One World* (SU 1967)
CSSM (1921–1956)
CSSM Occasional Papers (1884–1907)
John Eddison ed *Bash, a Study in Spiritual Power* (Marshalls 1983)
J M Laird *No Mere Chance* (Hodder & Stoughton and SU 1981)
Light of Life (Bombay: September 1976)
Peter J Lineham *No Ordinary Union* (SU New Zealand 1980)
On Special Service (1956–1967)
Outreach (1968–1983)
Peter Pattison *Crisis Unawares* (OMF Books 1981)
J C Pollock *The Good Seed* (Hodder & Stoughton 1959)
John and Moyra Prince *Lighting the Lamp* (SU Anzea Regional Council 1983)
John and Moyra Prince *Tuned into Change* (SU Australia 1979)
M Ray *Racontez les Merveilles de Dieu* (La Ligue 1967)
W B Roberts *Life and Death among the Ibos* (SU 1970)
Patricia St John *R Hudson Pope* (SU 1967)
Share the Word (SU International Council 1979)
David Winter *For All the People* (Hodder & Stoughton 1967)

Index